Nomadic Voices

Nomadic Voices

Conrad and the Subject of Narrative

Bruce Henricksen

UNIVERSITY OF ILLINOIS PRESS
Urbana and Chicago

Publication of this book was supported in part by a grant from Loyola University of New Orleans.

© 1992 by the Board of Trustees of the University of Illinois
Manufactured in the United States of America
1 2 3 4 5 C P 5 4 3 2 1

This book is printed on acid-free paper.

Library of Congress Cataloging-in-Publication Data

Henricksen, Bruce.
    Nomadic Voices : Conrad and the subject of narrative / Bruce
Henricksen.
        p.   cm.
    Includes bibliographical references and index.
    ISBN 0-252-01936-9 (cloth).—ISBN 0-252-06253-1 (pbk.)
    1. Conrad, Joseph, 1857–1924—Technique.   2. Narration (Rhetoric)
I. Title.
PR6005.O4Z7433   1992
823'.912—dc20   91-46316
                                                                      CIP

For
Janet, Frédéric, Jessica, and Teag

Contents

Acknowledgments

Much of this book has grown out of dialogue with students, and but for them it would not exist. The first chapter appeared in an earlier version in *PMLA* and is reprinted here with permission. Subsequent chapters were begun during a semester of sabbatical leave from Loyola University of New Orleans, for which I am grateful. Ann Lowry and the fine staff at the University of Illinois Press were supportive and meticulous, and Rob Schneider was a thorough and skillful copy editor.

This book is dedicated to my mother, who as a single parent provided education and love during a difficult time, and to my daughter and sons.

Note on Documentation

Parenthetical references are to the following readily available texts of
    Conrad's novels:

Heart of Darkness, ed. Robert Kimbrough (New York: W. W.
    Norton, 1988).

Lord Jim, ed. Thomas C. Moser (New York: W. W. Norton, 1968).

The Nigger of the "Narcissus," ed. Robert Kimbrough (New York: W. W.
    Norton, 1979).

Nostromo, ed. Martin Seymour-Smith (New York: Viking
    Penguin, 1985).

Under Western Eyes, ed. Boris Ford (New York: Viking Penguin, 1985).

Nomadic Voices

Introduction:
Boundaries of the Subject

There with Marlow's signature the letter proper
ended. The privileged reader screwed up his lamp,
and solitary above the billowy roofs of the town, like
a lighthouse keeper above the sea, he turned to the
pages of the story.

Lord Jim

Years ago Rene Wellek and Austin Warren distinguished between
"intrinsic" criticism and criticism that relates a literary work to "extrinsic" disciplines.[1] This distinction seems now to have been made
in another age and another world, where things were done differently. Now all disputes are border disputes, and no one is certain—
no one *should* be certain—where texts (literary or otherwise) end and
whatever remainder there might be outside of textuality begins. The
differentiation of literary discourse from other discourses, originally
motivated in part by the demands of academic politics, may have
helped literary study set up shop as a distinct discipline, but in denying the intertextual nature of cultural and social reality it imposed
serious constraints on the kind of knowledge criticism and scholarship
could produce. The relationship between the older paradigm of literary studies and the conservative politics of privileged readers is now,
at least to many, a foregone collusion. Today, if there is nothing outside the text—just as "the letter proper" and "the story" are both "in"
the larger text of *Lord Jim*—it is not because the text is an autonomous
artifact different in kind from ordinary language, but because the text
is itself a locus of social tensions and contradictions. The opposition of
the intrinsic and the extrinsic is, like Saussure's sign, arbitrary, which
is to say institutionally and historically determined.

My study, no less determined in its own way, reads Conrad from the perspective of this recent paradigm shift, from the point of view not only of current narrative theory (as refined by such figures as Mikhail Bakhtin, Roland Barthes, Gerard Genette, Jonathan Culler, Frank Kermode, and Paul Ricoeur) but also of such poststructural and postmodern concerns as the relationship between subjectivity and the constitutive discourses of society, the problematic grounding of narrative authority, and the agonistic relationship between grand narratives and the many voices their power would silence. It is not necessary to point to the ubiquity of the subject of "the subject" (or of this pun) in recent theory, and the breaking down of traditional boundaries separating the subject from its other parallels the redrawing of disciplinary lines within critical discourse. It is worth noting, however, that the various assaults leveled against the traditional subject of humanism, ranging from the direct attack of various Marxisms and New Historicisms to the less direct underminings of linguistic and semiotic deconstructions, have not buried the subject so much as repositioned it among diverse political and institutional economies.

Since the investments of the subject in an essentializing humanism are bankrupt, the agency of the subject, as it returns to our discourse like Freud's repressed, must return with a difference. Remembering that for Jean-François Lyotard the postmodern is not merely a period designation but also a name for tendencies latent in modernism itself, this book asserts that the necessity of this postmodern difference is apparent already in the texts of Joseph Conrad, overdetermined texts in which the discursive subject constantly deconstructs into diverse voices resulting from the networks of power in which the discursive subject is positioned. The concept of a narrator whose discourse imitates a speech act that might have been made by a real person in a lived situation has functioned to harmonize or regulate the play within the literary text of the speech diversity from the larger social text. Placing the traditional ways of thinking about narrators in brackets enables us better to hear these diverse, nomadic voices that are caught and bounded within the monadic subject.

The distortion resulting from conventional notions concerning narrators causes Jonathan Culler to say that "it is a major problem for the theory of fiction today, when narrative analysis has become so resourceful and, in dubious collusion with speech act theory, is attempting to convince us that a narrative is an act of a person. The theory of fiction needs to be alert to the inadequacies of this orientation, which strives to convert everything in language to a mark of human personalities." This anthropomorphism must be recognized,

Culler asserts, "not as an analytical perspective on fiction but as part of the fiction-making process."[2] In the spirit of Culler's warning, Bette London, in *The Appropriated Voice*, argues that the modernist belief in a unique self at the origin of discourse is the ruling construct of modernist aesthetics that must be questioned. But, she adds, "modernism's ruling constructs . . . are problematized *within* modernism—within the modernism we are empowered to perceive" by virtue of our own subsequent position.[3] The strategy of my reading, like that suggested by London, is to reinsert Conrad's texts into the current conversation, which has as its most compelling imperative the need to rethink identity and knowledge from the perspective of our ruling discourses and grand narratives. I will do this by focusing primarily on the problem of Conrad's narrators and the relationship of their discourses to the stories they tell. A secondary consideration will involve the way a narrator's regulatory discourse attempts to fix, "frame" or "subject" other characters in the story.

Therefore, while it is appropriate—perhaps in both senses that inhabit this spelling—to remember the critical tradition by which an author such as Conrad has come down to us, the mediating assumptions of this tradition (a sort of grand narrative in diverse chapters) must be questioned and appropriated in a reading that no longer accepts such certainties as unitary selfhood, the transcendent authority of the author, and the ordered autonomy of the literary text. But it is not my intention to impose an alien postmodern problematic on these modernist texts; rather, I hope to demonstrate that questions of ideology and the discursive subject or voice are the texts' own problematics. At the same time my reading would wrest, by means of what John Frow calls a "negative revalorization,"[4] Conrad's texts from the interests of an older critical hegemony that largely ignored these issues.

Having said this, I must add that my own reading, though not regretting the demise of this hegemony and of the humanism it supported, remains conventional in other ways that derive from my own temperament and education, which is to say that proceed from certain constraints that operate to maintain established paradigms, rooted within traditional critical practice. I write a book on a canonical figure —a white male from the "patriarchal" canon—and I offer "close readings" of separate novels, one per chapter. My defense of such conventional behavior is my belief that meaningful change occurs from within, through one's inhabiting certain structures and reshaping them to what extent one can. As Frow says:

To describe, from within a literary system, the interpretive limits set by the system is at once to describe a set of constraints and to interrupt the limits, the enclosing frame, by framing them within a larger closure. This process is neither revolutionary nor endless. The possibility of unsettling limits is always both given and limited by an actual condition of power. There is no outside of power. But to write, within discursive limits, with a recognition of what these limits are and of the forms of discursive objects and relations delimited by a discursive formation is to push at these limits, to lay them open to the inspection of a counterpower whose force is not completely contained or foreseen. Without this possibility no system could ever change, it could only collapse from its own inertia.[5]

Within the familiar structure of the critical book on a canonical author, I attempt productive misreadings that discover in Conrad's texts our own concerns with the necessary transgression of traditional boundaries, with the institutional and ideological constraints that operate upon the stories we tell, and with the need to abandon monologic discourses in favor of a more open and unconstrained global dialogue. As Lyotard argues, the limits that institutions impose on discourses are never definitive; "the limits are themselves the stakes" of our discourses, and "the boundaries only stabilize when they cease to be stakes in the game."[6] In addition to such specifics as the migration of Jim-stories in *Lord Jim* and the international aspect of conversation in *Under Western Eyes*, the general heteroglossia of Conrad's fiction and the repeated occurrence of framing devices within the literary text that gesture toward the text's external uses are examples of how Conrad's works prefigure today's transgression and remapping of boundaries in an increasingly diverse, disseminated, and multicultural discourse. In my readings, then, Conrad's texts, at least after *The Nigger of the "Narcissus,"* develop as increasingly direct but always modified challenges to the permanence of Western culture's hegemony.

In order to maintain a sense of the historically conditioned nature of these readings, it is necessary to place them in a sequence of prior interpretations and critical practices, each with its own relative legitimacy.

From the outset, biographical criticism, which New Critics tended to see as a soft-minded means of avoiding the complexities of the text itself, continued to assert its relevance to a proper reading of Conrad's fiction by virtue of Conrad's unique career as a Polish/Ukrainian immigrant writing in his third language and by virtue of his obvious reliance on personal experience in his fiction. This biographical chapter in the history of Conrad criticism now opens onto the postmodern and postindividual concern with the subject as a fragmented construction of the competing social voices of the larger and no-longer-outer world. Students of Conrad, therefore, remain deeply indebted to Frederick R. Karl and Zdzislaw Najder for important biographical studies. The biography of Conrad's seafaring days as it relates to his fiction is the focus of Norman Sherry's *Conrad's Eastern World*, and biography also occupies a significant place in Ian Watt's important study *Conrad in the Nineteenth Century*. The most recent biography at the time of this writing is Jeffrey Meyers's *Joseph Conrad*.[7]

Peter J. Glassman, adding a psychological dimension to biographical criticism, reads the early fiction, through *Lord Jim*, in the light of experiences of Conrad's youth and young adulthood that Glassman thinks were destructive to the normal development of selfhood and identity. Because of the death of Conrad's parents in his childhood, the political upheavals of his homeland, and his youthful flight to France and the sea, Glassman makes the startling assertion that "Joseph Conrad had no personality in the sense in which we normally intend the word." With this statement, Glassman approaches a dismissal of traditional notions of the author's authority and therefore anticipates the critical theory that refuses to see the literary work as the transparent medium through which a preexisting subject, the author, is expressed. With the death of the author comes the consideration of the text as a locus of competing social voices, as analyzed by Bakhtin, or as an elaborate, unauthorized play of signification of the sort Barthes envisioned in *S/Z*.

Relying less on personal biography and more on a rough-and-ready notion of the structure of the mind, Albert Guerard wrote his influential chapter "The Journey Within," seeing both "The Secret Sharer" and *Heart of Darkness* as allegorical descents into the inner reaches of the unconscious. To Guerard, the moral of "The Secret Sharer" is that we "cannot achieve wholesome integration of the personality until we have made the archetypal journey into the self."[8] Inheritors of psychological criticism might well examine narrative consciousness in terms of Bakhtin's concept of heteroglossia, as I will attempt to do in the chapter on *The Nigger of the "Narcissus,"* or in terms of Lacan's not-unrelated contention that the unconscious is the discourse of "the Other," a concept that influences my discussion of Marlow in the second chapter.

If biographical criticism has crossed the border into psychology in one direction, it runs headlong into politics in another. Eloise

Knapp Hay writes of the bitter political division within the family of the young Konrad Korzeniowski, whose father, Apollo, espoused revolution against Russian occupation and who died in political exile, leaving Konrad in the care of his conservative maternal uncle, Tadeusz Bobrowski, and thus in an atmosphere of disapproval of his father's cause and values. Such experiences give Conrad's fiction its decidedly political dimension, and perhaps its political ambivalence and hetero-glossia as well. Many readers have sought specific political allegories in his plots, and in response to the critical chestnut that Jim's leap from the *Patna* is a reencoding of Conrad's supposedly guilty flight from his homeland, Hay suggests that instead we equate Jim with Poland, discovering an allegory of Poland's attempted separatist "leap," of which Bobrowski disapproved and with which Marlow (now the Conrad stand-in) must come to terms.[9]

Avrom Fleishman agrees that Conrad's political imagination grows out of the experiences of his homeland, but he argues with Conrad's own designation of that land as Poland. Conrad was born in "an area of the Ukraine . . . which has at best only a marginal claim to being considered Polish," and his emigration "embodied the social problems of his generation," problems of personal and communal identity and of the legitimation of civil authority. To the questioning of the unitary self prevalent in recent theory and anticipated by Glassman, Fleishman adds the question of origins. For Fleishman, Conrad's origins in a landholding gentry are important—Conrad's revolutionary father was really not close to the aspirations of the people, a distance most of Conrad's fiction maintains. The tragic upheavals that divided his homeland and his family were experiences that led, in Fleishman's view, to Conrad's adoption of a conservative, Burkean ideal of the organic community, an ideal that stresses "the priority of the social unit to the individual self."[10] Watt follows Fleishman's lead when he discusses the value of gemeinschaft in Conrad's social model.[11] The threads connecting these studies concern the stability and nature of the subject and the subject's relation to society, issues I will pursue by examining narrative voices—and narrative structure itself—as discursive subjects of political power.

The impact of the political demands of the latter part of the twentieth century on literary studies in English has caused a reassessment of Conrad's own politics in terms of his attitudes toward developing nations and members of other races and cultures. The call to identify ethnocentrism and cultural biases in the Western literary tradition, a project enabled by techniques of deconstructive and suspicious reading, has revealed to many readers a Conrad who was in complicity with some of the more unpleasant attitudes and policies of his time. Chinua Achebe, for instance, equates Conrad with Marlow in *Heart of Darkness* and thereby mounts a scathing assault on Conrad's "racism," and Fredric Jameson, reading texts for their unconscious politics, attacks the conservatism of *Lord Jim* and *Nostromo*. Benita Parry's excellent study also originates in the imperative to reassess our major texts from a less complacently ethnocentric viewpoint; Parry reveals a Conrad struggling to contain profound political contradictions, as seen for example in what she takes to be the simultaneously radical and deeply conservative aspects of *Nostromo*. [12]

To examine Conrad's fiction in terms of the relationship between the individual and the social unit is to inquire into his representations of the moral identity of his characters and into his notion of ethical conduct. In my discussion of *Lord Jim* in the third chapter, therefore, I turn to Alasdair MacIntyre, who, in *After Virtue,* speaks to issues of conduct and virtue in a world that has lost its faith in grand narratives. To speak of matters of ethics and conduct is to believe that the self, however much it has become a subject in relation to the various forms of discipline and power within a society—however much it is socially constructed—can choose and act as a free agent.

In this regard, some critics have seen Conrad as a nihilist; others have seen a healthy, if not sanguine, humanist. These opposing voices in the critical tradition anticipate the more recent question of agency in a postmodern world that challenges traditional notions of self-hood and traditional groundings of belief. Albert Guerard, Thomas Moser, J. Hillis Miller, and Royal Roussel have emphasized the bleakness of Conrad's vision, especially in his early and most consistently ironic writings—*Heart of Darkness, The End of the Tether, Nostromo,* and *The Secret Agent.* According to Daniel R. Schwartz, however, "Conrad's pessimism and nihilism have been over-emphasized, while his humanism has been neglected." Although Conrad posits a morally neutral universe, for Schwartz's Conrad "man can for a time create his own islands of satisfaction and meaning." Murray Krieger, though he grants Conrad's nihilistic "tragic vision" its full scope, argues that Conrad ultimately opts for a more humanistic "ethical vision," a decision that is dramatized in Marlow's drawing back from the abyss into which Kurtz plunges.[13] But, as I will try to show, many of the assumptions in this humanistic tradition are precisely those that Conrad's texts hold up to skeptical examination.

The conflicting assessments of Conrad's political and moral vision speak to the complexities and tensions of the works themselves. With the passing of the New Critical insistence on the wholeness and harmony of the text, the various tensions, contradictions, and fault lines in Conrad's fiction—which exist not because of Conrad's clumsiness but because of inevitable and even enabling features of discourse—increasingly occupy critical attention. Suresh Raval begins one of the best recent books on Conrad with a look at Conrad's well-known formulation of his artistic intentions in the preface to *The Nigger of the "Narcissus,"* the intention to make the reader *see.* Raval persuasively argues that this manifesto has engendered a mistaken emphasis on the imagistic or impressionistic aspects of Conrad's art. The common interpretation of Conrad's ocular metaphor rests on a simplistic understanding of artistic representation and mimesis—on a crude differentiation between what is extrinsic and intrinsic to the text—and this interpretation invokes for its authority a romantic faith in the artist's sincerity. But for Raval, Conrad's imagism, when carefully probed, reveals "the multiple and contradictory features which somehow resist the translucent clarity of an image and the determinacy of a specific and fixed meaning."[14]

Raval is heir to a paradigm shift in critical theory that has been characterized as a "linguistic turn," a radical problematizing of the nature and possibilities of language and representation. Thus he argues that Conrad's narrators "often struggle with the inadequacy of language, striving for a sense of clarity which at times turns out . . . to be unattainable or illusory."[15] This theme has also been explored by William Bonney, who speaks of Conrad's "discontinuous narrative perspectives" and "discontinuous semiotics," and by James Guetti, who finds in Conrad the theme of "the unreality of imaginative structure of any sort."[16] My own analyses will often focus on the struggle of the text to contain the linguistic diversity of the various social discourses that inform the narrative discourse. To problematize language and representation in a literary text is not to ignore historical and social themes, since what is at stake is precisely the nature of their representation, and Conrad's fiction is consistently concerned with themes of morality and community, history and politics. Moreover, these themes are meaningless without reference to those related entities called the subject, the self, or the individual, and Conrad's fiction initiates a radical questioning of subjectivity and selfhood.

Charles Taylor, in his ambitious study of the history of selfhood as a concept in Western culture, enumerates four conceptual obstacles to the "scientific" study of the self, obstacles that derive from the inseparability of selfhood from language and the problematics of representation: (1) an object of scientific study is usually taken "absolutely" or objectively, not in its meaning for the observer; (2) in scientific study, the object's identity supposedly exists independent of descriptions of it; (3) in principle, the object of a science can be represented in explicit description; and (4) in principle, the object of a science can be described without reference to its surroundings. These features, each of which posits firm boundaries between the external and the internal, do not hold for the individual subject (or person) or the discursive subject (or text). One finds one's selfhood in relation to a larger community and to notions of the good that have existence "outside" the self before their internalization by the individual. Selfhood is defined by the significance other things have for the individual. This means that the self is constituted in interpretations and not objective descriptions: it is constituted within a language that can never make its assumptions fully explicit, and the language that can never be made fully explicit is internal to and constitutive of the self.[17] Taylor, then, deconstructs the Enlightenment concept of human beings as the ultimate "subjects" in reference to which an external world of objects must be comprehended and ordered.

As this essentialist, humanist view of the subject has fallen into disrepute in twentieth-century thought, it has given way to a second notion of the subject as constituted within power relations. Narrative authority, as London frames the issue, is "appropriated" by extrinsic interests. No longer a center that orders and governs reality, the subject itself is now seen as governed, as in references to a regime's "subjects." The notion of an autonomous self has become discredited especially among those who feel it carries an inappropriately depoliticized view of human agency. Conrad's texts are themselves products of a historical moment in which the older, humanistic notion of a transcendent, autonomous, and self-determining subject was becoming exhausted and the decentered subject was yet to be as fully theorized as it would soon be in works by such writers as Kafka, Koestler, Beckett, and their heirs. The same could be said of Bakhtin's texts, in which the self retains a center from which free action proceeds, despite the shaping (and subjecting) power of other voices.

Like Conrad's, Taylor's understanding of the subjected self questions certain deeply ingrained Western assumptions concerning the individual's possession of an authentic core that escapes or transcends the shaping powers of mere circumstance or of the external social gaze. Under these assumptions the self has a status similar to that of the heart, brain, or stomach—an objective status not dependent on language and interpretation. This model of the free and autonomous subject, by which our inner thoughts, ideas, and feelings are separated from a world of extrinsic objects—another version of the intrinsic/extrinsic opposition—serves to legitimate social and economic arrangements that involve concepts such as the natural rights of the individual and private ownership of property. But the actual effect of an industrialism that bound people to production was to fragment the subject by driving a wedge between the self that earns a livelihood in the economic system and the self that makes love, raises children, appreciates music, and so on.

The skepticism of many of Conrad's texts concerning the autonomous subject derives from their analyses of Western imperialism's impact on the self, analyses carried out despite the inability of those texts to escape reproducing imperialism's coercive discourse. This skepticism, with its reproductive undertow, is the primary thrust of *Heart of Darkness*, and the question of the subject's social construction remains the crucial concern of *Under Western Eyes*, which, of the five novels I study, is the one whose characters achieve the fullest measure of freedom in the face of the power discourses of others.

Taylor reminds us, in terms appropriate for the student of Conrad's work, that as natural as the familiar inside/outside partitioning of the world appears, the division is also a function of power relations:

> As solid as this localization may seem, and anchored in the very nature of the human agent, it is in large part a feature of . . . Western people. The localization is not a universal one, which human beings recognize as a matter of course, as they do for instance that their heads are above their torsos. Rather it is a function of a historically limited mode of self-interpretation, one which has become dominant in the modern West and which may indeed spread thence to other parts of the globe, but which had a beginning in time and space and may have an end.[18]

This internal "localization" of the subject tends to lose sight of the way the subject is formed by internalizing *external* discourses and *external* structures and hierarchies of a community and of the world. This latter fact is what Stein knows intuitively when he speaks of the problem of "how to be" in the context of finding Jim a position from which to be. That a certain mode of being must be positioned, as Stein and Jim are as dominant Westerners among Easterners, suggests the filiation between imperialism and romantic narratives of selfhood— narratives that exercise their power even as Conrad's texts question them. Because of the factor of positioning and because the subject is formed dialogically, models of the subject always imply a politics; the conflicting definitions of the subject cited above—the transcendent or self-determining subject versus the decentered subject—are confronted in Conrad's fiction in their political dimension, that is, as they relate to such matters as Western imperialist policies and the power of "material interests." The extent to which Conrad's texts stage this encounter, revealing the fragmentation of the bourgeois subject as a function of the dissolution of Western imperialism, is a measure of what we may call, in Raymond Williams's useful term, the "emergent" postmodernism of these texts.

Bakhtin and Lyotard have made crucial contributions to the project of returning narrative study to the political arena by way of questions of the subject. If the subject is constituted in dialogue with others, it is a political event. Furthermore, the language by which the subject is known often assumes a narrative form, positioning the subject in relation to a past and a future. The self, always a project subjected to historical conditions, is therefore within a story—a history (or "her story"). Thus Bakhtin and Lyotard agree that to every poetics of narrative there corresponds a politics.[19] While Bakhtin is primarily a literary critic, discovering the problematic relationship between social discourses and the self within the literary text, Lyotard is a philosopher of culture who discovers the problematics of narrative and the subject across what was once the border of literature, in the territories of scientific, social, and philosophical discourses.[20] To Bakhtin the novel embodies *glasnost;* in its own openness to difference, it is the genre most potentially representative of the open society, and "novelization" is Bakhtin's term for the writing of such openness. By demolishing distinctions between extrinsic and intrinsic discourses, the novel becomes the genre that is the shared space of society's competing voices and accents. This "dialogic" potential is contrasted in Bakhtin's vocabulary with "monologic" discourse, which represents authoritarianism in its attempt to dominate or repress rival viewpoints.

The way in which various social discourses often occupy or share single sentences, phrases, or even words in narrative discourse is demonstrated in Bakhtin's essay "Discourse in the Novel," a demonstration that also becomes a reflection on the dialogic rather than unitary nature of the human subject that is also formed, and therefore to a degree subjected, within the contestation of discourses.[21] The question of who one is can be rephrased as a question of who one talks to and where one positions oneself (in relation to what other speakers, and within what genealogy, what social space, and what narratives of the good). To have a self, in Bakhtin's texts as well as Conrad's, is to enter a conversation, to speak from a position and to an addressee. As the experiences of characters such as Kurtz and

Decoud in their very different ways are meant to show, one cannot be a self alone. In the process of the conversation that creates self-hood and positions the subject, one internalizes or shares the words of others. These various social voices and accents within a supposedly "single" utterance constitute what Bakhtin calls the "heteroglossia" of that utterance.

Bakhtin, whose career began during Conrad's lifetime, suffered internal exile under Stalin for his Christian beliefs. He lived a dialogue between Marxism and Christianity, and his concept of dialogism re-sisted the totalizing tendencies of Marxism much as Conrad resisted totalizing political systems. Conrad's childhood in Poland found him, not unlike Bakhtin, at the center of a dialogue between conservative and revolutionary values, and the political beliefs of Conrad's adult-hood seem often to mingle differing social voices in the novelistic manner Bakhtin describes. Bakhtin, like Conrad, works in the decon-structive tension between traditional theories of the centered self and a postmodern vision of the subject constituted in alien social voices. Bakhtin's emphasis on the multiple, polyphonic nature of the self and of discourse has politically disruptive implications, since the more tra-ditional and less problematic concept of the unitary self has been the enabling fiction not only of many novels but of various structures of authority in society. As the presumed origin, this monologic self controls and limits signification—a control exercised in the interpre-tation of individual texts but also in the construction of genealogies, histories, and institutions.

In his more specialized capacity as literary theorist, Bakhtin initi-ated a dialogue between a formalism that had become vapid and a soci-ology of literature that was too often crude and reductive. He insisted that criticism negotiate between the novel's architectural form and the historical discourses that constitute the novel's molecular struc-ture. Narrative study "must overcome the divorce between an abstract 'formal' approach and an equally abstract 'ideological' approach," and it must concern itself not merely with "private craftsmanship" but with "the social life of discourse outside the novel."[22] These ends are accomplished by deconstructing the monologic or unitary narrative voice, hearing instead the many social or ideological voices not only in the dialogue that is placed between quotation marks, but also in the microdialogues that constitute the narrator as discursive subject.

Bakhtin's monologic discourses, as David Carroll argues, corre-spond to Lyotard's grand narratives, those generalized stories that societies tell themselves in order to legitimate their policies and truth claims. Lyotard focuses on the narrative of Emancipation resulting from the French Revolution and on the narrative of Speculation originating in the German university system. For instance, to legitimate a field of research with the claim that the knowledge produced will contribute to the betterment of humanity is to invoke these grand narratives.[23]

But there are many grand narratives. Political doctrines of all stripes have been energized by apocalyptic grand narratives, from ancient political/religious movements to the powerful secularization of millennial narratives in Marxism. In just about any war one can recall, both sides have invoked grand narratives of the struggle between good and evil. The American civil rights movement of the 1960s gained power and moral authority by association with a narrative of an Exodus and a Promised Land. More generally, the lives of individuals are given a sense of identity and purpose through stories of success, failure, social or economic advancement, and spiritual rebirth. Narrative knowledge, then, is a powerful constituent in the lives of individuals, where it creates a sense of selfhood and identity while at the same time creating subject positions that people can and often must occupy in the narrative of a community's values and actions.

Firmly entrenched narratives can exert repressive regulatory forces while institutionalizing various forms of blindness (for instance, much research does not serve the betterment of humanity, and millennial narratives have often spawned barbarism). Like monologic discourse, the grand narrative can limit and discourage opposing, "politically incorrect" viewpoints. And when Lyotard calls for a dismantling of grand narratives in favor of *petits recits* ("little stories"), local stories that have a subversive or carnivalesque relationship to grand narratives, he is calling for a larger dialogics and a greater openness similar to what Bakhtin describes as polyphony and as the novelization of discourse. At issue is nothing less than the rethinking of the conditions of possibility for justice in a world where all legitimating narratives or theories (Lyotard asserts that all theories are disguised narratives) are suspect. Without such legitimating narratives, Lyotard acknowledges, "one is without criteria, yet one must decide."[24] Carroll further elucidates the nature of Lyotard's ungoverned discourse on justice: "The confrontation of opinions, of little narratives governed by no unique law, purpose, or end, defines the political for Lyotard, and narrative has a relative privilege in this area because it seems to be more overtly embedded in these conflicts than any other genre and in this sense more directly 'political' than other forms of discourse."[25]

Earlier I used the term "nomadic" to refer to various voices or accents from the larger social discourse that enter the language of a narrator or character. These nomadic intrusions can well be "official" aspects of a society's grand narratives. A second kind of nomadicism, then, is found in the little story, the oppositional voice that is not sanctioned by grand narratives—the stories told by Tekla and Sophia in *Under Western Eyes*, for instance, which find their way into the narrator's discourse only to deconstruct his cynical intentions.

Both Lyotard and Bakhtin emphasize the heterogeneity of narrative, a heterogeneity that is itself a reflection of the shared quality of social reality. But this privileging of diversity, and particularly Lyotard's privileging of the nomadic and ungoverned "little story" in its struggle for freedom from the domination of grand narratives, raises again the question of the nature of the subject and of the framing discourses with which it is delimited. Here, too, one must abandon models predicated on oppositions between the outside and the inside, since the subject is an appropriation and internalization of voices that come to one, like Leggatt or Haldin, from beyond the fragile boundaries one erects about one's "self." But the danger of such a view is that the self may seem to become simply an effect of discourse and language games. As Carroll again points out: "Neither Bakhtin nor Lyotard, however, sees this dissemination or dissipation of the social subject in negative terms, for it is not something to be mourned, not a loss to be regretted and whose recovery is nostalgically desired. Each on the contrary will attempt to think this dissipation affirmatively."[26]

Because my study often relies on Lyotard's suspicion of grand narratives, a distrust that he characterizes as "postmodern," I should clarify my use of that widely deployed term. I do not intend to find in Conrad a precursor to all that has been called postmodern, a term that is now ubiquitous in discussions of the late twentieth century—its music, architecture, popular culture, politics, technologies, philosophies, and so on. Often the term refers to a populist revolt against the complexities of high modernism; "talk poetry" revolted against the modernist aesthetic complexities of irony and ambiguity, and "pop art" staged a similar rebellion in visual media. As an antimodernist aesthetic, postmodernism sometimes celebrates the simulacrum—the work that exists in a regress of repetitions rather than as a single original, thereby expressing egalitarian rather than elitist values. Such a work aspires to the condition of Coca-Cola, which is great, Andy Warhol said, because each bottle or can tastes the same. Conrad's own complexities and elitist instincts would hardly anticipate such a postmodern antiaesthetic.

On the other hand, Thomas Pynchon, whose works have something of the elitist status previously enjoyed by the texts of James Joyce, is also called a postmodernist. Pynchon, then, suggests the ways that postmodernism can be defined in its continuities as well as its discontinuities with modernism. Furthermore, whatever position one takes on the relation between modernism and postmodernism can then be articulated, as Fredric Jameson points out, in either a progressive or a reactionary way. Thus, while Pynchon's continuities with modernism might find approval in a progressive perspective, Tom Wolfe's diatribe against modernism in *From Bauhaus to Our House* illustrates the way an assertion of discontinuity between the modern and postmodern can serve reactionary cultural politics. For Jameson, in fact, there are no less than eight positions in the modernism-post-modernism debate.[27]

The postmodernism for which Lyotard is a strong spokesperson is one that seeks to upset the stability of mastering positions by expos-ing discourses of power and exclusion. Such discourses often function as "myth" in Claude Lévi-Strauss's sense, offering imagined reconcilia-tions of real social contradictions. When such discourses are exposed, when their authority is undermined, one is left to experience other-ness free of the familiar distortions of prior representations. Today, the freeing of others from the domination of our signifiers is an impera-tive for membership in a multicultural world community. If, therefore, one takes the fall of the grand narratives of progress and mastery and takes the death of the subject as the dominant postmodern character-istics, there is an emergent postmodernism in Conrad's texts. When, at the end of *The Nigger of the "Narcissus,"* the narrator bids the crew farewell, this moment also commences the long goodbye to authori-tarian and monologic discourses that characterizes the rest of Conrad's career, a career that continuously points to "a crisis of cultural au-thority, specifically of the authority vested in European culture and its institutions."[28]

Another characteristic of postmodern fiction is worth remem-bering when we read Conrad. Linda Hutcheon's important study *A Poetics of Postmodernism* focuses on postmodern "historiographic meta-fiction," fiction that not only is extremely self-conscious, but that con-tains significant reworking of historical materials and persons—for instance, D. M. Thomas's *The White Hotel*, with its representations of Freud and of the horrors of Babi Yar, or Robert Coover's *The Public Burning*, which deals with the execution of the Rosenbergs.[29] Each of the Conrad novels discussed in the following chapters contains refer-ences to historical incidents or people, and each novel draws attention to its own devices in a metafictional way.

The historical context, then, for a discussion of the disruption of hegemonic discourse and the deconstruction of grand narratives in Conrad's texts is the decline of Western sovereignty. As Paul Ricoeur says in a passage that concludes by looking into our own future but that also suggests the world depicted in Conrad's *Lord Jim:*

> When we discover that there are several cultures instead of just one and consequently at the time when we acknowledge the end of a sort of cultural monopoly, be it illusory or real, we are threatened with the destruction of our own discovery. Suddenly it becomes possible that there are just *others,* that we ourselves are an "other" among others. All meaning and every goal having disappeared, it becomes possible to wander through civilizations as if through vestiges and ruins. The whole of mankind becomes an imaginary museum: where shall we go this weekend—visit the Angkor ruins or take a stroll in the Tivoli of Copenhagen? We can very easily imagine a time close at hand when any fairly well-to-do person will be able to leave his country indefinitely in order to taste his own national death in an interminable, aimless voyage.[30]

Conrad's increasing commitment to a politics and ethics of dialogic openness accounts for the difficulty of aligning him with political positions established and bounded within hegemonic Western discourse, since any such position would contain elements of monologic grand narratives of the sort his texts destabilize. Conrad is critical of both conservative authority and utopian revolution, of capitalism and of laborers who refuse to accept their lot. His attack on anarchism in *The Secret Agent* may seem to support liberal democracy, but this support is in turn undermined elsewhere by his skeptical examination of individualism and of the play of material interests within liberal democratic societies. Conrad is intuitively deconstructive in his foregrounding of the faults in various entrenched positions within social life. His own thought, so nomadic as to hardly seem to originate in a monadic subject, refuses to rest within recognized borders. As Raval says: "The attitude implicit in Conrad's political novels would reject Kantian as well as utilitarian principles that seek to articulate a rational plan of social action, just as it would reject the Hegelian as well as Marxist conceptions of determinate laws operating through history."[31]

In the chapters that follow, I will try to show the usefulness of Bakhtin's insistence on dialogism and heteroglossia and of Lyotard's opposition of grand narratives and little stories as ways to understand the contradictions and contests that occur within the discourse of Conrad's fiction. *The Nigger of the "Narcissus"* is a monologic novel with a narrative voice that serves a conservative historical metanarrative; as such it has affinities with *The Secret Agent*, in which each character is diminished and fixed by an overwhelming irony. The narrator of *The Nigger of the "Narcissus"* exercises a powerful control over the viewpoint of his characters, even to the point of rendering them incapable of speech at crucial moments. The movement in the subsequent novels toward something like a postmodern destabilizing of narrative authority is to be measured as a departure from the monologic tendencies of the narrator of *The Nigger of the "Narcissus."*

But to speak of "the narrator" in *The Nigger of the "Narcissus"* and *The Secret Agent*, and in *Nostromo* as well, is to invite the misleading assumption that the narrative discourse always comes from a single, unitary consciousness. Therefore, if one wishes to maintain the convenient notion of "the narrator" in these novels, one must do so under erasure, noting that the narrator is the product of a range of related viewpoints and nomadic discourses that have been internalized to form his conservative (but not entirely consistent or unitary) subject position. In other words, one encounters a fragmented discursive subject that cannot be satisfactorily unified by the formalist's conventions of reading. This heteroglossia provides a way of understanding what has been called the inconsistent or wavering point of view in both *The Nigger of the "Narcissus"* and *Nostromo*. Despite the monologism of the former novel, it has affinities with Bakhtin's nostalgia for a lost time of communal life and group solidarity. Bakhtin posits a "collective" time that is "differentiated and measured only by the events of *collective* life"—a life not unlike the lost organic society in the grand narrative that is implied by *The Nigger of the "Narcissus."* [32]

Marlow's narrative voice, particularly in *Heart of Darkness*, is also an arena of contestation, and the dramatization of Marlow's narrative situation foregrounds the pragmatics of a speaker's relation to an audience—with the question of how our "speech genres," as Bakhtin calls them, are formed as dialogic responses to specific situations and addressees. [33] The distinction in narrative theory between story and discourse, while impossible to maintain as one reads this novel, is nonetheless a useful tool for the analysis of this discontinuous narrative structure. In Lyotard's terms, Marlow attempts a discourse that would subvert imperialism's grand narrative of the enlightenment, progress, and emancipation brought by colonial activity. He would tell a nomadic tale in my second sense of the term. But Marlow finds it impossible to maintain a thoroughly oppositional position, and his "finalization" (another concept developed by Bakhtin) of Kurtz involves a return to one of the grand narratives of Western selfhood, what one might call the grand narrative of sin and redemption. Like the dream that shifts and recedes as it is represented in waking discourse, Marlow's oppositional truth sinks beneath the surface and is lost in the darkness of a secondary narrative revision.

Heart of Darkness and *Lord Jim* explore the nature of the self as it is formed but also subjected within social discourses, which is to say within conversations in a shared language and culture. This exploration takes the negative form of distancing central characters—Kurtz and Jim—from their culture of origin. Further, both novels exist in a space of conflicting forces. Both point forward to a postmodern vision of the dissolution of the subject as they examine the ethical dimension of human agency. As this dimension is traditionally formulated, to be an authentic person is to share in cultural exchanges and to act from one's subjective essence in terms of assumptions about the good. Kurtz's failure can be measured in these terms, and the insistence on the theme of hollowness in *Heart of Darkness* signals the disappearance of the subject of Enlightenment humanism. Thus Conrad's fiction rests on the edge of a paradigm shift in the discourses of the human sciences.

In *Lord Jim*, Marlow's discourse is more nearly "novelized," consisting of Jim-stories, gathered from various sources, that constitute a composite story of Jim's attempt to escape the finalizing and objectifying force of these stories told about him. Indeed, both Kurtz and Jim come to Marlow in various little stories from various sources, accounts that can only be imperfectly totalized in his single narrative. The subtlety of Marlow's discourse in *Lord Jim* lies in its posing of the question of whether Jim is to be understood (or "finalized") as an authentic subject or merely as a decentered ego. This question is reflected in Marlow's own discourse, which struggles to forge a kind of unity from the numerous stories of which it is cobbled together. Marlow's story, to the extent that it is *a* story, approaches Lyotard's notion of the *petit recit*, and his discourse is a meditation on the relation of its many embedded stories to colonialism's grand narrative of conduct and responsibility that Jim violates, and on the further relation of this violation to the emergence of Jim's selfhood.

Since, for Lyotard, to narrate is to assert one's political freedom, narration also imposes ethical obligations on the narrator; this ethical imperative haunts Marlow's narration of the stories of which he has first been the addressee. In fact, *Heart of Darkness* and *Lord Jim* (as well as *Under Western Eyes*) are studies in narrative pragmatics, that is, in the relations between narrators, narratives, and narratees. To study these pragmatics is to examine narrators as subjects who are situated within narrative and constituted in the responses they make to the narratives of others and in the way they position their own narratives.

But this relationship between the subject and the politics of narrative pragmatics is also occluded by the culturally dominant notion of an autonomous self, which Conrad resists. Charles Taylor describes this dominant notion: "Modern culture has developed conceptions of individualism which picture the human person as, at least potentially, finding his or her own bearings within, and declaring independence from, the webs of interlocution which have originally formed him/her, or at least neutralizing them. It's as though the dimension of interlocution were of significance only for the genesis of individuality, like the training wheels of nursery school, to be left behind and to play no part in the finished person."[34]

But the fashioning and subjecting of selves in the dialogic opening of each narrative to other narratives is at the heart of the political and ethical understanding of narrative, an understanding explored in Conrad's fiction by his probing of the limits and inadequacies of language itself. If justice demands for each person the right to narrate, narrative discourse is nonetheless a refracting, not a reflecting, medium, a "symbolic" realm placed between the narratee and an elusive "real." To tell one's story is not a simple matter, even if one is "free to speak" in the everyday sense of the phrase, since the available language exerts a shaping force upon that story even as it is brought into being.

Like *Lord Jim* in its multiplicity of little stories, *Nostromo* denies the possibility of a totalizing, monologic historical discourse, offering instead an image of separate "chronotopes," or time/space configurations. In *Nostromo* the question posed by the earlier novels about the validity of the individualist and postindividualist theories of the human subject is extended into an examination of the possibility of historiography. *Nostromo* scrutinizes the impact of imperial economic expansion on a client state that is characterized by preindustrial social formations and dominated by a foreign ruling class. The impact of capitalism on Costaguana is presented by means of a layering and juxtaposition of chronotopes and by means of an evocation of the differing time-spans in which differing historical narratives situate themselves. Charles Gould's conspicuously naive belief in the better life that will be purchased for this state by material interests—an example of Lyotard's grand narrative of progress and emancipation—contrasts with Conrad's own postmodern suspicion of grand narratives. The subsequent deterioration of Nostromo's self-concept is a moment in the demise of romantic notions of the self in favor of a vision of the decentered subject.

My study concludes by looking at Conrad's most dialogic and

polyphonic novel, *Under Western Eyes,* in which Razumov's consciousness emerges as conversation frees it from the monologic domination
of the discourse of the autocracy. In the process of this emergence, opposing social spaces are deconstructed through a sharing of discourse
that, despite the narrator's cynical beliefs to the contrary, points the
way to cross-cultural understanding, an understanding that is one of
the effects of thinking the dissipation or dissemination of the subject
affirmatively while experiencing the strangeness of our own Western
eyes. And despite all that has been said about Conrad's misogyny, in
both Nathalie and Tekla the novel allows its women their own voices
in opposition to the domination of male discourses. In its last pages,
as it modifies its own formal closure, *Under Western Eyes* refuses to
finalize its characters, leaving instead a vision of the open possibilities
of the future.

J. Hillis Miller argues that Conrad thinks through the nihilism
brought about by humanity's slaying of God, as Nietzsche's madman
describes it in *The Joyful Wisdom,* and that Conrad "prepares the way
beyond it." The slaying of God, according to Miller, is a result of the
privileging of subjectivity that separates human thought from all else:
"The ego has put everything in doubt, and has defined all outside
itself as the object of its thinking." Conrad experiences the implications of the slaying of God and points the way to a transcendence of
nihilism through the establishment of a "human world based on inter-
personal relations." This artistic vision "prepares for the daylight of
later literature."[35] While the question of the death of God occupies a
lesser place in my study, the story I tell of the movement from *The
Nigger of the "Narcissus"* to *Under Western Eyes* is also, like Miller's,
a story of a discovery—a discovery involving the deconstruction of
oppositions between the self and its other in favor of a vision of the
communal nature of selfhood and subjectivity, which is to say a vision
of ourselves as others among others.

These preliminary observations may suggest the differences between my study and Aaron Fogel's *Coercion to Speak,* which also discusses Conradian dialogics and which also locates its own assumptions in relation to Bakhtin. Fogel's study, like those by Parry, Raval,
and Bonney, positions itself within the poststructural problematics of
power discourses and subjugation. Fogel, therefore, refuses to accept
Bakhtin's affirmation of the open, liberating, and humanizing nature
of dialogue, opting instead for a darker vision bred of Fogel's attempt
to fuse the concept of dialogics with a Foucauldian view of power. For
Fogel speech is always forced, something wrung from the subject by

the power mechanisms in which it is entrapped. People are bullied and badgered into speech, and the exaggeration this view entails is indicated in Fogel's assertion that Kurtz's Intended "compels" Marlow to lie to her.[36] And while Razumov perhaps *must* write his spy report, the notion of coercion does not account well for the personal journal upon which most of *Under Western Eyes* is based.

It may seem discourteous to select a single critic with whom to disagree in these introductory remarks, but since Fogel and I define our approaches in ways that are superficially similar, it is appropriate to differentiate them at the outset, however briefly. He and I are in dialogue about the nature of Conrad's dialogics, and the "little stories" we tell are different. I should add that I find Fogel's study to be provocative and important.

My own writing was essentially completed before London's *The Appropriated Voice: Narrative Authority in Conrad, Forster, and Woolf* became available. Her chapter on Conrad deals with *Heart of Darkness*, and her concern with the forces by which the narrator's voice is appropriated parallels my own concerns in many ways. Her analysis of *Heart of Darkness*, however, arrives at conclusions that are different from—though not incompatible with—my own.

I should also say that the names of all critics and scholars occurring throughout these pages and in the notes represent critical positions, not people and colleagues. Like all critical studies, mine is nothing if not dialogic, and I have tried to indicate my debts to other participants in the cultural conversation through the conventional tags of quotation marks and endnotes. But these conventions can suggest in only a crude way the more deeply dialogic nature of my "own" words.

1

The (De)Construction of the Narrator in *The Nigger of the "Narcissus"*

> Only in individualist societies is it so important to control what individuals are and how they behave and think. There it is understood that the society's success or failure, its integration or breakdown, is ultimately determined by the competence and conformity of the individual. As a result much of the effort of modern society goes into constructing appropriate individuals.
>
> John W. Meyer, "Myths of Socialization and of Personality"

I

In the opening dialogue of *The Nigger of the "Narcissus,"* Mr. Baker, the chief mate, and Knowles, the night-watchman, have the following exchange:

> "Are all hands aboard, Knowles?"
> The man limped down the ladder, then said reflectively:
> "I think so, sir. All our old chaps are there, and a lot of new men has come. . . . They must all be there."
> "Tell the boatswain to send all hands aft. . . . I want to muster our crowd." (1)

Baker's depersonalizing speech—the synecdoche of "hands" and the generality of "crowd"—is answered by the friendlier tone of Knowles's "chaps" and "men." Beneath the surface of their conversation a submerged dialogue is heard between conflicting social attitudes and evaluations concerning the crew, who represent the working class in this novel. In the paragraph that follows, the narrator at first refers to the crew as "men," only to modify their humanity by saying they looked like "figures cut out of sheet tin" (1). Within a few lines they become "hands" in the narrator's own discourse, although his first use of that word could be read as indirect citation of the captain's language: "The captain was ashore, where he had been engaging some new hands . . ." (1).

Soon the narrator describes the "hands" as they settle in aboard ship. Other bodily parts are mentioned: "Shore-going round hats were pushed far on the backs of heads . . . ; white collars, undone, stuck out on each side of red faces; big arms in white sleeves gesticulated; the growling voices hummed . . ." (2). Everything is in the plural; no one is seen as a whole person; and no one yet has a name. The "growling" of the voices is hardly human, more the sound of a pack of animals, and "hummed" adds the suggestion of a machine. Snatches of conversation are quoted in which the pronouns "I" and "you," connoting individuality and personhood, occur, but the shifts from speaker to speaker are unmarked. To this point the narrator has conspired with Baker and the captain to rob the crew members of selfhood, and the persons designated by "I" and "you" are subjected by a discourse inimical to the interests of individual working-class men. Soon, of course, some of the crew will receive names and take on a certain individuality; such are the generic demands of the novel, which arose by way of affiliation with notions of the uniqueness of the individual person. This affiliation is problematized by The Nigger of the "Narcissus," not only in its representation of the crew, but more particularly in the question of the identity and subject position of the narrator himself.

Although Aristotle found plot or action to be more essential to tragedy than character, the novel has by and large reversed this hierarchy. As Roland Barthes observes, "In War and Peace Nikolay Rostov is from the start a good fellow, loyal, courageous and passionate, Prince Andrey a disillusioned individual of noble birth, etc. What happens illustrates them, it does not form them."[1] This concept of the subject as a permanent, stable, and unique psychological structure that transcends experience has, however, been challenged by recent developments in the human sciences; this challenge is a theme shared by such practices as psychoanalysis, linguistics, semiotics, deconstruction, and critical theory. For Jacques Lacan the self is always inhabited by alien discourses, like foreign cities within: "The best image to sum up the unconscious is Baltimore in the early morning." For Emile Benveniste the first-person pronoun is discursively necessary but representationally problematical. And it is the exhaustion of a particular concept of the self that Michel Foucault points to when, at the end of The Order of Things, he speaks of the disappearance of man. Since a theory of the text and of the discursive subject implies a theory of the human subject, Barthes, in discussing narrative discourse, poses the question of *who speaks,* concluding that traditional notions of authorship, character, and point of view fail to describe adequately the elaborate free play of voices and codes that constitute textuality.[2]

Mikhail Bakhtin, like these theorists, rejects a model of the self as a totalized and monological entity, although he retains a vision of a center of selfhood that responds to and selects from the various external social voices through which it completes itself. A mingling of social voices of the sort described by Bakhtin and Barthes is found in the narrator's discourse in *The Nigger of the "Narcissus,"* although it is not my argument that this mingling is a direct replication of Conrad's own mental landscape.[3] It will be convenient to refer to "Conrad's" texts, but my analysis attempts (with occasional and localized exceptions or border disputes) to maintain a distinction between the subject of the discourse and the real author. Similarly, it will be convenient to refer to "the narrator," even though I will often question that term's associations with notions of a centered, unitary subject. This questioning will focus on the heteroglossia—Bakhtin's term for speech diversity— within the narrative discourse of *The Nigger of the "Narcissus,"* which will be analyzed in relation to the familiar problem of Conrad's handling of point of view.

Conrad's first two novels depict extremes of isolation, but his third novel, *The Nigger of the "Narcissus,"* emphasizes the bonding of the crew, which must purge itself of disruptive individualism, of progressive values associated with the emancipation of labor and, most obviously, of the black "other." The narrator of this novel is suspicious more of the individualism that in his view supports revolution and anarchy than of the individualism that supports capitalism. Despite his disdain for material interests, his nostalgia for a traditional, organic social order (gemeinschaft) inadvertently supports capitalism by denying the sailors the right to oppose ownership. On the one hand, the narrator asks the reader to see the ship as a social microcosm: "Our little world went on its curved and unswerving path carrying a discontented and aspiring population" (63). On the other hand, the narrator often obscures the political implications of the story. This contrapuntal effect exists in spite of the monologic and totalizing impulses of the narrator, who wages a reactionary opposition to liberal grand narratives of progress and emancipation.

The interests of both ownership and labor are "material," and if individualism can underwrite capitalist authority, so can an assault on the sort of individualism caricatured in Donkin, with his *petit recit* of abuse and exploitation at the hands of ownership and management.

Thus *The Nigger of the "Narcissus,"* which privileges group solidarity over the individual, encourages the silencing of labor in favor of the interests of the larger social group and its managers. One might say this intention exists in the text's political unconscious, although in this novel the intention of constructing, by means of a conservative grand narrative, a subject (and subjected) position for labor hardly seems unconscious at all.

One of the most curious features of the novel is its linking of the black man, Wait, and the spokesman for the emancipation of labor, Donkin, as subtly affiliated threats to order. According to Patrick Brantlinger, themes in the popular literature of the nineteenth century gradually shifted "away from domestic class conflict toward racial and international conflict, suggesting how imperialism functioned as an ideological safety valve, deflecting both working-class radicalism and middle-class reformism into noncritical paths while preserving fantasies of aristocratic authority at home and abroad."[4] *The Nigger of the "Narcissus"* is situated precisely on the boundary of this turn or sublimation. Brantlinger then quotes John MacKenzie's description of the way racial and imperial topics had defused class antagonisms in the popular theater by the end of the century: "By then, imperial subjects offered a perfect opportunity to externalize the villain, who increasingly became the corrupt rajah, the ludicrous Chinese or Japanese nobleman, the barbarous 'fuzzy-wuzzy' or black, facing a cross-class brotherhood of heroism, British officer and ranker together. Thus imperialism was depicted as a great struggle with dark and evil forces, in which white heroes and heroines could triumph over black barbarism, and the moral stereotyping of melodrama was given a powerful racial twist."[5] The way Brantlinger and MacKenzie fix the formulas lurking behind *The Nigger of the "Narcissus"* is all the more remarkable in that neither mentions this novel specifically.

These culturally accepted formulas lend authority to the narrator's voice while simultaneously splitting and appropriating it (and him) for ideological purposes.

An assumption of readers who expect to find a sort of monologic authority in narrative, an assumption that inscribes within aesthetics the grammatical fiction of the transcendent subject or "I," is the belief that narrative point of view must reflect a single, unified consciousness. Faulting Conrad's novel for not adopting Henry James's aesthetic of the bourgeois subject, critics speak of Conrad's "gross violation of point of view."[6] This violation, however, is readable as a troping of the ideological tensions in the social life of discourse surrounding and informing the novel and as a deconstruction of the supposedly unitary self of the narrator. The monologic assumption is that a single narrative voice should dominate and harmonize the voices of the various characters, and that the novel is ultimately the great monologue of the narrator. But to conceive of point of view not merely as a quasi-visual perspective, but in terms of the microdialogue of attitudes and accents occurring within narrators themselves, requires a modification of the notion of a unitary point of view.

Narratology often distinguishes between point of view and narrative voice. Point of view indicates the position from which a story is told, and "position" can be understood in a number of ways; most obviously, it can refer to the physical position of a character and the perceptual limitations such positioning creates, but one can also write from the "point of view" of a character's moral sensibility, practical interests, and so on. Voice, on the other hand, refers to the teller of the story; it is possible to tell a story from a character's perceptual point of view—that of, say, Lambert Strether in *The Ambassadors*—but in a voice or voices that introduce independent evaluations and accents. In *The Nigger of the "Narcissus,"* point of view and voice are closely linked, since the shifts in point of view indicate the various voices or accents in the narrative discourse.

In *The Nigger of the "Narcissus,"* the wavering of the point of view, as traditionally defined in terms of spatial perspective, is a symptom of the heteroglossia that forms the narrator's voice—the discursive subject. The novel is therefore an early instance of the modernist and postmodernist concern with the fragmented self.[7] "Heteroglossia" refers here to the various social accents within the narrator's consciousness, since the narrator makes no serious attempt to enter into dialogue with his characters, and often in fact silences them. His discourse in relation to the characters is entirely "monologic" as Bakhtin uses the two terms.[8]

On the most obvious level, *The Nigger of the "Narcissus"* deconstructs the subject who narrates by juxtaposing a third-person narrative voice that refers to the crew as "they" with a first-person voice that says "we." These two pronouns, reflecting differing attitudinal accents, alternate in an apparently random way that has suggested authorial carelessness to many readers.[9] Furthermore, as R. D. Foulke observes, the first-person narrative voice is itself unstable, fluctuating "between immediacy and retrospection. At times he reports sensations as if they were happening; at other times he evaluates them in the perspective of what is to come."[10] If the "we" voice adopts the perspective of the crew, the third-person or omniscient voice creates a sense of distance, objectifying the crew and making the ship into a sort of panopticon in which nothing escapes narrative scrutiny. In *Discipline and Punish* Foucault stresses the preoccupation of nineteenth-century Western societies with social surveillance, and in *The Nigger of the "Narcissus"* surveillance is the service the narrative performs for imperialist ideology. Surveillance remains crucial in such later novels as *The Secret Agent* and *Under Western Eyes,* but in the latter, surveillance is less the function of the narrative than it is the evil the narrative exposes.

In *The Nigger of the "Narcissus"* surveillance is achieved by way of the wandering point of view, a formal element that the critical tradition, often insensitive to the politics of form, has largely castigated. This effect of surveillance through point of view is exemplified most clearly when, even though no actual observer could have been present, Donkin is seen hovering like a vulture about to plunder the sea chest of the dying James Wait. And elsewhere, conversations among the officers are reported that the "we" narrator, a member of the crew, could not have heard. Displaying a characteristic Bakhtin associates with the monologic discourse of Tolstoy, the novel violates formal consistency in the interest of surveillance—an interest Conrad announces in his preface when he states his intention to make us see. In this regard, Conrad's novel is like the *roman à thèse* described by Susan Rubin Suleiman, a genre written to promote a single social or moral thesis (such as the need for solidarity and hierarchy). Without mentioning Conrad's preface, Suleiman asserts that this genre appropriates from realism the impulse "to *make others see.*" She also describes the *roman à thèse* as the "doctrinaire" and "monological" product of historical moments characterized by "sharp social and ideological conflicts." [11]

Conrad's doctrinaire and monological narrator is himself inhabited by such conflicts. A crewman in real life might refer sometimes to his crew as "we" and sometimes as "they," but such shifts would mark an unconscious ambivalence toward the group. Furthermore, Conrad problematizes the narrator as a subject through the apparently random deployment of pronouns, a randomness that signals a wavering of social attitudes. It is such a nomadic mingling of social attitudes that concepts such as dialogism and heteroglossia (whether applied to novelistic discourse or to the human subject) prompt one to hear, and in this novel the two voices convey the ambivalence of the narrator's glorification of the sailors (so long as they remain obedient) from an aristocratic vantage point that precludes any real identification with them. In what follows I refer to the "we" and "they" narrators as distinct voices, but it should be remembered that such alterity exists within the no-longer unitary or monadic subject. [12]

The most interesting "violation" of point of view occurs in the final pages, when the narrative voice uses the pronoun "I" for the first time. It is as though the dialogic mingling of the two earlier perspectives gives birth to this fully dramatized and individualized narrator, and with his emergence the novel achieves an apparently unequivocal but actually ironic closure, ironic because this "I" narrator is unaware of his own dialogic nature and origins. The thrust of this novel toward the final presentation of the "I" narrator is similar to the narrative work Fredric Jameson discovers in his readings of Balzac, Gissing, and Conrad's Lord Jim and Nostromo, "the construction of the bourgeois subject in emergent capitalism." [13] Since The Nigger of the "Narcissus," moving from multiple and fragmentary voices to the singular, individualized narrator, analyzes and deconstructs this construction, the novel may be read as an anatomy of the unitary subject that exposes the subject's construction within imperialism's authoritative narratives. [14]

Ian Watt addresses the problem of the narrative voice's (or voices') mode of existence in The Nigger of the "Narcissus" when he refers to the choral function of the narrative: "There must be a plurality of voices, and not an individualized narrator, because the function of a chorus . . . is to achieve what Yeats called 'emotion of multitude.' " [15] Watt's plurality suggests Bakhtin's "diversity of social speech types," which constitutes the fabric of novelistic narrative by providing a mingling of "points of view on the world." [16] But within a few paragraphs Watt seems to contradict himself by falling back on the assumption that the entire novel issues from the consciousness of a single, marginally dramatized but unitary narrator. Nonetheless, his observation that the novel depicts society in transition is essential for an understanding of the novel's dialogic voices or viewpoints on the world.

The grand narrative, or metanarrative, underlying this novel, according to Watt, is a story of the historical shift between the two states named by the title of Ferdinand Tönnies's 1887 book Gemeinschaft und Gesellschaft. [17] Gemeinschaft (community) is a hierarchical social formation in which membership in such groups as family or village is obligatory and presumed to be "natural." Such a formation is similar to the lost collective or folk time Bakhtin speaks of in his essay on chronotopes. [18] Gesellschaft (society) is a horizontal social formation in which membership in such groups as trade unions or political parties is optional and in a sense "cultural." In gesellschaft, the interests of the various groups may be in conflict with one another and with the larger and now-residual community values. Gesellschaft is the social context of the modern novel, since, as Bakhtin argues, "the flowering of the novel is always connected with a disintegration of stable verbal-ideological systems and with an intensification and intentionalization of speech diversity."[19] Of course, the ideal community represented by the word "gemeinschaft" may never have existed in its theoretical purity, but such concepts, like Edmund Burke's "organic society," are necessary to a grand narrative that provides an ideological position from which to critique the present.[20]

The two social formations are in opposition throughout *The Nigger of the "Narcissus."* Individualism and special interests assert themselves when Belfast steals from the officers' table, when tools necessary for the maintenance of the ship are carelessly lost during the search for Wait, and when the helmsman leaves the wheel during the incipient mutiny. Such interests are suggested by the more individualistic tone of the "they" narrator, who experiences his own identity in opposition to the group. But older, communal claims assert themselves when the cook braves the storm to make coffee, when the crew fights the gale and forgets about Wait, and when Singleton stays at the wheel alone for thirty hours. The "we" voice suggests such community. An appeal to the special interests of the crew is heard in Donkin's call for mutiny, but the crew itself, recalling traditional values and refusing to define itself in opposition to management, rejects Donkin's leadership. The wavering of the point of view between the omniscient and the personal and between the plural and the singular reflects, within narrative form, the thematic opposition between a world perceived communally and one viewed from the perspective of a particular interest. The clash of these two social formations, together with the internal competition of voices within gesellschaft itself, generates the heteroglossia of the narrative. The self is formed socially and is never entirely removed from "extrinsic" social discourses; the instabilities of the narrator's self, evident in the wavering point of view, reflect the competing voices of his world.

The novel opens with the many conflicting voices of gesellschaft, Bakhtin's "speech diversity." We hear the crewmen bickering over prices with the Asiatics who have rowed them to the ship: "The feverish and shrill babble of Eastern languages struggled against masterful tones of tipsy seamen," and "howls of rage and shrieks of lament" are raised (1). Solidarity and imperial authority are asserted in the superiority, even when tipsy, of "masterful" Western tongues to Eastern tongues. But Belfast and Donkin immediately imply that the crew should define its interests in opposition to management, and Donkin further attempts to pit English speakers against "furriners" (7), irrationally threatening the very unity of the crew he wishes to organize against the officers.[21] The end of such a process, the novel seems to argue, would be a world in which individual will battles individual will, all legitimate order lost. Thus the heteroglossia of the ship creates a field of centrifugal and centripetal forces within the social unit that is forming across linguistic, national, and racial boundaries; Conrad's novel contains a speech diversity that reflects the inevitable ideological differences in a period of colonialism and expansionism, when, according to Bakhtin, "a national culture loses its sealed-off and self-sufficient character, when it becomes conscious of itself as only one among *other* cultures and languages."[22]

But not only is the reality to which the story refers many-tongued, the narrative discourse itself speaks in many voices. The term "story" in narratology refers to the events as they supposedly "really" happened and in their chronological order; "discourse" refers to the various effects of presentation, including plotting (which can violate chronology, repress events, and so on), point of view, and the narrator's evaluative language. The internal voices or microviewpoints within the narrator's discourse constitute evaluative accents that are structural responses to the competing voices in the world the narrative describes. Lyotard's concepts of the grand narrative and the little story must be understood as elements that can occur within the narrator's evaluative "discourse," not exclusively in the author's "story." The slippage in the use of the word "story" as one moves from literary narratology to Lyotard is unfortunate but should not be confusing.

The internal accents or voices in the discourse of the narrator of Conrad's novel—voices that, in London's terms, "appropriate" the narrative authority—include:

1. The ethnocentric voice, which elevates things Western, as in the opening reference to the "masterful tones" of even tipsy seamen in their relation to "the feverish and shrill babble of Eastern languages." The perception that one occupies a place of mastery or authority in the world is the founding assumption of most Western discourses on conduct and order in the nineteenth century—on what it means to be "one of us," as Marlow will say in *Lord Jim*. This perception provides a background rationale for the marginalization of Wait and the exclusion of Donkin, as well as for the glorification of labor in the service of capital; thus it could be taken as a kind of center around which the other voices revolve.

2. The literary voice, endowing the ship—and by extension the Western mercantile project—with symbolic significance by comparing it to a planet carrying "an intolerable load of regrets and hopes" (18). Under a powerful set of aesthetic assumptions, an invocation of the

literary code usually directs the reader to ignore the text's implication in matters of ideology and power. Sir Philip Sidney removed the poem from such entanglements by telling the story of the poet who "nothing affirms, and therefore never lieth," [23] and such depoliticizing of reading was further encouraged by notions of disinterestedness advanced by Immanuel Kant and Matthew Arnold. I. A. Richards's "Doctrine in Poetry" is an influential New Critical reformulation of the myth of the nonpolitical text. Terry Eagleton traces the Victorian age's version of this metanarrative back to the Romantic poets, who, despite their political activism, emphasized "the sovereignty and autonomy of the imagination, its splendid remoteness," a remoteness that offers the writer and the reader "a comfortingly absolute alternative to history itself." [24] While all literature obviously does not ignore political and social realities, the notion of a "literary" voice refers to that tendency in aesthetic theory to distance art from history.[25] This notion is consistent with the tendency of The Nigger of the "Narcissus" to obscure the question of the geopolitical role of the British Merchant Service.

3. The paternal voice, a mildly snobbish modulation of the literary voice. The paternal voice may seem hostile to community, as when it narcissistically wonders what books can mean to "big children" like Singleton (3), but its purpose is to create a subject position for labor within the capitalist order. It narrates a tale of God acting on sailors "paternally, to chasten simple hearts—ignorant hearts that know nothing of life . . ." (19). "They" are "obstinate and childish" (20). The word "children" recurs often in reference to the crew as seen by the "they" narrator, and the paternal aspects of the conservative grand narrative are inscribed in the title of the first American edition of the novel, Children of the Sea.

4. The idealizing voice, praising Singleton as the last of the heroic laborers, one who "steered with care" for thirty hours during the storm (55). This voice is close to the paternalistic voice, since Singleton is being praised by a superior; it is Singleton's childlike obedience that makes him worthy of heroic elevation. For the narrative discourse to discredit Donkin convincingly, the crew as well as the narrator must perceive his corruption. Singleton, obedient to the conservative will of this discourse, pronounces a "Damn you!" on Donkin and is rewarded with praise from the narrator for his "unspeakable wisdom" (80). Singleton's obedience to the will of the narrator is an especially clear example of the effect of monologic narrative intentions as Bakhtin describes them in his study of Dostoevsky. The ethical idealism governing this narrative voice in Conrad's novel assumes the existence of a transcendent realm of value by which action should be governed

and judged. Such assumptions, as is illustrated here, can serve political and economic arrangements. Ethical idealizations are, therefore, a form of reification, justifying specific human relations by encoding them in a metanarrative that serves hegemonic interests and that grants those interests an independent and universal status.

5. The historian's voice. A modulation of the idealizing voice, the historian's metanarrative eulogizes the sailors of the past, remembered by Singleton, who "knew not fear, and had no desire of spite in their hearts" (15). If "well-meaning" liberals would write a history stressing the hardships these sailors suffered (15), the novel's discourse offers a conservative counter-memory, a revision of liberal history that stresses the sailors' valor in a mythical era of adventure that is free of modern economic and social concerns.[26] This voice is a dominant accent of the "I" narrator who concludes the novel. As history is viewed under paternalistic and idealizing eyes, Singleton and Donkin become opposing ideologemes (the loyal worker and the cowardly agitator) in the conservative, monologic discourse of the novel.[27] The historian's voice resonates with the grand narrative of a Fall: the heroic sailors of the past were at one with their society, subjects who had no individual psychology that separated them from communal life; now, however, they are merely individuals and a threat to the solidarity of the community. The fact that the discursive subject's complicity with the material interests of shipping is a complicity with the capitalistic system that brought about the Fall is, perhaps, the central contradiction of that discourse.

6. The moralizing voice, damning Donkin for being "lazy" and "inefficient," for "cheating," for "cadging," and assuring us that Donkin's misfortune is "deserved" (5). This moralistic accent discredits the political position Donkin represents by depicting him as an inauthentic man of resentment (anticipating the Montero brothers in *Nostromo*), and it later accuses the crew members of a "sentimental lie" in their concern for Wait (96).[28] The attempt to put that concern in a negative moral category shows how moral categories can be used as disguised political weapons—what is dangerous in the sympathizing of the white working class with other racial or ethnic groups is that it could be the start of a new, revolutionary coalition. Setting itself *against* such "solidarity," the moralizing voice intersects and reinforces the accents of snobbery and paternalism in words such as "children." Hayden White's comments on historical narrative suggest that a moralizing voice may be essential to all narrative: "If every fully realized story . . . is a kind of allegory, points to a moral, or endows events, whether real or imaginary, with a significance that they do not pos-

sess as a mere sequence, then it seems possible to conclude that every historical narrative has as its latent or manifest purpose the desire to *moralize* the events of which it treats."[29]

7. The voice of law and order—a modulation of the moralizing accent—which warns that "discipline" and "the sense of hierarchy" are dangerously weak on merchant ships (9). To the extent that this conservative voice politicizes the story, it exists in tension with the depoliticizing tendencies of the literary voice. Discussing the "intimate relationship that Hegel suggests exists between law, historicality, and narrativity," White says that "we cannot but be struck by the frequency with which narrativity, whether of the fictional or the factual sort, presupposes the existence of a legal system against or on behalf of which the typical agents of a narrative account militate."[30] The narrative voice sometimes reports the legalistic discussions Donkin foments among the crew by calling attention to things "unjust and irremediable" (63), while at other times the narrative discourse sides with management and labels the crew "a community of banded criminals" (96).

8. The absent voice of liberal reform, to which the narrative seems to respond as though to an implied reader. The narrative discourse responds to those "philanthropists" who would be charitable to Donkin (6), and to those "well-meaning" reformers who would misrepresent the sailors of the past by dwelling on their hardships in an effort to harmonize history with reform ideology (15) and who do not recognize that the hard lot of a sailor is actually the gift of "justice," "perfect wisdom," and "eternal pity" (55). To the extent that the discourse is oriented toward such a liberal or reformist audience, even as a rebuttal, the voice of that audience is "present" in the discourse.

These voices constitute a spectrum of subject positions from which the story is enunciated, and they reveal the overdetermination of novelistic discourse by mechanisms of power. They are internal to the narrative discourse and, like the voices of the crew in the story, are dispersed between the boundaries of gemeinschaft and gesellschaft, the communal world and the fractured world. They constitute the various judgmental and ideological accents or microdialogues within a narrative discourse that, like Tolstoy's discourse as Bakhtin describes it, monologically dominates and manipulates the characters to form a political allegory. Such judgments seem inappropriate to the "we" narrator who is a crewman and also to a novel that claims to want to make us "see," since these judgments obscure our vision with a rhetorical haze. The suspicious reader must listen *to* the narrative's social discourses rather than simply see what it directs us to see. It may have been the verbal ambience of discourse that engulfs the story, transgressing the boundaries between story and world, that Conrad later had in mind when he wrote in *Heart of Darkness* that the true meaning of Marlow's tale was "outside, enveloping the tale which brought it out only as a glow brings out a haze . . ." (5).

Most of these voices or accents—the ethnocentric, the literary, the paternal, the idealistic, the historical, the moralistic, and the legalistic—are heard in the following descriptive passage, in which a moment is given literary heightening not only by its climactic positioning in the plot but through hyperbole: "lost forever in the immensity of their vague and burning desire." But at the same time, another voice disengages itself conservatively (saying "they" rather than "we") from the aspirations of the sailors, condescending to these aspirations from a paternalistic and moralistic platform. Captain Allistoun has just asked the disgruntled crew what it wants, and now he stands as both father and judge before childlike, fidgeting malefactors: "What did they want? They shifted from foot to foot, they balanced their bodies; some, pushing back their caps, scratched their heads. What did they want? . . . They wanted great things. And suddenly all the simple words they knew seemed to be lost forever in the immensity of their vague and burning desire. They knew what they wanted, but they could not find anything worth saying. They stirred on one spot, swinging, at the end of muscular arms, big tarry hands with crooked fingers" (82).

It is significant that at the moment the crewmen are asked to speak for themselves they become mute, as though their own voices must not be allowed to modify the visual image of their childlike helplessness. Here this conservatively biased narrative discourse, which at a crucial moment enacts (contra Aaron Fogel) a coercion to silence, offers another example of the monologic domination Bakhtin describes as being the antithesis of the freedom Dostoevsky grants his characters.[31] One recalls that an aspect of Singleton's quasi-heroic stature is his almost- complete reticence.

Although Fogel contends that Conrad is always sympathetic to labor, the narrative voice Conrad creates in this novel certainly is not; though Captain Allistoun tries to coerce the speech of the crew, the narrator's biases are served by representing the crew as wordless and confused.[32] Apart from Donkin, whom the discourse thoroughly discredits, only the narrative discourse itself is allowed to speak of the crew's interests and conditions. The narrator's view of these conditions is made clear in the opening paragraph of chapter 4, an encomium to the "privilege" of endless "toil" and "pain" bestowed by the paternal "justice" of the sea, a surrogate for the otherwise-absent and dubious authority from which such unashamed glamorizing of the sweatshop emanates. The sea, as invoked by the literary voice, conceals the origin of paternalistic power by becoming its surrogate. This symbolic manipulation shows how literary representation can exercise *its* power by denying its political status. Although Conrad's narrators will continue throughout his career to extol the virtues of work, they will not in the future portray it in contexts that so blatantly support exploitation.

In this narrator's depiction of the sailors as laborers, various social "languages" interact with one another. Such dialogism, Bakhtin says, bears a "subjective, psychological and (frequently) random character, sometimes crassly accommodating, sometimes provocatively polemical. Very often . . . this orientation toward the listener . . . interferes with the word's creative work on its referent."[33] This interference is seen in the narrative's polemics against Donkin and, at times, against the crew, as well as in the way the shifting point of view responds to external belief systems. For instance, the third-person point of view modifies the reform-minded reader's predisposition to sympathize with the crew's initial charity toward Donkin: "He knew how to conquer the naive instincts of *that crowd*. In a moment *they* gave him their compassion" (7, my emphasis). But the first-person plural brings the more conservative reader closer to the crew's confused subservience to Wait: "He demonstrated to *us* daily *our* want of moral courage; he tainted *our* lives" (29, my emphasis).

Such discursive judgments are structured into the plot, which acts as a mechanism of surveillance, discipline, and exclusion, first exposing, then expelling the enemies of order. One enemy of the European mercantile community, Donkin, represents an internal threat; the other, Wait, represents the threat from beyond the border—the threat of disorder generated by sympathy for the racial or ethnic outsider. This sympathy is moralistically criticized by a discourse that insists that such sympathy is paradoxically a form of self-pity. If the novel depicts a tension between a world conceived as a community and a world viewed through the lens of self-interest, a conservative version of communal values apparently triumphs with the expulsion of Donkin and Wait. The answer to the question posed early in the novel—"Is Wait really sick and will he die?"—of course, is yes: he is sick because dominant interests often pathologize the other, and he will die because the narrative will kill him. But the first-person narrator, who at the end of the novel replaces the "we" and "they" narrator(s), ironically undercuts these triumphant expulsions. He does so not only because of his *own* literal separation from the crew, but because his language reveals him to be inhabited by interests hostile to the welfare of the crew, the interests of a divisive individualism. It is as though he is an image or figure rising out of the unconscious of the preceding narrative discourse, a function rather than an origin of that discourse.

This shift in narrative voice, then, is not an arbitrary technical wavering but rather a troping of the drift toward individualism and fragmentation in the world the story depicts. The earlier narrative, with its movement between "we" and "they," alerts the reader to heteroglossia and signals oppositions one now finds within "I." By withholding the "I" voice until the earlier heteroglossia is established in our ears, the narrative structure prompts us to hear discord in this "I" when he finally appears.[34]

II

From the narrator's conservative perspective, the ship and its crew, while at sea, become a partially independent world with some chance for purity and community. But these hopes are infected by Donkin and Wait and further tainted by the ship's affiliation with the commercial interests of the land. The narrator occasionally alludes to these interests, but at other moments ignores them—we do not, for instance, ever learn what the ship's cargo is. This conflict gives rise to the mixed viewpoints of the middle chapters. But in the end the *Narcissus* is reunited with the sordidness of the land, and the babble with which the novel opens is now amplified. As the tug pulls the ship into port, "a low cloud hung before her—a great, opalescent and tremulous cloud, that seemed to rise from the steaming brows of millions of men. . . . On all sides there was the clang of iron, the sound of mighty blows, shrieks, yells" (101). The sea tale is framed by the land and especially by references to the babble and shriek of its many voices. This frame, while not literally external to the work, turns toward the larger world in which the novel is situated. But, as Frow says of frames in general: "The mere fact of the convergence of the internal structure and the contextual function of the text at the 'edge' of the text indicates that the frame does not simply separate an outside from an inside but unsettles the distinction between the two."[35]

Appropriately at this framing moment, the communal narrative voice gives way to an individual "I," unsettling the distinction between community and self. If the function of ideology is to construct subjects, *The Nigger of the "Narcissus"* lays bare this process by first establishing the discursive voices that weave together to form the ideological text from which an "I" emerges as a subject. This process denies the traditional assumption that the subject preexists its expression in language; language is now constitutive and does not simply represent a prelinguistic subject. This "I" is born out of the spectrum of subject positions mapped by the earlier heteroglossia. No sooner does this child of gesellschaft appear amidst the discords of capitalism than he tells us that he "disengaged [him]self gently" from the community of sailors (106), keeping figurative company with other, now-disengaged enemies of community—Belfast, Donkin, and Wait. His admission should give us pause, and within a few paragraphs of his birth and disengagement he becomes unreliable, describing the crew in a sentimental discourse reminiscent of Sea Scouts at summer camp, who give back "yell for yell to a westerly gale" (107).

His eloquent but blind praise of the crew reflects the noncoincidence between his selfhood and the world. Unlike the "we" and "they" narrator(s) he has supplanted, he knows nothing of the crew's errors, self-pity, and near mutiny, and he reproduces the "sentimental lie" (96) and the "chorus of affirmation" of falsehood (86) of which the earlier discourse had accused the crew. The "we" narrator had criticized the crew, saying, "And we were conceited. We boasted. . . . We remembered our danger, our toil—and conveniently forgot our horrible scare" (61). But the "I" narrator has conveniently forgotten such criticisms. He is one of those "well-meaning" people who rewrite history, although his ideology is different from that of the liberal reformers who would revise Singleton's memories to suit the labor movement. His rewriting of history is also a self-authorship that is influenced by ideological pressures prompting him to glorify the Merchant Service.[36] His final depiction of the crew as an idealized band of heroic companions is the logical result of the death and expulsion of the black other, the "fuzzy- wuzzy" who, according to the formula described by Brantlinger and MacKenzie, was used in popular literature to deflect awareness of domestic and class issues.

Whereas the ideologues of liberal reform alluded to earlier in the novel depict the supposedly devoted and faithful sailors of Singleton's memory as bemoaning their oppression, our new conservative ideologue depicts modern sailors (purged of the internal and external threats represented by Donkin and Wait) as happy and heroic. "Facts" are time-dependent, which is to say that what is remembered and what is forgotten can vary at different points in a life, in history, or (as here) in a narrative. But now it is not only liberal history that is revised; the "I" narrator's version of history is also a counter-memory to the one we have just read. Although he paints a different picture from the "hard and unceasing" toil (55) described earlier by the "they" narrator, the interests "I" serves are similar to those unconsciously served by his predecessors, and his voice is similarly paternalistic and "literary." Falsehood triumphed once among the crew; now, in the discourse of the crew's historian, it repeats that triumph. He imagines Donkin "discoursing with filthy eloquence upon the right of labor to live" (107), but his own eloquence, like that of the preceding narrators, is no less tainted by special interests.

His kinship with the earlier narrative voices arises from their all speaking for the interests of ownership rather than labor, each voice or accent being a constituent of the novel's "single" monologic grand narrative. The "we" voice is only too ready to criticize the crewmen (and therefore himself), particularly in their moments of self-awareness as alienated laborers, and he consistently sets his face against social change. His complicity with management and ownership is glimpsed when he romanticizes Captain Allistoun, who, as Foulke convincingly argues, is much more concerned with the speed of the passage than with the welfare of the crew, since he refuses to cut the masts (the recommended safety procedure for a ship on its beams, but one that would require time-consuming repairs before the passage could be completed), instead choosing to send a number of men into the danger of resetting the sails in the wind-lashed rigging.[37] Whereas the "we" narrator represses Allistoun's role in capitalistic domination, the "I" represses any mention of the crew's discontent, wrapping the men in a romantic haze and blinding his audience to the crew's deplorable working conditions. In other words, his strategy is different from that of the "we," but both narrators produce (or reproduce) a rhetoric that is implicated in the oppression of the sailors. And this is the same master served by the omniscient narrator who waxes literary about "the full privilege of desired unrest" (55) as people are dropping from exhaustion. "I" is unaware of these now-forgotten accents in the novel's discourse, and he presents himself unproblematically as the "brother" of the workers; he is, therefore, a locus of a tension between binding communal energies and the fragmenting power of special interests.

A person's ideological becoming is a process of selectively internalizing the words of others. This proposition from Bakhtin parallels his ideas concerning narrative. Just as a narrative is a point of interaction between an author and the belief systems of his or her culture and readership, so the self too is a hybrid, a place of interaction between an inner subjectivity and the other. Authorship, to Bakhtin, is therefore a metaphor for our self-fashioning; people, like novels, are dialogic, and we experience our being as a gift from others: "Consciousness is always co-consciousness."[38]

These ideas describe the "I" narrator's emergence from the discourse of the other narrators—in his kinship with these other voices as well as in his difference—and we may think of him as representing, if not Conrad himself, then the idea of the self-authoring author. Glassman points out the narrator's refusal or inability to join the crew in the end: "No one speaks to him. No one calls him by name. No officer gives him a parting word."[39] And Glassman directly equates, perhaps with too much pathos, the narrator's isolation with his author's: "For as we read *The Nigger* are we not invited to speculate how many times in his sea-going life Conrad must have taken to ship to flee from his own tormented idea of himself? And are we not meant to wonder on how many filthy quays of how many sordid ports Conrad himself must have stood while less complicated men rushed off to drink, chattering in English, without care or farewell for their alien mate?"[40]

Whether or not one identifies the "I" narrator with Conrad, it is clear that the narrator is a flawed storyteller, and his error is his inability to recognize his debt to other voices. There is something deluded in his "literary" pose of disengagement. He is speaking the discourse of an Other but is not aware that this Other, like Lacan's foreign city within, is the very economic system he seems to scorn. So while we hear the voice of sympathy for the "lost, alone, forgetful and doomed" crewmen (107), the "I"'s final romanticizing of the conditions of their labor implicitly supports their exploitation.[41] Thus he is a dialogic construct. Indeed, his own fiction of individuality and disengagement is found also in the discourse of capitalistic ownership, and it has ironic filiation with Donkin's rhetoric of individual rights and withdrawal from the social contract (a contract that benefits the upper strata of society far more than the lower), as well as with Wait's self-pity. The tale underlines this filiation by showing that Donkin, Wait, Belfast, *and* the narrator all become detached from the social unit. In narratological terms, the *story* of the narrator's separation undermines his *discourse* of solidarity.

As the "I" narrator emerges, the sailors wander from the Shipping Office to the Black Horse Pub, reenacting the exchange system of getting and spending. The Black Horse dispenses "illusions of strength, mirth, happiness" (106), offering the workman his hour of escape and his easy reward, from which, as Glassman observes, the narrator is excluded. Between the poles of the Shipping Office and the Black Horse Pub we see the Mint, "like a marble palace in a fairy tale" (107), suggestive of the unapproachable origin of the wealth that eludes the sailor, and we see the Tower, a place of discipline and punishment for those who run afoul of the system. These four buildings represent the cornerstones of a social and economic system—the Mint and the Shipping Office create money and dispense wages; the Tower and the Pub threaten discipline and offer consumable rewards.

The secret complicity of the narrative discourse, in its various voices and accents, with this system explains the "I" narrator's otherwise-curious whitewashing of the Mint in a rhetoric that bathes it in romantic light rather than in the darkness Conrad elsewhere associates with material interests—a darkness that swallowed the coins in the Shipping Office only a page earlier. Here, instead, it is the workers who are "dark": "And to the right of the dark group the stained front of the Mint, cleansed by the flood of light, stood out for a moment dazzling and white like a marble palace in a fairy tale" (107). This image of the Mint opposes the rhetoric we have heard concerning materialism, and the inconsistent handling of light and dark values recalls the earlier wavering between the "we" and "they" narrators; it is as though the "I" narrator has internalized their dialogue of viewpoints, which he now manifests in his visual description.

Within the narrative's manifest content and structure, then, the emergence of the "I" narrator reflects the pressure of bourgeois values in the narrative's political unconscious, or, as Bakhtin would say, its unofficial consciousness.[42] In producing this narrator, Conrad's plot completes the function Bakhtin accords to plot in general: "The plot itself is subordinated to the task of coordinating and exposing languages to each other. The novelistic plot must organize the exposure of social languages and ideologies, the exhibiting and experiencing of such languages."[43]

In Conrad's novel, this exposure is completed with the "I" narrator, who represents the paradoxes of the conservative author apparently trying to write sympathetically about labor in an age of capitalism and individualism. To Conrad, perhaps, he is an alter ego, a parodic reminder of the blindnesses that enable the author's vision. Gesturing in his rhetoric toward a story of a happy, harmonious crowd of brothers that never was, he nonetheless remains aloof from that crowd; his aloofness establishes a boundary and a position from which to maintain his ideological metanarratives, but it is also a function of the aesthetic code by which the "literary" is presumed to remain aloof from the interests of the workaday world, while often maintaining complicity with its ruling interests. His parting tribute to the sailors is a nostalgic attempt to rewrite their history according to the grand narrative and lost values of organic community, but in fact his own position of writing or telling is that of the disengaged contemporary author. He is the culmination of the tendency within the Romantic imagination to forge, as Eagleton says, an absolute alternative to history itself. His nostalgia seems to offer a critique of a fragmented capitalistic society, but it actually supports that system by obscuring real social contradictions behind fictional reconciliations: "Haven't we, together and upon the immortal sea, wrung out a meaning from our sinful lives? Goodbye, brothers! You were a good crowd. As good a crowd as ever fisted with wild cries the beating canvas of a heavy foresail; or tossing aloft, invisible in the night, gave back yell for yell to a westerly gale" (107).

The narrator has not, however, escaped the drift toward individualism and illusion that his rhetoric of solidarity would seemingly oppose, and in a deeply ironic and significant way his own illusion of the organic crew depends on his disengagement from the crew and on the capitalistic interests that have replaced organic community. That is, his position as conservative ideologue is grounded in some of the very realities of fragmentation and separation he laments. Our notion of a unitary author or narrator dissolves in the recognition that the text replicates the conflicts and contradictions of its society. The product as well as the producer of a text, Conrad's narrator is written by the discourses of his time, even as those discourses labor to conceal their authorship behind the fictions of "the literary," of the individual point of view, and of the unitary subject.

III

The three-phased drift in point of view—from the omniscient, to a blending of the omniscient and the subjective, to the fully individualized—can itself be read as a sort of metanarrative, a reflection of a hypothetical historical drift from organic community, to a transitional balance between gemeinschaft and gesellschaft, to a society characterized by the clash of special interests. Within this drift one hears the dialogic harmonies and dissonances of the various voices of those interests. Furthermore, the fictive narrator-author who emerges at the end of The Nigger of the "Narcissus" could be an uneasy and by no means literal mirroring of the authorial persona Conrad himself was adopting in the third of the "three lives" that Frederick Karl describes.[44] After the publication of Almayer's Folly and The Outcast of the Islands, the public in its misreading saw Conrad as merely a spinner of romantic adventure yarns, and the narrator, whose final romanticizing obscures the truth of the crew's behavior, is a fictive version of such an author.

This narrator may reflect Conrad's uncomfortable awareness of how the authorial voice is shaped in response to its readership. Although according to the preface the artist should make us see, the author who is shaped by public demand may be serving a societal will to blindness. To some degree this romanticizing narrator is a spokesperson for Conrad's own conservative ideology, but there is also an ironic distance between this narrator and the inferred author of this particular novel—"inferred author" being a term I prefer to the more familiar "implied author."[45] So if Conrad's own conservatism does enter the narrator's discourse, this would point to the inferred author's reservations about that ideology. One infers, therefore, an author who was uneasy with the conservative ideology expressed in the personal correspondence of the man Joseph Conrad around the time of the writing of this novel.

Wayne Booth exposes the chimera of authorial neutrality while criticizing the modernist opposition between telling and showing.[46] The fiction of objective seeing is an "alibi," in the sense Barthes uses the term in *Mythologies*, for a concealed ideology.[47] Conrad's need in the preface to hold a nonideological view of his often stridently ideological art is reflected in the oddly intransitive use of the verbs *to hear*, *to feel*, and *to see*, coupled with the intrusively author-itarian *to make*: "My task . . . is, by the power of the written word to make you hear, to make you feel—it is, before all, to make you see" (147). Putting vision at the head of the class of senses as the privileged representative of cognition and knowledge is traditional in Western literature and philosophy. But in "The Age of the World Picture," Martin Heidegger relates the notion of the world as picture to specifically modern forms of mastery and power, in which phenomena gain their very existence by virtue of representations—and therefore by virtue of the subject who represents: "The fundamental event of the modern age is the conquest of the world as picture. The word picture [*Bild*] now means the structured image [*Gebild*] that is the creature of man's producing which represents and sets before. In such producing, man contends for the position in which he can be that particular being who gives the measure and draws up the guidelines for everything that is."[48] The "to make you see" of the preface is a logical correlative of the monologic quality of the novel, which dominates its characters through surveillance and even through rendering them mute before the narrator's gaze.

However, the assumption of the preface that the auditory ("to make you hear") and the ocular ("to make you see") exist in an easy and natural congruence, inevitably revealing the same reality, requires examination. What one hears in this passage, if we supplement the word *power* with an accentuation of the word *make*—"by the *power* of the written word to *make* you hear . . . to *make* you see"—is a partial acknowledgment of the complicity of fiction, as a power discourse, with ideology and coercion.[49] The author is a "maker" in a sense Aristotle did not intend. But what is it he would make us hear, feel, and see? In his omissions the reader can hear and see the false consciousness of the neutral position, which labors to hide the ideological premises that might, like the Mint at the end of the novel, be illuminated if objects were supplied to the verbs *hear*, *feel*, and *see*. Does he wish us to see the undesirability of a sailor examining his conditions? Does he wish us to see the heroism of a captain who risks the lives of crewmen for a faster passage and therefore increased profits?[50]

Such omissions, which make seeing seem ideologically neutral, are similar to the false consciousness that we see (I belabor the word intentionally) in Arnold's "literary" concept of disinterestedness as it occurs in his crusade to hellenize the middle class so as to legitimize its authority over the lower classes.[51] Thus we hear something—a will to power and mastery—in the text of Conrad's preface that undercuts the objective theory of art it intends to convey when it privileges the sense of sight, a privileging that is found (not coincidentally) in the modernist concept of fictional point of *view*. A dialogic theory of the text and the self, by which reading is figured as hearing rather than seeing, provides at least a partial escape from the coercive power of the artist's vision.

The detached and superior position from which Conrad's narrator views the laboring class in the novel can also be heard in the passage in the preface where Conrad visualizes stopping by a roadside to watch a laborer in a field:

> Sometimes, stretched at ease in the shade of a roadside tree, we watch the motions of a labourer in a distant field, and after a time, begin to wonder languidly as to what the fellow may be at. We watch the movements of his body, the waving of his arms, we see him bend down, stand up, hesitate, begin again. It may add to the charm of an idle hour to be told the purpose of his exertions. If we know he is trying to lift a stone, to dig a ditch, to uproot a stump . . . we may bring ourselves to forgive his failure. We understand his object, and after all, the fellow has tried. . . . We forgive, go on our way—and forget.
> And so it is with the workman of art. (147–48)

Fogel would say that "we" refers to the lazy reader politely disguised, but there may also be something of the real Conrad, the would-be country gentleman, in this "we." The text's comparison of the artist's work to the laborer's may seem charmingly democratic, harmonizing with the call (elsewhere in the preface) for "solidarity" and lost communal values. But less charming is the glimpse of the fin-de-siècle aesthete, languid and idle, curiously watching some "fellow" whose work he appropriates in a self-congratulatory and self-dramatizing trope. In this trope, the laborer himself has not truly been "seen" at all, but only used. The preface, then, also exhibits a dialogic opposition between a voice of community and a voice of elitism and individualism.

The notion of an objective seeing, as Heidegger suggests, is a mask or alibi for the subject's power position, as is an aesthetic of narrative that calls for a single (and thus inevitably biased) point of view. Here the notion masks the conservative ideology of Conrad's text. Such a positioned point of view, a reflection within literary practice of the ideology of individualism, emerges in the final pages of *The Nigger of the "Narcissus,"* almost as though the text wished to reveal its devices and to abandon its pose of objectivity. What I have called the "literary voice," by which the politics of the novel's representations are aestheticized, now becomes personified. Thus there is a deconstructive tension between the novel's conclusion, with its individualized and faulty seer, and the themes of solidarity and objective vision in the preface (although the preface also contains elements discordant with those themes), as well as between the "I" narrator and the earlier choral voices of the novel's own discourse. These tensions reflect fault lines in the larger social text, generated by laissez-faire capitalism, between communal and individual interests.

The author concept that emerged as a product of capitalist ideology and its attendant aesthetics is itself a fictional reconciliation of oppositions. On the one hand, the author is economically dependent on an audience, and produces a product for sale. The sad frequency with which Conrad's letters voice his desperate concern about money suggests how economic necessity can turn the author into a commodity, a salable personality catering to societal needs. Specifically, Conrad feared becoming merely a spinner of adventure yarns— a genre that, as Brantlinger shows, was co-opted by imperialist ideologies and libidinal dreams in which the exotic other is a territory suited to the unbounded indulgence of desire.[52] On the other hand, the author mythology that grew out of Romanticism projects the image of the writer as a detached and superior individual who, although unacknowledged like Shelley's legislative poet, imaginatively leads the culture rather than simply reproduces its fantasies of domination. The concept of "literature" maps a space from which the artist's voice can ostensibly exercise its authority, however occupied it is by alien voices in reality. This leadership—and Conrad anticipates many of the authors of the next generation—would return us to a lost, precapitalist community, despite the daily dependence of these artist-leaders on the capitalist system.

The ambivalent relation of the "I" narrator to the crew in *The Nigger of the "Narcissus"* can be read as reflecting the modernist storyteller's ambivalent relationship to his or her society—a relationship also figured in the persona who muses upon the distant laborer in the preface. The narrator's farewell to the crew further anticipates Conrad's own future career as an elitist or high-culture artist enacting the modernist, antipopulist stance while also desiring popular success and attempting popular formulas. As Jameson says, the contradictions of the cultural politics of modernism were such that modernism's negations depended on that which they repudiated: "Zola may be taken as the marker for the last coexistence of the art novel and the bestseller to be within a single text."[53] According to one definition, postmodernism has subsequently tended to resolve the contradiction in which Conrad was caught in favor of popular culture and an assault on modernist pretensions.

The structural feature—the alleged wavering of point of view—that has so bothered readers of *The Nigger of the "Narcissus"* is, then, not merely a naive violation or cavalier disregard of a formal rule by a young writer. It is a structural element, etched in the novel's discourse by history, by the position of the artist in capitalist society, and perhaps, as biographical critics have thought, by Joseph Conrad's personal experiences. By virtue of this structure, the disengaged storyteller emerges out of the social discourses and metanarratives dispersed throughout the novel; this process of inscription is analogous to the way human subjects are formed out of the discourses of capitalism in Western societies. The novel's violation of the rules concerning point of view exposes the dialogic and polyphonic nature of discourse and consciousness. *The Nigger of the "Narcissus"* reveals the paradoxes of the discursive subject as a storyteller who must maintain the fiction of a disengagement that offers a perspective from which to "see" or "hear" society's speech diversity, while being always already inhabited and constituted by that diversity. The sharing of this paradox of detachment and engagement—and thus the problem of narrative authority—by the narrator of *Under Western Eyes*, the last novel of Conrad's major phase, shows that the paradox remained a central concern of his art.

2

Discourse and Story in
Heart of Darkness

The explicit appeal to narrative in the problematic of knowledge is concomitant with the liberation of the bourgeois classes from the traditional authorities. Narrative knowledge makes a resurgence in the West as a way of solving the problem of legitimating the new authorities.

Jean-François Lyotard, *The Postmodern Condition*

As for the narrative constructions of our lives, there is no need to speak at length about the possibilities of delusion which attend us here.

Charles Taylor, *Sources of the Self*

I

Conventionally, a narrator is thought of as a person, a monadic subject whose identity precedes the narrative act. In *The Nigger of the "Narcissus"* this notion is reversed, and a narrator is formed in the act of narration, illustrating the contention of V. N. Volosinov and Mikhail Bakhtin that "consciousness is a social-ideological fact" arising out of social situations and speech acts rather than preceding them.[1] The subject of the enunciation is not posited as an origin, but rather as an effect of discourse. The individualized "I" of the final pages of *The Nigger of the "Narcissus"* emerges out of the ideological voices that traverse the earlier narrative discourse, directly anticipating Marlow.

Unlike his predecessor, Marlow is a dramatically conceived "character" from the outset. But *Heart of Darkness* also struggles with themes of fragmentation that the conventions of literary narrative as Conrad found them were poorly equipped to handle. Marlow asserts that "I have a voice too, and for good or evil mine is the speech that cannot be silenced" (38). However, as such critics as Bette London and Vincent Pecora have argued, the extent to which Marlow's voice can be termed his own is precisely the issue the novel raises.[2] And this novel, too, reaches closure by reinstating conventions that contain the lie of coherence and unity, but in *Heart of Darkness* the lie within the conventions is thematized explicity.

Steve Ressler offers a convincing portrait of Marlow as a person harboring deep-seated feelings of guilt and inauthenticity. These are intimated early in the novel with Marlow's inadequate explanation of his motive for going to Africa, his uneasiness about how he got the job, and especially his feeling of inauthenticity when his aunt defines him as an "emissary of light" (15). Marlow's pretenses and inauthenticity explain his subsequent identification with Kurtz, which is appropriate in ways that escape Marlow's own understanding. Marlow's sense of self has been vindicated by his belief in Kurtz as a man equipped with moral ideas, and, Ressler argues, "what ends for Marlow is the possibility of forging for himself a new future or gaining a renewed sense of his future through emulation of the great man, the large figure of daring and energy."[3] London's approach echoes Ressler's in stressing Marlow's initial, guarded confession of bad faith. Her questioning of Marlow's authenticity and of the ideological and communal structuring of his voice results in the best feminist reading of this novel to date, a reading that traces the subterranean connections between the male bonding Marlow initiates with his listeners and the ideologies of imperialism and racism. Marlow's voice, she concludes, "is the product of a negotiation of the cultural coordinates of race, gender, and nationality."[4]

Conrad's words in his best-known political essay, "Autocracy and War," encourage the examination of his narrators as socially constructed voices: "The psychology of individuals, even in the most extreme instances, reflects the general effect of the fears and hopes of its time" (85). Conrad's novels offer versions of this psychology that challenge received notions about the nature of the individual in society, and *Heart of Darkness* extends the radical questioning of the tradition of the novel of character begun in *The Nigger of the "Narcissus."* Henry James's criticism of the failure of *Heart of Darkness* fully to dramatize Kurtz is itself a failure to understand the implications of this novel's representation of a fragmented "character" who must be assembled by the discursive and ideological stategies of other discontinuous subjects such as Marlow, his narratees, and Conrad's readers.[5] The fact that Kurtz achieves a recognizable identity only as he is constructed in the speculative metanarratives of others is a crucial aspect of this novel's meditation on the subject and the community in which the subject is situated.

It is useful to examine Marlow's identity from the standpoint of the relation between story and discourse, particularly as that discourse in turn attempts to construct an identity for Kurtz out of the sparse story fragments available to Marlow. Since the story/discourse relationship is a function of the dialogic or other-directed nature of Marlow's speech act, it offers a way of mapping the self-actualization that accompanies Marlow's tale. Although Marlow is a "single," designated character, unlike the pastiche of voices that narrate most of *The Nigger of the "Narcissus,"* he is nonetheless marked by inconsistencies and social contradictions. Further, Marlow's discourse is often as monologic and authoritarian as that of his predecessor; like the narrator of *The Nigger of the "Narcissus,"* Marlow silences the other at crucial points in his narration. Not only do Africans and women have no significant voice, but Kurtz himself, whose conversation Marlow looks forward to, actually says next to nothing when the time arrives. Kurtz's speech (and his poetry) is reported in vague paraphrase—in indirect citation that acts as a form of control or repression. Since Marlow himself is a recipient of many of these indirect citations, the novel reveals an ambient field of power relations within the social discourse, a field in which conventional boundaries between self and other, one's own words and the words of others, break down.

Dennis Brown argues that J. Alfred Prufrock's voice is constructed out of contrasting social discourses, and something of the same is true of Marlow's.[6] Prufrock drowns in the voices of others as the poem ends, and Marlow drowns in the ambient metanarratives of the larger social discourse. In terms of the way selfhood is represented in narrative, *The Nigger of the "Narcissus,"* with its undesignated and shifting narrative voices, is to "The Waste Land" as *Heart of Darkness* is to "The Love Song of J. Alfred Prufrock."

The invitation to look for meaning not simply "in" the story of *Heart of Darkness* but in the pragmatics of the narrative situation occurs in the framing narrator's famous remark: for Marlow "the meaning of an episode was not inside like a kernel but outside, enveloping the tale which brought it out only as a glow brings out a haze, in the likeness of one of these misty halos that, sometimes, are made visible by the spectral illumination of moonshine" (9). In this elaborate metaphor, the sun as source or origin is like an absent author, but also and more profoundly it suggests whatever absent origin or power legitimates our narratives; the moon, like a narrator, is only a reflector of this absent source. The halo is a refraction of the moon's reflection, and it "exists" only in a problematic sense and only from a certain angle of vision or reception; only an audience in a certain position can "see" the halo.

Thus the imagery posits an absent origin, a reflecting medium or text, and the highly mediated nature of our own perceptions. It does all this while interjecting doubt as to the presence of any stable core of truth or reality in Marlow's story. Didier Coste could have had Marlow in mind when he described the pragmatics of narrative by saying that in narrative "the message is . . . the meaningfulness that is turned by the participants and witnesses of the act of communication into evidence that this act has taken place. The narrative message, the tale told, is not therefore a 'content'; it is not contained within a text."[7] Meaning is beyond the borders of the text, occurring in the space between discourse and audience; it is an ambient halo in which a story lives as it travels through other verbal atmospheres, and it is dependent on our angle of vision, which is to say on strategies of interpretation that result from our own social, institutional, and historical positions.

Meaning is never the possession of the supposedly solitary utterance or story, since every utterance depends on past utterances and is in turn directed toward present and/or future audiences and is therefore inhabited by them. Meaning is as much outside as inside the utterance. As Bakhtin says:

> Everything that is said, expressed, is located outside the "soul" of the speaker and does not belong only to him. The word cannot be assigned to a single speaker. The author (speaker) has his own inalienable right to the word, but the listener also has his rights, and those whose voices are heard in the word before the author comes upon it also have their rights (after all, there are no words that belong to no one). The word is a drama in which three characters participate. . . . It is performed outside the author, and it cannot be introjected into the author. . . . There can be no such thing as an isolated utterance. It always presupposes utterances that precede and follow it. No one utterance can be either the first or the last. Each is only a link in the chain, and none can be studied outside the chain.[8]

In an often-quoted letter to Cunninghame Graham, Conrad says that "the idea" in *Heart of Darkness* "is so wrapped up in secondary considerations that You—even You!—may miss it."[9] This remark refuses to close down interpretation, and, like the framing narrator's metaphor, it invites a decentered reading. Cunninghame Graham, a socialist, would naturally focus on the novel's critique of imperialism, and few readers schooled in the mimetic assumptions of realism could fail to see the story of the "pilgrim's" and of Kurtz's moral bankruptcy as the primary consideration. But if we bracket these primary considerations, then Marlow's own discourse, its reception, and their ideological implications emerge as the crucial secondary considerations. The "story" is not unproblematically reflected in the narrative "discourse," since our symbolic forms, codes, grand narratives, and *petits recits* create the world they report on. Narrative and its codes are ideologically saturated, and to study Marlow as a dialogically constructed narrator is to examine the complex relationships and unstable boundaries between narrative and world.

When, in the final paragraph of *The Nigger of the "Narcissus,"* the narrator eulogizes the crew as being "as good a crowd as ever fisted with wild cries the beating canvas of a heavy foresail" (107), his discourse seems to have forgotten the many criticisms of this crew that were overtly voiced earlier in the novel. It has a problematic relation to the story just told. His is now a convenient memory, creating an official ideology of a romantic, heroic, and dedicated labor force. The framing narrator who begins *Heart of Darkness*, despite his suggestive problematizing of the issue of interpretation, is also a mythmaker whose retrospective grand narrative of colonial history serves the interests of imperialism. He invokes "the great spirit of the past," then eulogizes "the great knight-errants of the sea," Sir Francis Drake and Sir John Franklin, together with all the "adventurers" whose ships returned to England "full of treasure" (8). His discourse creates a glorified past that is usable for the purposes of imperialism.

Marlow speaks in dialogic relationship to the romanticizing (and propagandizing) frame narrator. His first words in *Heart of Darkness*, "And this also has been one of the dark places of the earth" (9), initiate a *petit recit*, an alternate story, in response to the grand narrative of the framing narrator, who has just delivered his eulogies to Drake and Franklin out loud to his friends on the *Nellie*. Thus Marlow's story finds its significance dialogically in relation to what lies beyond it, while also unsettling the distinction between the story and its outside. And if *The Nigger of the "Narcissus"* moved from a realistic story to an ideologically freighted romanticizing of the past, the opening of *Heart of Darkness* seems (deceptively) to move in the opposite direction. While the discourse of the earlier novel supported the interests of trade and imperialism, Marlow begins by announcing an oppositional position, countering the frame narrator's romanticism with his own realism—his little story of the Roman antihero.

Brook Thomas associates Marlow's response with Foucault's concept of "counter-memory"—the memory that recuperates what official memory needs to forget (the blindness that has enabled its particular vision) in the process of creating its myths and narratives of self-justification.[10] Marlow's version of history is less clearly useful to present political and economic interests than are the "abiding memories" of the frame narrator, memories that constitute a sort of official history (8). Marlow's counter-memory brings to light what those official interests have repressed or ignored, occupying the subversive position of Lyotard's *petit recit*. In Bakhtin's terms, if the framing narrator presents an "official" consciousness, Marlow's is an "unofficial" consciousness. But in *Heart of Darkness* the boundary between these two discourses will prove to be unstable. Marlow's apparently oppositional discourse does not entirely escape the pressures of official memory, and in crucial ways it ultimately submits to them, following more subtly the pattern of the emerging ideologue found in *The Nigger of the "Narcissus."* As Brown says, *Heart of Darkness* "constitutes a provisional attempt at deconstructing Western selfhood."[11]

The illusory nature of the subject is, to many theorists, an inevitable consequence of the nature of ideology. For instance, Diane Macdonell's discussion of Louis Althusser argues in a Bakhtinian vein that "ideologies are never simply free to set their own terms but are marked by what they are opposing" and that "opposing ideologies are shaped by each other." Often "what is thought within one discourse is an effect related to what is unthought there but thought elsewhere in another."[12] Ideologies and discourses are dialogically formed. Marlow's unofficial discourse is haunted by opposing official ideologies, creating contradictions he is unable to reconcile.

In his "semantic history" of imperialism, Richard Koebner claims that by 1899 "the word imperialism had been split into two opposite interpretations and evaluations" in the British political arena.[13] This split is found in Marlow's social attitudes and in his attitudes toward the subject in imperialist society. At times he believes in a subject that is constructed by societal discourses, those voices he refers to as "principles" (38) enforced by "neighbors," "the policeman," and "lunatic asylums" (49), with their promise of surveillance and threat of confinement. Without these formative societal pressures, the person is hollow—a blind force of greed and lust symbolized by Marlow's first glimpse of Kurtz with a mouth that looks as though it "wanted to swallow all the air, all the earth, all the men before him" (59). But at other times Marlow betrays a lingering belief in the unitary, transcendent, and self-governing subject of bourgeois individualism, the subject whose presumed essential validity underwrites the colonizing of less-developed "subjects."

Brown observes that "the tale [*Heart of Darkness*] is littered with sketchy representations of the unitary self—many of them parodic."[14]

Important among these is the accountant, and Marlow's attitude toward him is curiously ambivalent. He is a hairdresser's dummy, to be sure, but Marlow is not ironic when he admires the strength the accountant displays in keeping up appearances in the wilderness. From the idealizing point of view of Western ideologies of the self, there *should* be an essence beyond appearance, and from this point of view the accountant is inauthentic. But, on the other hand, Marlow is also suspicious of such idealizations. If we are dummies dressed in the codes and discourses of our times, the accountant is a successful one. He tells Marlow that Kurtz is a "remarkable" man, and many times later in the story Marlow pays a certain respect to the accountant by repeating the adjective "remarkable" when discussing Kurtz.

Thus the "same" Marlow who is so critical of the hollow rhetoric of imperialism is nonetheless colonized by this rhetoric. He accepts the idealized image of Kurtz propagated in the stories that have been told about him by these other characters, and even after his encounter with Kurtz he hopes to salvage certain aspects of that idealization. Marlow's own subject position in the power struggle within the trading company has been dictated by the discourse of others, which has placed him in the "gang of virtue" (28). Although Marlow acknowledges his lie in silently accepting this characterization, a deeper irony is found in the fact that Marlow's virtue, because of his entanglements with the imperialist project, truly *is* suspect. As Marlow defines Kurtz by weaving a fabric of his own (and others') story fragments about Kurtz, he himself is similarly defined by the stories of others.

On the conscious level, Marlow wants to reject the grand narrative of "the cause of progress," which he knows to be a lie, and to find a little story—an alternate organizing myth—that will lend coherence to his experiences. But it is difficult to discover or produce a little story that is not already colonized by the grand narratives it tries to oppose. One must speak the language society makes available. Marlow is struggling with a language game, although, according to Lyotard, "there is no possibility that language games can be unified or totalized in any metadiscourse."[15] In the end Marlow returns to a grand narrative—not that of progress through material expansion and conquest, but one that tells a story of sin and redemption by which imperialism forgives itself and grants itself absolution. Like Prufrock, he drowns in other voices.

In the meantime, Marlow searches for the narrative encoding that will satisfy his need for coherence without bowing to official tales. Lyotard sheds light on such a quest: "Most people have lost the nostalgia for the lost narrative. It in no way follows that they are reduced to barbarity. What saves them from it is their knowledge that legitimation can only spring from their own linguistic practice and communicational interaction." [16] As Marlow tests these alternate forms of knowing, these alternate linguistic practices, his irony is often unstable and ambiguous, resulting from the difficulty of escaping colonization by (or from the uncritical sharing of) imperialist discourse. The various stories or story elements Marlow tells that are meant to solve interpretive problems about Kurtz simply generate new ones. Since Kurtz's history remains a matter of speculation, it is impossible to know and evaluate him with the kind of narrative knowledge that questions of identity and selfhood normally require. To make sense of a present action is to place it in a narrative, to connect it to a past and a future and to a project. But Kurtz is curiously without a story that we can know with any certainty, and this fact raises the secondary consideration of what a subject is without a position within a story available to the community.

As Suresh Raval argues, when Marlow says that Kurtz's eloquent essay was written "before his—let us say—nerves went wrong," Marlow's "let us say" hints that this story of cataclysmic change, like a sudden illness, is a polite but suspect fiction. [17] It is a metastory that functions as an alibi, allowing one not to question the larger grand narrative of progress through imperialism. Marlow's discourse on Kurtz and the imperialist enterprise is a pastiche of metastories or explanatory narratives, such as the medical story of psychological change (parodied in the doctor who measures Marlow's head) and the cultural story of the conversion of one who "went native." This latter metastory is particularly offensive in its ethnocentric ideology, since it transfers the blame for Kurtz's conduct to the "savage" culture Kurtz adopted rather than locating it in Western culture. John A. McClure observes that Kurtz's call to "exterminate all the brutes!" is itself a brutally logical closure to this metastory. [18] If Marlow's "let us say" casts doubt on the medical metastory, his portrayal of the sepulchral city and the "pilgrims" deconstructs the civilized-savage opposition. On the other hand, Marlow's careless use of the words like "savage" and "nigger" reinstates the opposition, indicating his ambivalence concerning the metastory about "going native." This ambivalence offends many Third World readers, and Chinua Achebe sees in the novel only racism, not the larger arena in which various discourses, including that of racism, contend.

Conrad's texts are committed to the truth of contradiction, and *Heart of Darkness* presents contradictions not only in the various attitudes, voices, and metastories that inhabit Marlow's discourse, but in what has come to be called the story/discourse opposition in narrative structure. Jonathan Culler shows that the usefulness of the story/discourse opposition in narratology lies in its unstable, self-deconstructing nature.[19] The terms are most interesting precisely when we have difficulty maintaining the boundary separating them. What is the true story about Kurtz, and how do the explanatory metastories embedded in Marlow's interpretive discourse influence our perception of that truth? Is he a great man gone bad, or someone who was always a schemer and role player and who has finally shown his true colors? Is he an apostate who abandoned a supposedly superior culture for a supposedly savage one? Or is he a sick man? Is the story we think we see a product of Marlow's interpretive discourse, or is it objectively available?

Marlow's discourse is, paradoxically, a set of metastories originating in the discourses of others and filling the void left by the absent "true" story of the historical Kurtz.[20] When Marlow speaks of Kurtz's nerves going bad, he offers, with a skeptical qualifying phrase, an interpretive metastory that renders Kurtz's literal story more understandable to a "civilized" audience conditioned to accept medical narratives concerning behavior. Kurtz may have always been a Babel of diverse voices, visually symbolized, perhaps, in the motley clothing of his disciple, but Marlow does not make this version of the story explicit. Nor does he critique the European's ideology and subject position so much as marvel over his transformation when separated from home. Thus the metastory of transformation limits the oppositional force of Marlow's discourse.

Marlow is uneasy with the idea of a heteronomous subject constituted within social discourses, and in spite of the evidence of his experiences he seeks ways of reaffirming a traditional, humanistic concept of the transcendent subject. In this regard, Marlow is inhabited or colonized by his bourgeois audience's investments in notions of a unitary, inner-directed self; therefore, he opposes mere "principles" to what he calls "deliberate belief" (38), and "hollowness" to "inborn strength" and "restraint" (43). These latter terms are vestiges of an idealist discourse that speaks of an essential human nature—a discourse that regulates human behavior by positing norms of naturalness and universality. Marlow's belief in beliefs, however, is difficult for him to maintain, and a few pages after positing the opposition between principles and beliefs, he deconstructs it by equating "superstition, beliefs, and what you may call principles." Ironically, this passage shows that what Marlow has called beliefs cannot be distinguished from principles. That is, Marlow abandons his belief in beliefs just as he has accused others of abandoning their principles, "at the first good shake" (38).

The contradictions and slippages in Marlow's discourse go to the heart of bourgeois ideology as it evolved from the eighteenth century. As the middle class replaced absolutist power, it needed to work out its own solution to the problem of authority. According to the grand narrative of Rousseau's *The Social Contract*, the ideal citizen surrenders to the general will. The law or authority must, in a society committed to individualist endeavors, be internalized in each person. As Terry Eagleton observes: "Each subject must function as its own seat of self-government. . . . the bourgeois subject is autonomous and self-determining, acknowledges no merely extrinsic law but instead, in some mysterious fashion, gives the law to itself. In doing so, the law becomes the form which shapes into harmonious unity the turbulent content of the subject's appetites and inclinations. The compulsion of autocratic power is replaced by the more gratifying compulsion of the subject's self-identity." [21]

Rousseau states, in words Conrad may have had in mind when choosing his title, that the new law must be one "which is not graven on tablets of marble or brass, but on the hearts of the citizens." [22] Marlow's faith in restraint, inner strength, and deliberate belief indicates his desire to believe in the possibility of the inner-directed self, which the Marxist tradition skeptically calls the bourgeois subject, and to believe in the authentically encoded heart. His experiences, however, have taught him that most people's principles are not deeply ingrained. Ultimately, Marlow's entire preoccupation with the questions of inner authenticity—of substance versus hollowness and belief versus principles—may be politically and morally irrelevant, for these distinctions lose force if they merely defer the question of what ends are served by the beliefs/principles. Away from the police and public opinion, which can "frame" the subject in many ways, the manager gives the law to himself when he advocates hanging the Russian, since "anything can be done in this country" (34). And the turbulent content of Kurtz's appetites and inclinations surfaces all too readily in the absence of external constraints.

What is significant is the impact such behavior has on others, a significance that must not be lost in an interminable discourse on origins. Raval is correct in emphasizing the skepticism with which Conrad "deals with contradictions that plague not only lives of individuals but also individuals in their relation to their community." [23] But Marlow's sense of responsibility to a larger community is flawed, as demonstrated when his experience of the grove of death engenders no second thoughts about piloting the steamboat. In fact, while piloting the boat, he meditates on the virtue of not looking too deeply into things.

Marlow inadvertently demonstrates the policing power of appeals to the self-governing subject in his own admiration of the "restraint" and "inborn strength" of the cannibals, who do not eat their exploiters. This "law," apparently etched in the hearts of the cannibals, serves the interests of their exploiters and keeps the cannibals in captivity. Marlow is shocked at the obviously imposed "laws" by which other Africans are defined as enemies and then shelled, as criminals and enslaved, or as rebels and killed. But when the Africans, employed by whites for low wages, appear most like an exploited underclass in a capitalist society, Marlow applauds the restraining (enslaving?) nature of this inner law. Many slave owners were shrewd enough to give religious training to their slaves, and the advantaged still build protective barriers around their own interests with discourses encouraging the poor to internalize restraints against coveting and stealing. Marlow's idealism readily conspires with exploitation.

Terry Eagleton argues that any project to create this inner-directed subject "is likely to be deeply ambivalent" (27). This is because it is difficult to determine whether the subject really has internalized the law or is merely being directed by external forces: "There is a world of political difference between a law which the subject really does give to itself, in radical democratic style, and a decree which still descends from on high but which the subject now 'authenticates.' Free consent may thus be the antithesis of oppressive power, or a seductive form of collusion with it."[24]

The problem is that, until the subject is tested in extremity, as is Kurtz, one cannot know which of the above categories is really operative—in Marlow's terms, beliefs and principles look the same to the outside observer. Marlow accuses his listeners on the *Nellie* of a comfortable ignorance of such issues, guided as they are by public opinion and by fear of scandal, police, and lunatic asylums. He is expressing a radical skepticism concerning the shift of power from external authority to the heart of the bourgeois subject. He does not treat his auditors as inner-directed, authentic selves, but as subjects coerced into a collusion with external power by power's many depoliticized disguises in bourgeois society. But he can't be sure which is the case, any more than he can explain how beliefs differ from principles or why some people apparently have "inborn" qualities that others lack. Nor does he seem aware of how these idealistic notions themselves function to police and regulate behavior.

Freedom, it would seem, is unrepresentable. As Eagleton says, describing the relationship between political and aesthetic judgment in Kant: "All that is most precious falls outside the representational sphere. If this preserves what is most valuable from succumbing to the determined status of apples and armchairs, it also threatens to strike vacuous the very essence of the human subject. If freedom is finally unrepresentable, how is it to exert its ideological force, given that ideology is itself a question of representation?"[25] Marlow's oppositional discourse, his critique of the current state of Western civilization, is occupied, even undermined, by his nostalgia for official ideological assumptions concerning the inner-directed subject. Furthermore, this discourse reflects an undecidability, an epistemological impasse, concerning the nature of the subject. Fleishman analyzes this impasse in terms of Conrad's nostalgia for a Burkean organic society, a nostalgia that makes Conrad's characters into "object lessons in the failure of individualism."[26]

In the absence of a truly organic society, imperial and colonial policies depend on discourses that endow ethnic points of view with the halo of essential truth, of "deliberate" beliefs. This ideology commits Marlow to a work ethic, a belief that in work you can find "your own reality" (31). Navigating a steamboat on a strange river requires complete immersion in one's work, a constant scrutiny of the surface of the water. Marlow is grateful for this: "When you have to attend to things of that sort, to the mere incidents of the surface, the reality—the reality I tell you—fades. The inner truth is hidden—luckily, luckily" (36). Again, Marlow's discourse is fraught with contradictions. Is work a discovery of reality or an avoidance of it? Marlow's appeal to work forgets that the accountant was also dedicated to work, as was Kurtz. In an organic society, work is valued only as it relates to communally accepted values and goals, but in the gesellschaft of Marlow's experience a meaningful discourse on values and goals is absent. Further, what does it mean to celebrate "the mere incidents of the surface" in a total discourse that proclaims to navigate to the heart of things? Can this be thought as a significant deconstruction? Or is it merely that in getting ever deeper into the surface of things, Marlow is content to embrace the outer-directed selfhood he elsewhere caricatures?

Marlow's discourse is double-voiced, probing the contradictions and the emptiness of colonial policies in the manner of a nomadic *recit*, all the while swimming, and ultimately drowning, in fictions and positions that impede that same critique and that in fact collude with official practices. A literal instance of this contradiction and collusion is Marlow's repair and navigation of the imperialists' boat: Marlow's escape into work results in his serving the colonial effort his discourse otherwise exposes. Here Marlow's character replicates the enabling blindness of *The Nigger of the "Narcissus,"* which celebrated the work and the solidarity of the crew (a solidarity possible only after certain crucial exclusions) by repressing the fact that this labor and solidarity serve the interests of the merchant navy of an imperial power. Likewise, in *Heart of Darkness,* the journal on seamanship that Marlow finds, and that gives him such a sense of relief (since here is a writer devoted to the accomplishment of a task at hand), is writing that ultimately serves colonial endeavors. It differs from Kurtz's notorious essay mainly in being less aware of the interests it serves.

Conrad's novel—or the halo it creates in a postmodern atmosphere—is very much about discourse and its discontents and about conflicting discourses inhabiting the "same" space, whether that space be a person, a narrator, an essay on savage customs, or a national policy. Kurtz scrawls the words "exterminate all the brutes" at the bottom of his double-voiced essay on civilizing the Africans, an essay that oddly anticipates its "opposing" final discourse in its opening grand narrative that posits the white man as a superior, godlike being. The book on seamanship contains a marginal discourse by another voice in a language Marlow cannot read and mistakenly identifies as cipher. These writings in the margins enact a dialogic unsettling of the limits of the texts. Similarly, surrounding the "voice" of Kurtz, in other margins, is the "immense jabber" of the wilderness (48). What is disturbed here is the opposition between reason and sanity, so crucial to the regulation and policing of civilized life—an opposition Derrida has disturbed in his response to Foucault, "Cogito and the History of Madness." The papier-mâché Mephistopheles at first "jabbered" (29), then "talked fluently" (30). The Logos has fled, and all of these errant discourses are haunted by the question asked of Marlow back in Brussels, "Ever any madness in your family?" (15).[27] The world Marlow depicts is an engine for the production and containment of a madness that is manifested in the gulf between language and its posited objects or truths.[28]

In fact, the "savagery" that supposedly infects Kurtz is figured as a kind of discourse that inhabits Kurtz dialogically, just as "civilizing" discourses inhabit those who remain in Europe. In a demonic parody of the Wordsworthian scene of instruction (as in "There Was a Boy"), Marlow says of Kurtz that the wilderness "whispered to him things about himself which he did not know, things of which he had no concept till he took council with this great solitude—and the whisper had proved irresistibly fascinating. It echoed loudly within him because he was hollow at the core" (57–58). And Fogel contends that "even the mist that pervades the landscape is an image of rhetoric."[29] This metastory, with its scene of demonic instruction or seduction, is paradoxically another version of the civilizing process, the internalization of the discourse of another. Thus Marlow's language inadvertently deconstructs the civilized/savage opposition, one of those deliberate beliefs Marlow nonetheless wants to retain.

The metastory of the mysterious, inscrutable intentions of the wilderness is on one level a way of shifting blame away from Europe for the decayed conduct of Kurtz and the "pilgrims." Like the medical narrative of Kurtz's change, it saves the grand narrative of imperialism from direct criticism by locating the cause of Kurtz's deterioration in another story. It is a part of the colonial alibi, but it also is an aspect of the novel's critique of ideology. Principles of conduct and morality find strong support in the belief that they are in rapport with the laws of nature, as in Wordsworth. Marlow's inscrutable and possibly hostile wilderness disallows the grounding of ideology in nature, since when nature whispers too loudly in Kurtz's soul things fall apart. With this metastory climaxing Marlow's meditations on the wilderness, *Heart of Darkness* undermines the belief in nature as a metaphysical foundation for social order, separating the language of value from nature. The supposedly vague, adjectival language—"brooding," "inscrutable," "unspeakable," and so on—that bothered such early critics as F. R. Leavis in fact represents this metaphysical uncertainty.[30] How does one represent with concrete or "objective" language that which is absent or unrepresentable?

Marlow's discourse on the wilderness, then, can both support and undermine official ideology, and this is just one of the ways his discourse is "inconclusive" (11) to the frame narrator, who "listened on the watch for the sentence, for the word that would give me a clue to the faint uneasiness inspired by this narrative" (30). The uneasiness his audience feels with Marlow's narrative reflects the uneasy alliances that form Marlow's own selfhood. One of Conrad's defter touches is the way the frame narrator's reference to the "uneasiness inspired" by Marlow is echoed in Marlow's assertion that the manager of the central station, one of the hollow men, "inspired uneasiness" (24). Marlow's listeners are largely silenced by Marlow's discourse, just as he is dominated by the manager's; this parallelism equates Marlow with those whose hollowness he would expose.

The unease of Marlow's narratees is dramatized by their occasional interruptions of his story; these interruptions foreground the pragmatics of the storytelling situation and the dialogic relationship between teller and listener, pointing to Marlow's struggle to fashion a tale that his audience (with the ideological biases of lawyers, accountants, and company directors) will understand. The contradiction between this demand and the oppositional and antihegemonic truth of his experience, a truth itself untotalizable and contradictory, is a secondary conflict in the novel, perhaps the one Conrad alluded to in his letter to Cunninghame Graham. Thematizing the question of storytellers and their audiences while reminding us of the "coercion to see" in the Preface to *The Nigger of the "Narcissus,"* Marlow asks: "Do you see him? Do you see the story? Do you see anything? It seems to me I am trying to tell you a dream—making a vain attempt, because no relation of a dream can convey the dream-sensation. . . . No, it is impossible. It is impossible to convey the life sensation of any given epoch of one's existence—that which makes its truth, its meaning— its subtle and penetrating essence. It is impossible. We live, as we dream—alone" (30).

All that Marlow thinks he knows about Kurtz prior to their encounter comes to him through narrative transactions with others. And Marlow's own story on the *Nellie* refers to his previous telling of a false and truncated story to Kurtz's Intended. At every turn Marlow's story is about stories, the literal ones we tell to one another and the metastories that fill explanatory roles in our discourses and ideologies. The significance of a narrative such as Marlow's exists not only in the story—the events that supposedly literally occurred—but also in the discourse—the manner of the story's telling and the relationship of this manner to the audience.

II

Plot is an element of discourse, not story, since plotting alters or revises the story through reordering, selection, and emphasis—processes that are all dictated pragmatically by a narrator's relation to an audience. The present discussion of Marlow's discourse and its various plottings extends the suggestion made by Peter Brooks in *Reading for the Plot.* Of *Heart of Darkness,* Brooks says:

> The text, then, appears to speak of a repeated "trying out" of orders, all of which distort what they claim to organize, all of which may indeed cover up a very lack of possibility of order. This may suggest one relationship between story and narrative plot in the text: a relationship of disquieting uncertainty, where story never appears to be quite matched to the narrative plot that

is responsible for it. Yet the orders tried out in *Heart of Darkness* may in their very tenuousness be necessary to the process of striving toward meaning: as if to say that the plotting of stories remains necessary even where we have ceased to believe in the plots we use. Certain minimum canons of readability remain necessary if we are to be able to discern the locus of the necessarily unreadable.[31]

The moment when the relationship between discourse and story is most crucial is when Marlow interprets Kurtz's final words, the words Marlow lied about to the Intended. What Marlow says to his friends on the *Nellie* is that Kurtz was a "remarkable man": "He had summed up—he had judged 'The horror!' He was a remarkable man. After all, this was the expression of some sort of belief; it had candour, it had conviction, it had a vibrating note of revolt in its whisper, it had the appalling face of a glimpsed truth—the strange commingling of desire and hate. . . . It was an affirmation, a moral victory paid for by innumerable defeats, by abominable terrors, by abominable satisfactions. But it was a victory!" (69–70).

The question, as Robert Kimbrough puts it, is, "What do you think that Conrad thought that Marlow thought that Kurtz thought?" when Kurtz said, "The horror! The horror!"[32] These words could refer to almost anything; they are a writerly, free-floating text. Marlow has no evidence to warrant the assertion that Kurtz's soul gained a kind of victory or redemption (such things, though crucial, are unknowable), and he seems to have been swayed by an eloquence and theatricality— "it had a vibrating note"—that he is suspicious of everywhere else. We have a minimal story element, the fact that Kurtz uttered these words, and then we have, as a kind of halo surrounding them, Marlow's interpretive discourse—a grand narrative of victory and salvation.

Throughout, the novel offers reasons to suspect Marlow's interpretations. Even on the level of style and description, the novel presents choices between alternate interpretive discourses and encodings. *Heart of Darkness* is a sequence of false and revisionary encodings. Ian Watt has referred to the moments of "delayed decoding," moments when incorrect first impressions must be corrected—"sticks" soon appear as arrows, the "cane" that kills the helmsman becomes a spear, and "balls" become shrunken heads. But any decoding is always also another encoding. While certain encodings yield more useful knowledge than others in a given situation, Watt assumes the possibility of a language that will represent reality as it "really" is, decoded and cleansed of any obfuscations brought about by the medium of representation. But Marlow's vague and inconsistent use of the terms "real" and "reality" throughout the novel problematizes the boundary between reality and discourses upon it.

McClure suggests that the problematic relationship between narration and truth is figured in the act of navigation,[33] as when Marlow says: "You lost your way on that river as you would in a desert, and butted all day long against shoals, trying to find the channel, till you thought yourself bewitched and cut off for ever from everything you had known once—somewhere—far away—in another existence perhaps" (35). But even on the ocean passage to Africa, before he becomes his own navigator, Marlow feels that his voyage, occurring in psychological as well as physical space, takes him away from established facts: "For a time I would feel I belonged still to a world of straightforward facts; but the feeling would not last long. . . . the general sense of vague and oppressive wonder grew upon me. It was a weary pilgrimage amongst hints for nightmares" (17).

Perhaps the facts have no firm, independent existence, but are constituted by discourses, by paradigms of thought and epistemes; in recording this feeling, Marlow records his distance from the sustaining assumptions of Western society. To narrate without this familiar structure of facts and referents is indeed to navigate strange waters and traverse many borders.

Despite Marlow's implicit warnings, Juliet McLauchlan, like many critics before her, echoes Marlow's interpretive choice concerning Kurtz's final words. She writes: "Marlow calls Kurtz's judgment: 'an affirmation, a moral victory paid for by innumerable defeats, by abominable terrors, by abominable satisfactions. But it was a victory.' This quotation leads directly to consideration of the nature of the inner conflict which culminates in Kurtz's victory."[34] Critics in the humanist tradition who have been colonized by Marlow's discourse share Marlow's need to salvage a belief in transcendent values, with all their regulatory power.[35] Thus McLauchlan affirms her own belief in "Kurtz's undoubted victory, a confirmation of the validity of his ideals, intentions, even words."

In attaching a signified to "The horror! The horror!" and grounding this utterance in a culturally approved grand narrative of moral judgment, Marlow may intend to reveal the power of that culture to remain the colonizer of Kurtz's heart even after his wilderness experience. Or he could mean, more imperialistically, that the culturally approved narrative is "natural"—a universally true story of the heart's journey, even if the heart belongs to a man who has been cut loose from all the external constraints cultures employ. This difference, like the question of salvation, is crucial but undecidable and unrepresentable.

Marlow plays with a sort of Christian emplotment, in opposition to Conrad's own militant agnosticism, in his many references to devils and infernos, and he resorts to the concept of redemption early in the novel, when he refers vaguely to "the idea" that can redeem colonialism from being mere conquest. This, of course, is the "official" belief that saturates his apparently oppositional discourse, and it has both a Kantian and a Hegelian ring.[36] Lyotard discusses the status of Kant's Idea in *Just Gaming*, a book that examines the nature of justice. In Kant, the regulating Idea in which the concept of justice can be grounded is that of a "totality of practical, reasonable beings."[37] But how, Lyotard asks, can a discourse on justice be grounded in a postmodern age that does not accept the story, the grand narrative, of this totality? Or, to recall the doctor who gave Marlow his physical examination, what is the status of justice when, instead of reason, there is madness in the family? As Lyotard puts it, how can we judge without criteria and in terms of a social bond that "is not made up of a single type of statement, or, if you will, of discourse, but that is made up of several kinds of these games"?[38] What is the status of justice when there is no truth?

For Hegel, the Idea is the plan of providence embodied in world history. To the extent that Conrad's early modernist text encourages a skeptical response to Marlow's vague evocation of the Hegelian providential Idea, it points beyond modernism to Lyotard's postmodern problematic.[39] Raval glosses the status of the Idea in Hegel as follows: "For Hegel, world history reveals the plan of providence; at any given stage of history, the community of men is in conformity with reason at that stage. Hegel thus conceives of history as a succession of communities which in later stages embody more and more adequately the Idea."[40]

This concept of history, which places Hegel in the organicist tradition of Burke, informed the side of the British debate on African policy that argued that British expansion was a manifestation of divine will.[41] Marlow wants to believe in the organicist tradition and in the role of a providential colonialism within it. Through most of his journey he thought Kurtz embodied this idea, since Kurtz had supposedly gone to Africa "equipped with moral ideas of some sort" (33). Marlow knows from the start that profits and self-interest are crucial, but he assumes these can be justified if they coexist with other humanitarian activities—with an idea "you can set up, and bow down before, and offer a sacrifice to. . ." (10). But Marlow's story constantly undermines the Kantian Idea of a totality of reasonable beings (there *is* madness in the family) and the Hegelian Idea of a historically unfolding plan of providence (in Africa, one *can* do whatever one wants).

Kurtz's essay on reforming savage customs is ominous in its opening idealism, revealing, in its statement that whites must approach Africans "with the might as of a deity" (50), a will to power underlying the idealism. The dark power that such idealistic grounding produces is imaged in Kurtz's painting, which represents justice coming not from light but from darkness. Thus Marlow is forced to confront the postmodern experience of the dissolution of the idealist grand narrative in which the discourse of values has traditionally been grounded. His problem, much like Lyotard's today, is how to denounce the totalizations of imperialism and yet maintain a sense of ethics and justice, since these seem to require grounding in universalizing beliefs. This issue recurs in *Under Western Eyes*, where the relationship between Haldin's act of assassination and its motivating (and redeeming?) "idea" is at issue, an idea that is also treated skeptically. Nathalie says that Haldin "told me once to remember that men serve always something greater than themselves—the idea." Razumov responds by saying, "In you everything is divine" (326), recalling the more cynical association of idealism with god-playing in Kurtz's essay.

Eloise Knapp Hay observes that Marlow's early reference to the grounding idea justifying colonialism is oddly deconstructive. Just as Marlow speaks in the voice of the civilized person who would bring light to the savage, he adopts imagery and rhetoric (bowing down and sacrificing) that seem to embody savage idolatry.[42] Hay fails to add that Conrad's irony does not rule out reference to Christian worship, and in fact Marlow concludes his tale by bowing to the Christian grand narrative in his talk of repentance and victory. The question is, can justice ever be derived from reason, or must its prescriptions be taken on faith? If Marlow's imagery implies subterranean connections between the "civilized" and the "savage," then Western idealism is undone even as it is given voice, as the imagery suggests that references to great ideas can underwrite brutal institutional practices. Marlow's worship of a saving idea parodies the "unspeakable" rites and practices of which Kurtz will later be accused, and Marlow's failure to specify the idea he worships parallels his later failure to specify Kurtz's rites and his vagueness about Kurtz's plans and "ideas." This lack of specificity in Marlow's discourse, an effect within his narrative of the ungrounded nature of ideological signification, is not a failure of language, as Leavis claimed, but a crucial element of the experience of ungrounded discourse that the novel creates.

Kurtz's "ideas," if they ever really existed and were not mere elements in a convenient pose, have given way to self-interest, and Kurtz has apparently pursued his ends with cartridges and the shrinking of heads. In this novel, and in *The Secret Agent* and *Under Western Eyes*, terrorism thrives in a world where master narratives have been abandoned, where "principles won't do" (*HD*, 38), and where the regulatory power of public "opinions" has replaced "the Idea."[43] What offends Marlow so much about the manager of the Central Station is his sober willingness to see Kurtz's terrorism as a possibly acceptable but poorly timed "method." Thus madness is contained within the manager's reason, whereas Kurtz's actual terrorism is extenuated for Marlow by his more complete loss of reason.

In order to maintain a position from which justice can be articulated, from which Kurtz and the manager can be judged, Marlow interprets the events of Kurtz's life and death in a familiar grand narrative of fall and redemption. But one cannot really refer to what Marlow is interpreting as "events," since Marlow only has available to him a few story fragments and a few opinions about Kurtz—a brief encounter with a dying man who crawled into the jungle and with a fool who liked his poetry. Kurtz is not a character in the traditional sense; perpetually displaced and decentered, a shadowy effect of the discourse of others, Kurtz anticipates the dissolution of character in later fiction. Marlow turns these fragments called "Kurtz" into narrative by lending them a vague and hypothetical history—a greatness from which Kurtz may have fallen, a redemption he may have found. By virtue of this discursive gesture, since to have a self is to have a story, Kurtz is lent a bogus or tentative selfhood in Marlow's enunciations. This is a conservative gesture on Marlow's part, a retreat from the postmodern world of little stories into traditional certainties about the subject and its destiny that are embedded in larger, presumably universal narratives. Of the two metastories explaining Kurtz's supposed change, Marlow is clearly skeptical of the medical story of the man whose nerves went bad, and he is not convinced of the cultural story of the man who went native. But Marlow is himself the author, which is to say the willing conveyor, of the consoling story of redemption, victory, and salvation.

Perhaps Conrad himself would have been skeptical of Marlow's discourse of redemption. He says, in a letter to Marguerite Poradowska, "I astonish and perhaps scandalize you by my joking about criminals while you think me capable of accepting or even admitting the doctrine (or theory) of expiation through suffering. . . . It is a doctrine which . . . discloses the possibilities of bargaining with the Eternal. . . . Each act of life is final and inevitably produces its consequences in spite of all the weeping and gnashing of teeth and sorrow of weak souls who suffer as fright grips them when confronted with the results of their actions."[44] One wonders if this would not be Conrad's own response to Kurtz's final cry. In fact, there is something in Marlow's emplotment that parodies the work of Conrad's father, who, according to Avrom Fleishman, "wrote in the train of Zygmunt Krasinski, a major poet whose social idealism was a Christianized version of the Hegelian progress toward a rational state."[45]

Marlow's finalizing response, his grand narrative of redemption, is what, in the terms of Murray Krieger's analysis of *Heart of Darkness*, keeps Marlow within the Kierkegaardian "ethical" realm.[46] Dying, Bakhtin observes, is an event for others, not for the one who dies, for after one's death others will finalize and summarize one's life. As Gary Saul Morson and Caryl Emerson remark, describing Bakhtin's views on death and finalization, "When someone dies, he at last becomes fully available for a finalizing image because he can no longer change himself; it is an event in the lives of those who survive and who contemplate and finalize that being's life. Finalization is only possible from the outside."[47] Or as Conrad writes in *Under Western Eyes*, "The dead can live only with the exact intensity and quality of the life imparted to them by the living" (290). Marlow's discourse is a refracting medium, not entirely transparent and certainly not a simple mirror held up to nature; it is an imaginative structure whose powers to represent and configure the real are the novel's true problematic, and never more so than in the discourse's representation of Kurtz's death.

Marlow finalizes Kurtz by recourse to the grand and tragic narrative of sin and redemption, presenting Kurtz's last words as the generically familiar deathbed confession. As if to underline the generic choice of tragedy (earlier the towns along the coast had "farcical" names), Kurtz's death occurs offstage and is reported by a messenger—"Mistah Kurtz—he dead" (69). These generic choices are ideologically freighted, reaffirming Western values by means of a recurrent grand narrative (sin and redemption) and a dominant genre (tragedy) of our culture.

Marlow is like one of Hayden White's nineteenth-century historians, whose emplotments correspond to one of four archetypal story forms: romance, tragedy, comedy, or satire. White argues that the choice of one of these forms is dictated not by the story events themselves but pragmatically, by the reader's expectations and by considerations of acceptability: "The encodation of events in terms of such plot structures is one of the ways that a culture has of making sense of both personal and public pasts." Furthermore, White argues, such encodations arise out of the dialogic relationship between the historian and his or her public, revealing the historian's willingness to share with the public an understanding of the forms "that significant human

situations *must* take by virtue of his participation in the specific processes of sense-making which identify him as a member of one cultural
endowment rather than another."[48]

What happens in Conrad's fiction, according to William Bonney,
is the staging of a confrontation between "semiotic patterns that are
culturally antecedent to Conrad and Conrad's reconstitution of them
in his own works."[49] Or, as Bakhtin writes, referring specifically to
spoken utterances such as Marlow's:

> The speaker's speech will is manifested primarily in the *choice of a
> particular genre.* This choice is determined by the specific nature of
> the given sphere of speech communication, semantic (thematic)
> considerations, the concrete situation of the speech communica-
> tion, the personal composition of its participants, and so on. And
> when the speaker's plan with all its individuality and subjectivity
> is applied and adapted to a chosen genre, it is shaped and devel-
> oped within a certain generic form. Such genres exist above all
> in the great and multifarious sphere of everyday oral communi-
> cation, including the most familiar and the most intimate.

Such genres develop "in continuous and constant interaction with
others' individual utterances," Bakhtin claims: "This experience can
be characterized to some degree as the process of *assimilation*—more
or less creative—of others' words. . . . Our speech . . . is filled with
others' words, varying degrees of otherness and varying degrees of
'our-own-ness,' varying degrees of awareness and detachment."[50]

Kurtz's death becomes an event in the lives of others and is
shared with others by virtue of its encoding in a familiar speech (and
literary) genre—it is a tragedy of sin and redemption. Thus his story
implies that the grand narrative of Western Christianity is true and
that there is salvation for even the worst imperialist. This comforting
writing of Kurtz's death is the result of Marlow's "drawing back" (69)
from the abyss Kurtz stepped over. Thus, while McClure's analysis of
Marlow's confrontation with imperialist ideology is excellent in many
ways, his version of Marlow's "end" is mistaken. McClure is right to
say that Marlow has learned "the radical provisionality of his own
everyday world." But it is not clear that in the end Marlow "breaks out
of the positivistic, self-confident conceptual universe of Victorianism
into the relativistic, doubt-ridden world of modern consciousness."[51]
I believe Marlow is correct in reporting that he drew back—but back
into the conceptual world McClure has him abandoning. As Hay says,
"The logic of ideas in history is discovered partly through Marlow's
effort not to face it in *Heart of Darkness.*"[52]

Conrad's letter to Cunninghame Graham referred to earlier asserted that the real intentions of the novel would emerge in secondary considerations involving its ending. Marlow tells his listeners on the *Nellie* that the particular ending spoken to Kurtz's Intended—also generically familiar, a tragic and romantic love story—was a lie. The decision to tear the words "Exterminate all the brutes!" from the bottom of Kurtz's essay on repressing savage customs created another lie concerning an ending. The relationship between closure and truth is thus problematized, and readers who are suspicious of grand narratives and of the tropological nature of "truth" and "history" might extend such suspicion to Kurtz's deathbed confession and the triumph that Marlow reads into "The horror! The horror!"

The notion of Kurtz's redemption serves ideological needs by locating Kurtz's failure—and, by extension, that of Western imperialism—within a larger providential order. This is in keeping with Marlow's nostalgia for the Hegelian Idea, which uses the passions of humans in unknowable ways for the ultimate good. This appropriation of Kurtz's dying words to a comforting grand narrative corresponds to the phenomenon of finalization as described by Bakhtin.[53] Finalizing Kurtz in the grand Christian narrative of sin and redemption is more subtle than simply tearing away a part of his writing, but it has a similar purpose in its serving the interests of the living. Again, this is like the deconstructive oppositions White sees in historical texts: "The dialectical tension which characterizes the work of every master historian usually arises from an effort to wed a mode of emplotment with a mode of argument or of ideological implication which is inconsonant with it."[54] Conrad intentionally foregrounds not only the tension between narrator and story but that between narrator and audience, revealing a pragmatics by which the reader must always impose his or her own metanarratives and interpretive strategies in an attempt to wrest meaning from a text that always warns us of the arbitrariness of interpretation.

There is a scarcity of "story" and an abundance of "discourse" in what Marlow says about Kurtz's death. Marlow provides a few disconnected story elements concerning Kurtz, but his knowledge is so fragmentary that most of what we think we know is a "writerly" construct of either Marlow's discourse or our own. We know that the Russian mentions cartridges, but we only infer that Kurtz shot people or had them shot. We know there are shrunken heads around his hut, but we only infer how they got there or why—Marlow says Kurtz turned the heads inward so they would "adore" him, but Marlow actually knows nothing of the reasons for their placement. One's knowledge of another's heart is never clear. We know Kurtz wrote an essay, then scrawled a postscript, but we do not know (although Marlow makes a vague guess) when these events occurred in relation to other verified or inferred events. The reader writes many ghost chapters, fills many gaps, and discards many alien associations in totalizing and refamiliarizing Marlow's defamiliarized and inconclusive narrative.[55] And, like Marlow's original act of narration, this refamiliarization calls upon ideological beliefs (our own little stories or grand narratives), since these beliefs provide the discursive structure with which to make a story.

In *Beyond Culture* Lionel Trilling called attention to the ambiguity of "The horror! The horror!": "To me it is still ambiguous whether Kurtz's famous death-bed cry . . . refers to the approach of death or to his experience of savage life."[56] These, of course, are not the only options—Kurtz could, for instance, simply be pitying himself in overly dramatic terms for the interruption of his plans. Nonetheless, Trilling sees Kurtz as a hero of the spirit. Similarly, Raval's excellent exercise in skepticism, while acknowledging interpretive uncertainty, capitulates to a reading that credits Kurtz with profound insight and conversion. Raval notes that "Kurtz's final judgment could have nothing extraordinary about it," but he goes on to opt for a reading that grants Kurtz an achieved insight into "his experience of savage life." When he says Kurtz died knowing "that his eloquence and idealism are only masks which hide the truth" and that this truth concerns "culture" and the impotence of "the ideal of the self" (35), he dominates and colonizes Kurtz's subjectivity with his own desires, making Kurtz into a quasi-Marxist critic of language and ideology.

Historically, *Heart of Darkness* has seduced readers into accepting and then elaborating on certain assumptions of Marlow's discourse, as though to view this discourse with complete detachment would be too dark altogether. Conrad seems to have achieved the perfect writerly text, since each reader can make Kurtz aware, in his death, of whatever truth is most dear to that reader. The history of the interpretation of Kurtz's dying words can be read as the history of an idealizing search for heroes of subjectivity in English and American cultural commentary. Like all deaths, Kurtz's is an event in the lives of those who survive, and his words belong also to them. To write something heroic or uplifting into Kurtz's final words is to seek to recuperate bourgeois subjectivity and culture by inserting Kurtz's words into one of the grand narratives of that culture. This finalization of Kurtz shifts emphasis away from a critique of imperial exploitation, just as Marlow's admiration of the cannibals' "restraint" shifted emphasis from the political to the subjective. With this finalization, then, what was oppositional in Marlow's discourse drowns—like Prufrock's inner voice—in the official words of others.

But other interpretations of Kurtz's dying words would be entirely compatible with the banality of a man who died raving about his own great plans and ideas. One can accept the interpretive rule of significance—that the best interpretation yields the most significance from the text—and still insist that the greatest (and darkest) significance is in Kurtz's utter banality, even at his end.

III

Marlow's emplotting of Kurtz's death might be added to the trial orderings Brooks discusses in *Reading for the Plot*, orderings in which "story never appears to be quite matched to the narrative plot that is responsible for it." [57] The people on the *Nellie* hear their trial ordering of Kurtz's death before they hear the lie Marlow told the Intended, and this encourages the assumption that the plotting offered on the *Nellie* is the real story. The lie to the Intended was not premeditated, but was dictated by the fluid circumstances of Marlow's encounter with her. It remains uncertain whether Marlow had planned from the start to offer the particular finalization of Kurtz that he does on the *Nellie*, or whether this decision might also have arisen during his narration. Marlow's prefatory story about the young Roman, which arose as a spontaneous response to the frame narrator's jingoistic hyperbole, anticipates the Kurtz story but says nothing about the Roman's final repentance and victory, only his ending in savagery. By the time Marlow gets to the point of discussing Kurtz's death, his discourse has been interrupted more than once, and he has become frustrated with his inability to reach his audience in a meaningful way, as one can hear in his impatient questions: "Do you see him? Do you see the story? Do you see anything?" (30).

The silences that mark this frustration are part of Marlow's discourse, revealing the incommensurability of the story he would tell and the story his audience is willing to hear. [58] After one of his silences, and in apparent response to a listener's objection that he is being absurd, Marlow exclaims: "Absurd! This is the worst of trying to tell. . . . Here you all are each moored with two good addresses like a hulk with two anchors, a butcher round one corner, a policeman round another, excellent appetites, and temperature normal—hear you—normal from year's end to year's end. And you say, Absurd! Absurd be—exploded!" (48).

Perhaps Marlow's decision to eulogize Kurtz was made at some point *after* his audience began to find his story "absurd," since the absurd is that which remains unassimilated by our familiar grand narratives. London discusses such moments in the text as indicating Marlow's need to assert a sort of masculine dominance over his audience, particularly in view of his having taken a feminine position in relation to Kurtz.[59] I believe she is correct to find a politics in the margins of the discourse, in the exchanges between Marlow and his auditors, although the political implications that I find are less conditioned by gender considerations than are London's.

We all know how, in our own "natural" narrative transactions, the promptings and proddings of our listeners help to shape the speech genre of the story we are telling. At the outset Marlow presented his story as a *petit recit* in opposition to the grand historical narrative of exploration, progress, and the just cause of imperialism; but in the pragmatics of the narrative transaction this oppositional intention has not been well received, and he now speaks from within the audience's grand allegorical (in the medieval sense) narrative of personal redemption.[60] As exemplified in the medieval system of levels of interpretation, culture offers only a finite set of metaencodings for the myriad literal stories people produce. Marlow may deny and expose one of these encodings, the metastory of progress and colonial altruism, but he must do this from within another of these culturally prescribed grand narratives.[61]

Aaron Fogel speaks only of Marlow's lie to the Intended as an example of "forced speech," but his argument, had he chosen to deal with *Heart of Darkness* at greater length, perhaps would have led him to discuss the elements of coercion to speak on board the *Nellie*.[62] Although coercion may be too strong a word to describe Marlow's narrative decisions, Fogel's thesis is certainly provocative: "Conrad's art presents persons having effects on each other as agents. There is not good ground for suggesting that he believes that discourse produces us, rather than vice versa. But insofar as he also denies that "true" speech is what is produced freely, or from within, or in deep, intimate conversation, he seems 'antihumanist.' Speech instead is 'force.' "[63]

Conrad dramatized the narrator's speech undergoing changes during the speech act in *The Nigger of the "Narcissus,"* which ends with a narrator who is distinct from the various voices that speak through most of the story. And the Marlow we meet in *Youth* also changes as he speaks (and drinks); his final sentimentality, which is also an interpretive discourse, is loosed by intoxication. Although narratives are usually read under the assumption that a stable and fixed intention governs the text from beginning to end, there is no reason to suppose that texts imitating oral speech might not imitate the revisions of intention that often exist during actual speech, revisions "coerced," or at least prompted, by the pragmatic speaking situation, particularly the silences and frustrations of listeners. Within *Heart of Darkness*, the changed intention—the changed genre—of Kurtz's scrawled conclusion to his essay on the improvement of the "savages" establishes the theme of a text that reaches closure only by radically altering itself.[64]

Marlow talked of the "impossibility" of conveying the truth of his African experience, comparing it to an entirely private "dream-sensation" (30). In *The Interpretation of Dreams* (published at about the same time as *Heart of Darkness*), Freud defines "secondary revision" as the alterations and reinterpretations of the dream that occur when the dream is remembered and/or reported in the codes of waking thought and speech. The dream, like Marlow's experiences, is only known as a translation into a different medium occurring in a different "state" of consciousness, and the reported dream may be further altered by the patient's perceptions of its reception (by the pragmatics) in the therapeutic setting. The latent dream is as purely subjective as mental activity can become, occurring in a state where the codes and constraints of normal life are relaxed or absent. It is therefore knowable and representable only in a very problematical sense, and dream analysis ends up interpreting secondary representations of the dream—the daytime discourse upon, and emplotment of, the dream—rather than the "true" dream itself.[65]

For Freud's purposes this substitution has a theoretical but no great practical consequence, since the secondary discourse tells us much about the subject and his or her orientation in the social realm— be that subject a dreamer or a narrator. This waking discourse is a fabric of official ideologies that encircle and contain (that "censor," in Freud's own political metaphor) the unofficial ideology of the latent dream thought. The opposition between the original latent dream and the revised manifest dream is therefore like the unstable narratological opposition between story and discourse. In comparing his story to a dream, Marlow lends his own authority to our analysis of the revisionary nature of his discourse, an analysis that finds Marlow revising his "nightmare" within the daytime codes and values—the grand narratives—of the European community, even as darkness, a harbinger of sleep and dreams, descends around the representatives of that community on the *Nellie*.

It is traditional now, thanks largely to Albert Guerard, to read *Heart of Darkness* as Marlow's inner journey and to see a transformation in Marlow from the young adventurer into the contemplative Buddha for whom "the glamour's off" (11). To suggest that covert changes may occur in Marlow even as he narrates extends this interest in Marlow as a dynamic character. To see such changes as negotiations among social discourses is not to deny the inner journey, since the inner self is constituted from these discourses. In Lacan's famous saying, the unconscious is the discourse of the Other. In the act of narration, Marlow's inward navigation returns to the public genres and modes of perception by which our culture constructs subjects.[66] Thus, when Conrad says that "secondary considerations" concerning the novel's ending contain the heart of the story, he may well mean something like the process of secondary revision. After referring to secondary considerations, Conrad's letter to Graham says that the beginning of *Heart of Darkness* "chimes in with your convictions," presumably Graham's objections to imperialism. But Conrad adds, *"Mais après? There is an après."*[67]

This *après* may be Marlow's retreat into the supporting assumptions of imperialism. His desperate quest for such support is noted by Hay: "It is typical of Marlow's dilemma that while he claims to be concerned above all with self-knowledge and truth, he progresses toward deception and denial; while disdainful of the staves which all the European civilizers carry in the Congo, he obsessively frets that they and he himself lack anything to support them; and while priding himself on the power of his English belief in an idea, he can find no "real" idea in his head to support him when he needs it."[68] This excellent characterization of Marlow falls short only in not seeing that his discourse on Kurtz's redemption, as a sort of secondary revision, *is* the final, supporting deception toward which he has progressed.

One change in Marlow is acknowledged by Marlow himself in his overt story—the illness he carried with him from the Congo. Marlow's illness was alluded to at the outset by the framing narrator, who referred to Marlow's yellow complexion and sunken cheeks (1), and Marlow tells us that upon his return his temperature was seldom normal (70). Marlow's illness, which occurs in the literal "story," parallels the metastory of illness that was offered in Marlow's discourse as a possible explanation of Kurtz's change.

Illness in the individual, as Richard Ohmann shows in his analysis of American literature from 1960 to 1975, is often a displaced representation of illness in the society.[69] The illness can be either mental or physical: "Through the story of mental disorientation or derangement, then, these novels transform deep social contradictions into a dynamic of personal crisis, a sense of there being no comfortable place in the world for the private self. These books are narratives of illness."[70] One aspect of the society's illness is the sham nature of most of the work it requires people to perform. It is fitting that as Marlow reaffirms an ideology of individualism in his finalization of Kurtz, and as he performs the tasks of the conquerors who are responsible for the grove of death, he himself should suffer the physical encoding—the sickness— of the social relations this ideology engenders and justifies.

Although Conrad says in the preface to *The Nigger of the "Narcissus"* that the author's job is to make us see, perception has complex origins; the word through which perception is mediated is a shared word, and this dialogism shapes the narrator's vision and re-vision. Conrad's preface also says that the artist "descends within himself, and in that lonely region of stress and strife, if he be deserving and fortunate, he finds the terms of his appeal."[71] If that lonely region within is inhabited by the discourse of the Other, one's "appeal" is found there because it is a place where the inside becomes the outside, where nomads meet and distinctions between the intrinsic and the extrinsic vanish. By confronting the shared words of the unconscious, one again becomes social, but this can only be a "cure" if the society itself is healthy. Thus the journey Guerard likens to psychic exploration is a discovery of illness that is both one's own and more.

My emphasis on the problematic, shared nature of Marlow's discourse, especially my refusal to grant ultimate authority to the grand narrative of redemption with which he interprets Kurtz's last words, may be unsettling (or absurd) to many readers. Since it denies traditional "givens" of the story and leaves less that we know for sure, it may seem to be an exercise in the occlusion of meaning. But I prefer to see it as an examination of the *conditions* of narrative meaning—and of a text written to invite an examination of those conditions. Therefore, when Marlow says, "I have a voice too, and for good or evil mine is the speech that cannot be silenced" (38), one experiences a level of irony that escapes Marlow's control, since the voice that cannot be silenced is not entirely his own; his words are also the speech of others. Furthermore, as Fogel observes, Marlow's incessant discourse doubles the coercive power of Kurtz's speech and, by extension, colonialism's coercive discourse.[72]

The word "discourse" echoes throughout *Heart of Darkness*. It is as an eloquent, discoursing voice that Kurtz first attracts Marlow: "I made the strange discovery that I had never imagined him as doing, you know, but as discoursing" (48). If "doing" is the action in a story, Marlow privileges discourse over story. This privileging occurs also in Marlow's comment on Kurtz's essay: "There was the unbounded power of eloquence—or words—of burning noble words. There were no practical hints to interrupt the magic current of phrases" (50–51). But at one point, in the darkness, Marlow himself seems to be merely a disembodied voice to the framing narrator, who searches for the "clue to the faint uneasiness inspired by this narrative that seemed to shape itself without human lips in the heavy night air of the river" (30). For the framing narrator, Marlow the person has disappeared, leaving only language suspended in darkness. All the suspicion of language that Marlow creates reflects back on his own discourse, also a source of unease.

Jonathan Culler's demonstration of the difficulty of maintaining a distinction between story and discourse is a narratological application of the epistemological notion that facts are constituted by paradigms and discursive formations rather than the reverse. His analysis of *Oedipus Rex* and *Daniel Deronda* shows that story events that are usually assumed to be simply reported *in* discourse are in fact produced by the demands *of* discourse.[73] While it is impossible to do away with the perspective by which fictive events "really" happened, it is just as impossible not to recognize the perspective by which discourse subverts this assumption. Concluding his discussion of *Oedipus*, Culler says:

> Oedipus himself and all his readers are convinced of his guilt but our conviction does not come from the revelation of the deed. Instead of the revelation of a prior deed determining meaning, we could say that it is meaning, the convergence of meaning in the narrative discourse, that leads us to posit this deed as its appropriate manifestation. . . . Instead of saying, therefore, that there is a sequence of past events that are given and which the play reveals with certain detours, we can say that the crucial event is the product of demands of signification. Here meaning is not the effect of a prior event but its cause.[74]

Kurtz's atrocities in the social world and his victory in the spiritual world are similarly "the product of demands of signification" made by Marlow's discourse. Marlow's redemptive finalizing of Kurtz (and the reader's acceptance of it as an event "in" the story) is demanded by his need to redeem "the idea" of colonialism, as well as his pragmatic need to make contact with his Western audience. We say that Kurtz said "The horror! The horror!" because he saw the light, but we say it because it is too dark to think otherwise. Thus Marlow's discourse, which ostensibly critiques the official grand narrative of colonialism, is marked by what Freud called transference, a relationship occurring when a discourse repeats, in an altered or displaced manner, those processes that are its object of inquiry.

As Frank Kermode argues in *The Sense of an Ending*, our fictions serve to console us, not simply to tell us the truth; they respond to our need "to live by the pattern rather than the fact."[75] In *Heart of Darkness* the narratees, in need of the consolations of propaganda, conspire with Marlow's discourse to transfer a consoling "truth" to Kurtz's story.[76] The way in which this aspect of Marlow's discourse arises out of the social immediacy of his situation is suggested by Volosinov and Bakhtin:

> Every sign, as we know, is a construct between socially organized persons in the process of their interaction. Therefore, *the forms of signs are conditioned above all by the social organization of the participants involved and also by the immediate conditions of their interaction.* When these forms change, so does the sign. And it should be one of the tasks of the study of ideologies to trace this social life of the verbal sign. Only so approached can the *problem of the relationship between sign and existence* find its concrete expression; only then will the process of the causal shaping of the sign by existence stand out as a process of genuine existence-to-sign transit, of genuine dialectical refraction of existence in the sign.[77]

Culler addresses the audience's constitutive activity when he speaks of the logic by which an event determines discursive responses and of the alternate logic by which discourse requires us to posit prior events, the logic by which discourse *creates* story. Culler says that "these two logics cannot be brought together in harmonious synthesis; each works by the exclusion of the other; each depends on a hierarchical relation between story and discourse which the other inverts."[78]

If Marlow's grand narrative concerning Kurtz's last words is a product of certain needs, could one argue the same for the last words themselves, for the literal story? Did Kurtz "really" utter them? Barbara Herrnstein Smith argues that literary discourse is an imitation of some other form of discourse; novels imitate histories or autobiographies, and so on: "As a general class, literary artworks may be conceived of as depictions or representations, rather than instances, of natural discourses. . . . The various genres of literary art—for example, dramatic poems, tales, odes, lyrics—can to some extent be distinguished according to what types of discourse—for example, dialogues, anecdotes of past events, public speeches, and private declarations—they characteristically represent."[79] *Heart of Darkness* is an imitation of what

William Labov has called "natural narratives"—stories told by real people in real social situations.[80]

One characteristic of a natural narrative is that it contains "evaluative" discourse, language designed to make the story seem worthwhile to its audience. Marlow's interpretive language concerning Kurtz's victory would be an example of such audience-oriented evaluation. But Labov also points out that often a storyteller will invent things that supposedly take place *in the story,* but that did not actually occur, simply for their evaluative effect, as when someone says, "And then I thought, 'My God! We're all going to be killed!' " The person probably didn't think this at all, but presenting it as part of the story makes a discursive or evaluative point.

In commenting on Labov, Culler says that "one can emphasize the reportability of a story by attributing an evaluative comment to one of the participants and narrating this comment as an event in the story."[81] In other words, not only does reading sometimes require that we reverse the hierarchical relationship between story and discourse, it requires at times that we deconstruct this relationship entirely. By virtue of a sort of catachresis, the characteristics of discourse get transferred to story in a manner that occludes the boundary between story and discourse. Marlow's own comparison of his story to a dream allows this speculation, for the kind of discursive distortion that the official censorship mechanism works on the latent dream thought affects the dream "story" itself, not simply the waking, interpretive discourse that is produced upon the remembered dream.

It is possible, then, that "The horror! The horror!" is just such a distortion, a piece of official evaluative discourse transferred into the story to make the story acceptable to its narratees as a sign of Kurtz's repentance. Culler quotes Labov as saying: " 'Pointless stories are met with the withering rejoinder, "So what?" Every good narrator is continually warding off this question.' "[82] One recalls Marlow having to ward off the charge of absurdity; one way to do it is to invent profound dying words for Kurtz. The archetypal example of this kind of undecidable relation between story and discourse occurs in Freud's analysis of the Wolfman's story of his "primal scene" experienced at age one-and-a-half. Freud ultimately concludes that it is impossible to know whether this scene really occurred, or whether the Wolfman simply needs to believe that it occurred. If the latter is true, then the Wolfman was finding something available in the public discourse and writing it into his own story so as to generate an explanation of later feelings by supplying a specific cause. Marlow may be similarly occupied in "making" sense.

Ronald Schleifer, discussing Roland Barthes's theory of writing, also questions the reality of Kurtz's final words: "Even Kurtz's 'voice'– imitated in Marlow's discourse—might not be so clear as it seems: what Marlow takes as Kurtz's whisper, 'The horror! The horror!' and elaborates ('writes' out) in such obsessive detail, might only be the stretorous breathing of a dying man, what Barthes calls the 'grain' of the voice. It might be 'misquoted.' "[83] I assume that many readers will decline to agree that the words "The horror! The horror!" were not actually spoken. Brooks is correct to say that "certain canons of readability remain necessary," and the willful turning of events in the story into the lies of an unreliable or politically implicated discourse without good evidence would make reading impossible. Perhaps showing how the analogy between literary narrative and natural narrative could be used to question such pivotal "facts" of the story simply illustrates the limits of Barbara Herrnstein Smith's idea that literature imitates nonliterary discourses such as natural narratives. But the story at the heart of any narrative discourse is a dark thing, achieving its shape and contour by the light of conventions of reading. Or perhaps the story is like the blinding but absent sun in the frame narrator's famous characterization of the relationship between Marlow's tales and their meanings. In any case, if one admits even the possibility that "The horror! The horror!" comes from the evaluative needs of Marlow's discourse, then the comfortable distinction between story and discourse deconstructs.[84]

This distinction originates in the conventional semantic notion of language as a set of signifiers referring to extralinguistic referents. These referents become, in narratology, the "kernels" of the story, as Seymour Chatman calls them.[85] If, however, we adopt the Bakhtinian position that each utterance is an overdetermined response to a large set of conditions and constraints—such as the speaker's perception of audience, the motives and interests of the speaker and audience, the setting in which the utterance occurs, and the question of what is permitted and what is discouraged by dominant ideologies—then the need that the story/discourse and the signifier/referent oppositions filled ceases to exist, since the utterance is now understood in terms of these conditions and constraints and not simply in terms of "the referent."[86] These social conditions produce "genres of speech performance" determined by "the extraverbal milieu" and "other people."[87] Marlow's generic encoding of Kurtz's death is a classic example of such a speech performance.

These conditions and constraints engender Marlow's discursive assertion of Kurtz's redemptive victory, and they may also engender his "story" element—"The horror! The horror!"—on which this discourse hangs. Story and discourse dissolve into one another as an effect of the reconciliation Marlow seeks between himself and the values of the culture he began by critiquing. If this reconciliation seems at odds with Marlow's opening intentions, then something has happened to molest those intentions.

"Molestation," as Edward Said employs the term, is what happens to undermine narrative authority, and it is "central to a character's experience of disillusionment during the course of a novel." Since so much of Kurtz's story, whatever it really is, "is posited outside of Marlow's discourse," we are inevitably left questioning Marlow's authority. Thus, Said contends that "by the end of the tale we are aware of something that Marlow has given birth to that eludes empirical verification, even as it rests most securely upon the fact that Marlow has delivered it. Here, in most of its senses, authority is involved, except that we are required to accept that authority as never final." [88]

Endings are necessary fictions that console us by giving a shape and a significance to time. These fictions often refer not to some immediately available reality but to other fictions, and our sophisticated modern fictions have, Kermode says, "a real relation to simpler fictions about the world." [89] This highly mediated or deferred relation to reality is a version of the "molestation" of narrative authority Said describes. Fictions do not simply imitate the truth of experience but conspire with historical reality to confer truth upon experience. Kermode recognizes that this "truth" can be political as well as personal or spiritual when he speaks of the temporal fictions upon which both Marxist and fascist ideologies have rested. [90] Marlow's discourse sifts through shards and fragments of other fictions, of stories we tell to explain ourselves and our culture as they change in time. In navigating the Congo River, Marlow served imperial interests, and in the end his narration navigates back to some of the founding beliefs of imperial culture, recuperating an eschatology that offers an otherworldly redemption and victory to even the worst of imperial Europe's sons.

3

Lord Jim and the Pragmatics of Narrative

When once the truth is grasped that one's own personality is only a ridiculous and aimless masquerade of something hopelessly unknown, the attainment of serenity is not very far off.

Joseph Conrad, Letter to Edward Garnett

And the idea that I think we need today in order to make decisions in political matters cannot be the idea of totality, or of the unity, of a body. It can only be the idea of a multiplicity or of a diversity.

Jean-François Lyotard, *Just Gaming*

Conrad interrupted his writing of *Lord Jim* to complete *Heart of Darkness*, and many intertextual relations exist between these novels. They are linked not only by Marlow's presence and the attendant foregrounding of the pragmatics of narration, but by themes of cross-cultural encounters and imperialism, and by—above all—issues concerning justice and the subject. Jim and Kurtz both turn their backs on Western culture, both seem to discover new selves, and both adopt relationships to people of another culture. But Jim's career (as posited in the conventional or friendly reading of the novel) of benevolent lawgiver and arbitrator in Patusan, although ultimately a failure, is in most respects the opposite of Kurtz's cynical exploitation. Suresh Raval says that "if Kurtz has surrendered himself to the archetypal passions, Jim has surrendered himself to an impossible ideal of the self."[1] And Avrom Fleishman nicely sums up the parallels between Jim and Kurtz and the way these parallels establish the opposition between the exploiting conqueror and the benevolent colonist. Jim, Fleishman optimistically asserts, becomes a significant and positive political force within his new community, and Jim's constructive political action stands in contrast to the mere "work" performed in *Heart of Darkness*. [2]

If these differences compel us to hear a different Marlow in *Lord Jim*, this is not surprising from the standpoint of dialogics and pragmatics, since Marlow has a different audience in the two novels—the bourgeois businessmen of *Heart of Darkness*, defined specifically by their economic functions, as opposed to the less narrowly identified and perhaps more intimate friends of *Lord Jim*. Each audience elicits from Marlow a separate discourse with its own assumptions and purposes. On the other hand, the more positive picture of the impossibly idealistic white man among the Malaysians recalls Marlow's worship of the saving "idea" that would justify colonialism in *Heart of Darkness*, and perhaps Marlow's desire to give Jim the benefit of every doubt is a continuation of his turn back to consoling interpretations implied when he grants Kurtz a heroic "victory" and redemption at the moment of his death. That Jim's career in Patusan, despite all of Marlow's generous assessments, is ultimately a political failure speaks of the presence in these texts of Kant's awareness of the incommensurable gulf between the Idea and its embodiment in institutions and practices.

By embedding the Kurtz story, or story fragment, in the individualistic and ahistorical assumptions of a grand narrative of sin and redemption, Marlow turns the discourse away from history and social criticism; once Kurtz is pronounced victorious, Marlow has nothing more to say about the Africans and what has been inflicted upon them. The question of justice for Marlow gives way to a question of what happens to the soul of the sinner rather than what is done for earthly victims; society's illness, as seen in such distortions of the concept of justice, becomes encoded in Marlow's body as literal illness. Fredric Jameson argues that a similar concealment of the real violence of imperialism occurs in *Lord Jim*. [3] Although there is much to object to in the imperialism depicted in *Lord Jim*, the objections do not find voice in Marlow's discourse to the extent that they did in *Heart of Darkness*. Marlow likened his story in *Heart of Darkness* to a dream, and Jameson assumes that in *Lord Jim* some of the message of the dream has receded into the unconscious, requiring an archaeological recovery from the novel's "political unconscious."

Probing this place of the Other's discourse involves a foregrounding of those aspects of Marlow's tale inherited from, and shared with, the larger cultural and societal discourses in which he lives, just as in *Heart of Darkness* Marlow's inner journey led him to rediscover connections with public myths. Martin Green has demonstrated the affiliations between imperial politics and English adventure stories, beginning with *Robinson Crusoe*. The adventure story, Green says, is the "generic counterpart in literature to empire in politics."[4] Bette London argues that the "generic codes of melodrama, mystery, suspense, romance" are implicit in Marlow's voice in *Heart of Darkness* and that these codes constitute some of the many ways Marlow's voice is occupied by the ideological assumptions of imperialism, racism, and sexism.[5] One of the most interesting differences between *Heart of Darkness* and *Lord Jim* is that the generic codes become revealed in *Lord Jim*, codes that construct a culture's assumptions concerning truth and authentic experience. The foregrounding of stories and storytelling in *Lord Jim* not so much conceals—*pace* Jameson and others who find in Conrad only an imperialist progagandist—as reveals the connections between adventure stories, other culturally naturalized forms of narrative, and a failing imperial project.

If the word "discourse" haunts Marlow's own discourse in *Heart of Darkness*, the word "story" plays a parallel self-referential role in *Lord Jim*. James Batchelor, in his book-length introduction to *Lord Jim*, explores this novel's numerous connections with other stories, many of which have the affiliation with imperial politics asserted by Green, London, and Patrick Brantlinger. Batchelor reveals how narrative materials are circulated, transferred, or smuggled across borders from one discursive sphere to another. The novel's central irony of the unnecessary betrayal is also found in *The Red Badge of Courage*, since both the battle line in Stephen Crane's novel and the bulkhead in Conrad's do not break after all. And despite Conrad's disdain for Robert Louis Stevenson, the way that Conrad's story and two of Stevenson's novels share similar kernels of plot was apparent to an early reviewer of *The Pall Mall Gazette*, who wrote: "When Jim, the burly German Captain, and his two engineers come up from the sea, as Marlow describes it, we are faintly conscious of some old familiar acquaintances. It is out of *The Wrecker* that these people have strayed; or is it, perhaps, *The Ebb-Tide* that has been brought to our recollection by their faces and characters and destinies?"[6]

Both of these novels by Stevenson deal with an upper-class English outlaw. *The Ebb-Tide* depicts three Englishmen who are destitute in the Pacific islands. In the second part of the two-part narrative they become active adventurers of the sort who assault Heyst and Lena in *Victory*. The narrative technique of *The Wrecker*, with its central character who tells his tale to the narrator, resembles Conrad's technique in *Lord Jim*. The upper-class Englishman, Carthew, is treated sympathetically even though he is involved with others in the murder of the crew of a stranded ship, after which the murderers pose as survivors. Carthew goes unpunished, and, as Batchelor says, "he is, as Stevenson does not, but easily could, write, 'one of us.' "[7] In "The Secret Sharer" Conrad also treats the crime that apparently must be exempted from normal justice. As Nietzsche argued, good and bad are terms we give to what belongs to us and what belongs to others. Marlow seeks to "make all possible allowances" for Jim because he is "one of us" (45), and in "The Secret Sharer" the young captain's crime of abetting Leggatt's escape paradoxically functions in a positive way to prepare the captain for command, whereas the captain of the *Sephora* who wishes to enforce the law is depicted as weak and foolish.[8] The example of Stevenson shows that the question of making ad hoc "allowances" for certain of "our" people was a theme Conrad shared with the larger cultural conversation of late Victorian England. And Conrad's themes of conduct, law, and the ability or inability of "our" people to maintain their selfhood in the absence of normal societal constraints is found also in Stevenson's less fully realized novels.

Batchelor sees antecedents to the bonding between Jim and Marlow in James Fenimore Cooper's Natty Bumppo and Chingachgook, a bonding that in both cases "is almost incommunicable, and which stretches the novelist's linguistic and dramatic resources."[9] This bonding exists in the absence of a social world in which the characters can feel at home, an absence underlined in *Lord Jim* by the Malabar Hotel scene—with the strategically placed references to the banality of the tourists in whose ambient discourses Jim speaks of his own identity— and again later by Marlow's own ode to home. On a more general level, both *Heart of Darkness* and *Lord Jim* take part in a dialogue with (and not a rejection of) Kipling's cheerleading defense of "the idea" of British colonialism, while at the same time *Lord Jim* has roots in travel books such as Alfred Wallace's *The Malay Archipelago* (1869). Wallace was a naturalist whose account of the discovery of a certain butterfly is written into Stein's story. Furthermore, influences on *Lord Jim*, both general and specific, have been identified in stories by Maupassant, Flaubert, Turgenev, and Dostoevsky, as well in the philosophy of Schopenhauer.[10] More distant origins exist in heroic, romantic, and tragic literatures. One of these dialogic connections is revealed in Dorothy Van Ghent's excellent discussion of Jim and Oedipus.[11]

This textual rhizome does not exist only in what we artificially call the "literary" domain. Jim, as we know, was modeled on such historical figures as James Brooke, who lived among Malaysians during the first half of the nineteenth century and gained fame as a benevolent lawgiver, and Jim Lingard, whom Conrad had met.[12] The "Brooke myth" was manipulated by Brooke himself, together with his admirers and hired biographers; since most of what was written about Brooke came from within this circle of mythmakers, the boundaries between history and fiction remain blurred. Brooke had come to represent among Westerners the ideal imperialist, and the Brooke myth is a particularly clear example of how the social discourse is already aesthetically encoded. Lingard comes to us represented in the more human form of a mere egoist. Also, the *Patna* episode appropriates from the pages of the news the *Jeddah* incident of 1880, which was widely discussed in the British press precisely in terms of issues of conduct and Western ideals, and Jim resembles the first mate of the *Jeddah*, Augustine Podmore Williams. Williams, like Jim, was the son of an English clergyman, and Conrad and Williams were both in Singapore in 1883, where they could have met. Captain Brierly's suicide was apparently suggested by the suicide of Captain Wallace of the *Cutty Sark*.

Gustav Morf argues that *Lord Jim* also has roots in Conrad's more personal experiences and psychology. In Morf's discussion the personal and the historical intersect, as he sees Jim's betrayal and ongoing sense of guilt as a displacement of Conrad's departure from Poland— itself a sinking ship—and of Conrad's ensuing self-criticisms.[13] (Morf observes, in an interesting moment of pre-phenomenological reading, that to an imperfect eye the "n" of "Patna" might look like the "ri" of "Patria.") It is also possible to see in the Marlow-Jim friendship a rewriting of Conrad's relationship with Stephen Crane. Crane, who died in 1900—the year of the publication of *Lord Jim*—was many years Conrad's junior, as Jim is Marlow's.[14] In all these ways and more, *Lord Jim* is a mingling and sharing of stories told elsewhere, making the novel one of Western culture's self-portraits at the turn of the century. As Raval says, the resonance and power of Jim as a fictional character reside "in the complicated mediation between fact and fiction that he represents."[15]

What we might therefore call the communal authorship of *Lord Jim* is reflected in a displaced manner within the novel as it replicates the circulation of stories, their border crossings, within the social discourse; the inside of the novel mirrors the outside, and Jim mediates "fact" and fiction within the fictive world of the novel. Marlow's story is made of many stories that he gathers in diverse places and times, and each element of Jim's story is also someone else's story—Captain Brierly's, the French lieutenant's, Gentleman Brown's. Marlow's discourse and point of view are dialogically inhabited by the words (in the form of either direct or indirect citation) and by the points of view of these others.

Marlow's story is itself told by an external narrator, and the unity of this story is further problematized when the narrator introduces Marlow by suggesting, with his "perhaps," that Marlow has told Jim stories at various other times and places, with each telling, perhaps, carrying its own pragmatic spin: "Perhaps it would be after dinner, on a verandah draped in motionless foliage and crowned with flowers, in the deep dusk speckled by fiery cigar-ends" (21). Possibly, then, what is presented as a direct quotation of a specific utterance by Marlow is actually an abstraction or typification, a text compiled from Marlow's variant tellings. Everywhere beneath the surface unity of "the" novel and "the" story of Jim lie fragmentation and multiplicity. If postmodernism, suspecting the regularization implicit in notions of totality and harmony, privileges dispersal, pastiche, and fragmentation, then *Lord Jim*, while unified by the centrality of Marlow's voice—but a voice plagued with doubts and uncertainties—anticipates a postmodern dispersal into perpetually decentered textuality; it can be read as a critique of singular metanarratives that would totalize and finalize their objects.

The very form and structure of the novel, then, reflect the central problematic of the unitary subject in Western culture while exemplifying the nomadic circulation of "little stories" within the social discourse. *Lord Jim* reveals the implications, for a theory of the subject and society, of what Didier Coste and other narratologists call "the narrative paradox."[16] Narrative affirms change while at the same time asserting that the self remains in some essential way unchanged—different yet the same. The narrative paradox is therefore a basic paradox that any discourse on selfhood must confront as it deals with the question of the shape of a life as a whole.

Or, to put it differently, it is only within a narrative form of knowledge that the subject can be understood in relation to past and future states. If such paradoxes are basic to narrative, this fact may account for the privileging of narrative over lyric and drama as the dominant genre in a society in which the subject has emerged as a problematic. More specifically, narrative offers a vehicle for exploration of the contradictions inherent in the bourgeois subject, which seeks to assert its wholeness and singularity outside of social relations and in spite of a reality of flux and instability. Claude Lévi-Strauss described myth as providing an imaginary reconciliation of real social contradictions; similarly, in its function as the organizer of unity and difference, narrative attempts to reconcile the contradiction between the unitary subject and the changing, historically conditioned subject. For Marlow the narrative paradox is further complicated by the multiplicity of the various Jim-myths and Jim-stories that come to him after his encounter in the Malabar Hotel.

The narrative paradox is foregrounded in *Lord Jim* with the contrast between Jim's cowardice on the *Patna* and his courage in Patusan. Many readers have felt that the novel does not negotiate the change or the paradox successfully, and that it shifts from the mode of psychological realism into the mode of romance and adventure literature in the Patusan story. Further, the novel's criticism of the romantic imperialist and of adventure literature's collusion with imperialism that is implied in the opening depiction of Jim and his self-concept derived from "holiday literature" may be undermined when the second half of the novel itself becomes an imperialistic adventure story; it is as though the novel's critique ends up reproducing the object of its criticism.

But in the Patusan story Marlow himself becomes self-conscious of the genres in which he speaks, thereby encouraging an examination of how the truth about selfhood is dependent on—and produced by—conventions of narrative encoding, on, as Marlow says, "the convention that lurks in all truth" (57). It is the force of such conventions that turns the self into a subject of social discipline. That there seem to be two stories and two genres placed side by side in this novel is, in other words, a form of the narrative paradox that is readable as a commentary on, first, the cultural fiction of the unified subject that must reconcile oneness with change and, second, the way selfhood must always be subjected to mediating narrative codes. If Marlow has ideological reasons for making all allowances and ultimately vindicating Jim, this vindication occurs in another speech genre and in another code from the one in which Jim's guilt was perceived. On a larger narrative scale, this genre shift is like the reassessment of Kurtz accomplished by narrating his death in the new (to Marlow's discourse) genre of the sin-and-redemption story.

In direct conversation, Jim seeks to tell his own story and thus to establish his status as a free agent whose project is unfinished. *Lord Jim* is profound and troubling because it suspends, throughout Marlow's intense meditation, undecidable questions concerning the relationships between the subject and the social bond. Jim's example raises "doubt of the sovereign power enthroned in a fixed standard of conduct" (31). Without such a sovereign power, society and the self drift into a crisis of legitimation wherein all codes become arbitrary and eventually lose authority. At times Marlow seems to see the self as a subjected and illusory product of conventions, as when he says of Jim's struggle in the Malabar, "It was solemn, and a little ridiculous, too, as they always are, those struggles of an individual trying to save from the fire his idea of what his moral identity should be, this precious notion of a convention, only one of the rules of the game, nothing more, but all the same so terribly effective by its assumption of unlimited power over natural instincts, by the awful penalties of its failure" (50). At this moment, whatever Jim is, Marlow is certainly one of us. He raises again the question informing *Heart of Darkness*: whether people can live from an authentic center in which the law has been fully internalized, or whether the self is nothing more than a version of the codes and conventions of a culture, an effect of various cultural and social language games.

The hint that the latter may be the case is given early in the novel when Jim is said to have been weaned on "light holiday literature" (4); here Conrad's framing narrator explicitly thematizes the shaping influence of societal discourses as they come to the individual already aesthetically encoded in entertaining narratives. Jim's internalization of these discourses in his fictional world mirrors the way Conrad's novel internalizes discourses from the "real" world—the Brooke myth, for example. That Jim's struggle for authenticity will occur in and be shaped by narrative structures is suggested by Marlow's next words: "He began his story . . ." (50). Central to Lyotard's argument in *Just Gaming* is the belief that no single account or story can claim full authority, but must be viewed as a supplement to others, since each person's right to a narrative voice—to respond with one's own moves in the language game—is an essential political right. This is a right Jim seizes for himself, although his little story does not subvert the grand narratives of his culture so much as it attempts to align him with those narratives once again. Despite this qualification, Lyotard's articulation of the relationship between justice and the "little story" is anticipated with uncanny accuracy in Conrad's fiction.

Therefore, although Marlow briefly entertains the opinion that Jim's struggle is ridiculous, he shares Jim's need to save from the fire a metastory of Western humanity's moral identity. An affirmation of this moral identity is crucial to the ideology of colonialism, and in this novel Marlow is more sympathetic to colonialism than he is in *Heart of Darkness*. But if Marlow's oppositional discourse in *Heart of Darkness* is haunted by its *official* other, Marlow's more hegemonic discourse in *Lord Jim*, so openly nostalgic for the values of home and the codes of the British Merchant Marine, is nonetheless haunted by *unofficial* stories. We can understand Marlow's sympathetic identification with Jim because Jim's struggle is a version of his own. Jim's struggle is enacted on the stage of history; Marlow's, perhaps, is actualized only in the meditations of his narratives. "It behoved me," Marlow says, "to make no sign lest by a gesture or a word I should be drawn into a fatal admission about myself which would have some bearing on the case" (65).

Jim's need, as he tells his story in the Malabar, is to affirm that he is something other than he appears to be in the finalizing discourses and stories society has produced about him. In conversation and correspondence with others, Marlow encounters Jim within the narratives that circulate among the colonialists in Eastern ports and towns, monologic narratives in which he is objectified and finalized by the gaze of these others. This subjecting of Jim's self to the discourse of others occurs at the hearing into the *Patna* incident, concerned as it is with "facts." But Marlow's own gaze, which Jim encounters during the inquiry, holds promise of another "hearing": "Jim's eyes, wandering in the intervals of his answers, rested upon a white man who sat apart from the others, with his face worn and clouded, but with quiet eyes that glanced straight, interested, and clear" (20).[17]

After the inquiry, Jim's objectification by others is enacted by Chester and later by Gentleman Brown. Chester claims also to live in a world of fact and to "see things as they are"; he is sure he knows all that Jim is and finally will be. Chester's failure to finalize and use Jim at the outset of the novel is answered by Brown's degree of success in the end, which frames the story or stories of Jim's freedom with references to the inevitable finalizing of the self as it becomes subjected to the will of others. Jim's life is a struggle to write his own story and to escape the "facts" as produced by alien discourses and stories; therefore, Jim's career captures Alasdair MacIntyre's sense of life as a self-authored quest.[18]

Marlow's discourse upon Jim's story is more cautious than his discourse in *Heart of Darkness,* in which (despite internal contradictions) he confidently tells us who was hollow, who had restraint, and so on. But in *Lord Jim* Marlow adopts an interrogative mode, a different speech genre, that questions both Jim and himself. With regard to Marlow's thoughts on the selfhood of others, *Lord Jim* is an inversion—or another "secondary revision"—of *Heart of Darkness.* Jim is an enigma whom Marlow sees in glimpses through an always-rising and always-enveloping fog; the grounds of Marlow's sympathy for Jim remain unclear. Jim simply looks right—he is one of us—and, perhaps like Brierly but to a lesser degree, Marlow is therefore made uneasy about himself. One of the novel's more subtle effects is the way Gentleman Brown's undermining of Jim is anticipated in many of Jim's remarks to Marlow—especially the repeated question, "What would you have done?" The many doublings, echoings, and sharings intimate that all of the Europeans are implicated in one another's behavior. Furthermore, Marlow's discourse balances two of the most fundamental factors influencing the subject—one's conversation with one's community, and that community's discourses concerning the good. These factors are, of course, inextricably entwined.

Marlow wavers between seeing Jim as a man morally courageous enough to face his error in the context of a clear vision of the good and seeing him as a romantic fool concerned only about public opinion. The novel, a masterpiece of concealment, maintains, throughout its long meditation on conduct, social codes, and cultural allegiances, a sense of the inscrutability of the inner self, an inscrutability maintained in Marlow's refusal ever to finalize Jim as he had Kurtz. This concealment makes the reading of Lord Jim a uniquely active, "writerly" process. Because the questions of who we are and how to be can only be posed, never definitively answered, Albert Guerard says, anticipating the reader-response paradigm, that Lord Jim forces "upon the reader an active, exploratory, organizing role," compelling her or him "to collaborate in the writing of the novel." [19]

Marlow's sympathy with Jim's struggle to affirm his selfhood is a function of Marlow's distrust, shared with his inferred author, of the possibility of public justice. Marlow knows that there are "issues beyond the competency of a court of inquiry" (57). This knowledge, so potentially disruptive to public justice, is nonetheless necessary in order to maintain a certain concept of the integrity of the self. It is this paradoxical knowledge that the young captain in "The Secret Sharer" must internalize by way of his own violation of the law, a violation that this story presents as a stage in the captain's growth. Leggatt is also one of us—a "Conway boy" [20]—and therefore is above the law like the captain, his double; the secret this story shares with its reader is that laws are instruments of social regulation to be wielded by a ruling class, not ultimate values in themselves. Of course that class must police itself and maintain standards of conduct when its transgressions become public, lest its appearance of legitimacy erode, and it is further desirable that its officers internalize the laws without question, as did the French lieutenant in Lord Jim.

This policing is the function of the inquest in Lord Jim. As it is concerned only with "facts," the inquest cannot take account of the deeper reality of the inner self—the world of feelings and sensibilities that authenticates Jim in Marlow's eyes. The official investigation can only subjugate. Marlow's meditation on Jim is a meditation on the question of whether the law can be truly internalized in the subject or whether it must always remain an imposition of external authority. Societies require assemblies in which policies are debated and procedural rules are enacted, but Marlow probes the limits of such jurisdictions. Marlow's quest for a redeeming subjective quality in Jim may be the alternative of a man who has lost faith in public procedures, but it also bespeaks an ultimate belief in class or racial privilege, re-encoded in a metanarrative of subjective worth; this grafting of class privilege to a discourse of valorized inner qualities leads Marlow to assert at one point that "those who do not feel do not count" (136). The novel's dilemma is that although the authenticity of feelings always escapes representation and although the privileging of certain forms of subjectivity enacts a concealed politics, the alternative is Chester's form of representation; he sees "things exactly as they are" (99) but does not see the inner man, concluding that Jim "is no earthly good for anything" (102).[21]

But Marlow does not embrace an entirely private code of sensibility: "The real significance of crime is in its being a breach of faith with the community of mankind" (95). Like his author, Marlow wants to believe in "the sovereign power enthroned in a fixed standard of conduct" (31), a power that creates "community" (31) and "the fellowship of the craft," which depend on "the strength of a wider feeling" (79). To yearn for a community governed by a fixed code of conduct and then to ground that code so elusively and subjectively in "fellowship" and "feeling" is to live at the center of the problematic of bourgeois individualism and its relation to order and justice, particularly as order and justice involve one's relations to other ethnic and cultural groups whose subject positions and very selves are different from one's own. These social contradictions cause Guerard to see in Conrad himself "the idealist, the skeptic, and the outlaw."[22]

Kant argued that one must not derive value from fact, and Marlow's story is a search for a grounding of value beyond the "facts" produced by the metanarratives driving the public inquest and subsequently interpreted by Chester. The way the novel establishes the problematic of the subject and public order caused Guerard to distinguish between the novel we read first and the one we reread. *Lord Jim*, Guerard argues, is designed to pull the reader into Jim's camp on a first reading and to encourage criticism of Jim on a second reading (131–40). Guerard's need to posit "two" novels dramatically illustrates the way Conrad's one novel has balanced an opposition that lacks resolution within the totalizing tradition of Western humanistic criticism. Guerard's reader, after all, is a member of the community that Jim's problematic represents, and the phenomenology of reading that he describes would probably not apply to Third World readers (such as Chinua Achebe), who might not perceive the first of Guerard's two novels. Critical phrases such as Guerard's "the reader" also perform a sort of social regulation when they smuggle in the biases of a particular group of readers.

In a novel rich in oppositions, the most crucial is the one between the public inquiry into Jim's misconduct and the other inquest, the other telling and hearing, that goes on between Marlow and his companions. These two hearings pose the opposition between seeing Jim as a subject within public discourses or as a self who escapes the positioning of those discourses. Marlow conducts his inquiry in a narrative mode, and *Lord Jim* reveals the ability of narrative to produce or represent (which may be the same thing) a form of subjectivity that the other discourse of the official hearing cannot. Stein says that the central question is "how to be" (129), and memory is crucial to the structure of what we think we are, both as individuals and collectively. We are what we think we have been, and as we selectively narrate and interpret our past, we produce our future. In this sense Marlow's narration, as it did—or tried to do—in *Heart of Darkness*, again stands as a "counter-memory" or "unofficial" consciousness. Furthermore, Marlow's narrative, and the framing narrator's presentation of it, is persistently self-referential, asking that we consider the purposes of narrative and the codes and conventions that enable those purposes. "Try as I may," Marlow says, "for the success of this yarn, I am missing innumerable shades—they are so fine, so difficult to render in colourless words" (58). But Marlow does not tell us what the criteria for success would be; perhaps, to recall Guerard's reader-response thesis, we might say that the successful story is one that involves an audience in determining the definition of success and therefore in self-scrutiny.

Kant's notion of a universal subjectivity brings into being a "community of moral subjects," since in the deepest aesthetic experiences "morality and feeling for once come together."[23] Successful narration, in Kantian terms, would be linked to the formation within the aesthetic experience of a sense of community, a community where the troubling oppositions between external authority and inner selfhood (between principles and beliefs, as the opposition was formulated in *Heart of Darkness*) are resolved. But Terry Eagleton asks how something can "be at once a judgment, which involves subsuming particulars to a law of the understanding, and yet no more than a feeling."[24]

The Kantian aesthetic, Eagleton concludes, attempts to universal-ize a realm of subjective feeling, and in so doing is "the very paradigm of the ideological," the ideological being understood as the encoding of "emotive attitudes relevant to the reproduction of social power."[25] The refrain of self-reference in Marlow's narrative, then, encourages us to examine that narrative's encoding of such emotive attitudes. Fredric Jameson finds such attitudes covertly concealed in the "unconscious" of the narrative. But in revealing and foregrounding its codes, the novel invites rather than conceals an examination of its own position in a cultural network that is inevitably ideologically freighted.

Overtly, Marlow's tale is an assemblage of stories he has heard and read (in personal letters and newspapers) about Jim. Its telling has no official or public function, but rather epitomizes the osten-sibly unconstrained conversational sharing in an individualist society. It occurs on "a soft evening" when "a lot of men [are] too indolent for whist" (58), and the comparison with a card game should alert us to how the pleasures of the aesthetic text disguise the normative function of the stories people tell one another. The fact that stories are more than merely entertainment for indolent men is made clear in Jim's need to tell his own story, and to a lesser degree in the references within his story to how the other *Patna* officers invented *their* story while waiting to be rescued. "What did I care what story they made up?" Jim asks (76). And later he dismisses their account: "They told their story. . . . The story didn't matter" (81). Their story, fabricated for public consumption, foregrounds the ideological function of stories.

The possibility that Marlow's own story has its covert intentions and its covert connections with the more public and formal discourses on "how to be" is suggested when Marlow, in commenting on his own desire to spare Jim from "a formal execution," tells his auditors that if they do not have some notion of his hidden motivations, "I must have been very obscure in my narrative, or you too sleepy to seize upon the sense of my words" (93). This metacommentary occurs at the point where Marlow tells Jim of Brierly's wish that Jim leave town and evade the rest of the public hearing. Marlow confesses that his own desire to avoid public judgment grows out of "the secret sensi-bility of my egoism. I am concealing nothing from you, because were I to do so my action would appear more unintelligible than any man's action has a right to be, and—in the second place—to-morrow you will forget my sincerity along with the other lessons of the past" (93). For Marlow, sincerity, another subjective and unrepresentable quality, underwrites the abandonment of the group's procedures of regula-tion when those procedures threaten to make revelations that are too damaging to the group. Marlow's ranking of his own "sincerity" in a category with "lessons of the past" and his presentation of this sincerity as a valid grounding for decisions about values and conduct illustrate the difficulties of ethical discourse in individualist societies. Perhaps the selective memory, or the active forgetting, that Marlow predicts will obscure his sincerity is not so much a lapse as a necessity enabling public deliberation on the "fixed" codes of conduct.

At this point, having inadvertently revealed his sincerity's potentially antisocial tendencies, and having worried about his audience's inability to comprehend his story—his auditors are all too prone to socialize with "the usual respectable thief of commerce" (26)—Marlow anticipates rewritings of Jim's story in a manner analogous to the way a story of greed and exploitation in *Heart of Darkness* becomes rewritten as a spiritual allegory. "The time was coming" when a "legend of strength and prowess" would form around his name (106), and Jim's achievements would become "fit materials for an heroic tale" (138). But Marlow questions the appropriateness of narration in a heroic genre, since the heroic posits people solely in their relations to society and to external codes. A heroic narration is appropriate, Marlow says, to minds "struck by the externals" of Jim's success (138).

MacIntyre's account of heroic societies provides a relevant gloss on Conrad's reasons for implicitly contrasting Marlow's narrative with the "heroic" narratives about Jim that circulate in the outside world, beyond the veranda and evening of Marlow's utterance. MacIntyre observes that in heroic societies, values were given and one's place was predetermined, as were one's privileges and duties: "A man in heroic society is what he does"; a person and his actions are identical, and one "has no hidden depths. . . . To judge a man therefore is to judge his actions." Courage is a central virtue in heroic society: "To be courageous is to be someone on whom reliance can be placed," and "morality and social structure are in fact one and the same in heroic society."[26] If these characterizations are accurate, then it is apparent that Marlow's references to the legends forming around Jim in Patusan constitute a meditation on the differing assumptions of heroic society and bourgeois society.

Lord Jim proceeds, or recedes, as a structure of prolepses and analepses,[27] and the content expressed by this formal feature concerns historical continuity. Past or residual values such as honor and courage coexist with either the dominant or emergent values represented by Chester and Gentleman Brown. Marlow's craft as a seaman is rich in tradition, but he lives with the knowledge that those past traditions may be increasingly less-necessary fictions, the quaint metanarratives of another time:

> Surely in no other craft as in that of the sea do the hearts of those already launched to sink or swim go out so much to the youth on the brink, looking with shining eyes upon that glitter of the vast surface which is only a reflection of his own glances full of fire. There is such magnificent vagueness in the expectations that had driven each of us to sea, such a glorious indefiniteness, such a beautiful greed of adventures that are their own and only reward. What we get—well, we won't talk of that; but can one of us restrain a smile? In no other kind of life is the illusion more wide of the reality—in no other is the beginning *all* illusion—the disenchantment more swift—the subjugation more complete. (78–79)

Words such as "glorious," "beautiful," and "adventures," with their literary overtones, suggest how ideology occupies aesthetics. The subject's internalization of the appeals to glory, beauty, and adventure (the sea only reflects back what shines upon it from the subject's eyes) motivates him to a labor whose reality is ostensibly repressed in Marlow's discourse ("we won't talk of that") but is actually lurking in words such as "greed" and "subjugation." The phrase "a beautiful greed of adventures" is the verbal achievement of a society (not just a narrator) that has thoroughly inseminated heroic and aesthetic discourses with capitalism's single most acceptable motive.

Marlow's discourse reminds us of the inappropriateness of the heroic story others tell—it is, seemingly, a genre bespeaking a primitive and superstitious mentality, containing a metanarrative even more quaint and more ancient than the codes of conduct Marlow clings to. The heroic cannot be reconciled with the notions of selfhood produced by bourgeois society, and Dorothy Van Ghent is therefore correct to compare *Lord Jim* with Sophoclean drama, although she does not actually discuss Sophocles as a critic of heroic values. But MacIntyre speaks of Plato and Sophocles in terms of a project "to expel the Homeric inheritance from the city-state." Plato's dialogues, according to MacIntyre, intentionally point "to a general state of incoherence in the use of evaluative language in Athenian culture," and one could easily say the same for Marlow's monologue, which is dialogically inhabited by the contradictions of his own culture. Sophocles, in *Philoctetes* and in *Antigone*, confronts us with "two incompatible standards of honorable conduct, two rival standards of behaviour," and it is "Sophocles who systematically explores rival allegiances to incompatible goods."[28]

This fracturing of the heroic worldview in Sophocles and Plato makes them legitimate antecedents to Conrad's novel, which hovers between judgment by sympathetic identification and judgment by law, and between a view of the self as transcendent potential or as the totality of one's acts. As Van Ghent says, both *Oedipus* and *Lord Jim* ask whether the self is deducible from circumstances. The "subtle but tangible distinction between the human agent and his destiny allows the classical dramatists to orient clearly what we may call the metaphysical significance of the hero's career, the universal problem and the law of life which that career illustrates."[29] The Sophocles connection that Van Ghent explores also explains the generally satiric attitude toward the heroic that occurs in the second part of *Lord Jim*.

And yet, despite Marlow's awareness of the inappropriateness of a heroic discourse on Jim—"already the legend had gifted him with supernatural powers" (162)—Marlow himself is momentarily seduced by the heroic encoding or metanarrative. After scoffing at the legend, calling it "bally rot," Marlow says to Jim, "My dear fellow, you don't suppose *I* believe this" (162), but a moment later Marlow himself describes Jim's laughter as "Homeric" (163). Having imagined a heroic version of Jim's story, Marlow then tells of "the popular story" (164) that, by the rules of a sort of generic declension out of Northrop Frye's *Anatomy of Criticism*, seems to have shifted from the heroic to the romantic: "Jim with the touch of one finger had thrown down the gate" (164). In the romance, Jim's lover, Jewel, becomes "a fabulously large emerald." This story, or Jim-myth, travels "slowly down the coast," living its own life with its own pragmatic variations; it even has its local "scribe" from whom Marlow hears it (171).

The heroic societies suggested by Jim-legends and Jim-myths are like the Burkean "organic society" that Fleishman finds as the underlying value in Conrad's political thought, but the evocation of these myths and legends in *Lord Jim* also looks ahead to Bakhtin's discussion of the evolution of modern narrative out of earlier, less individualized social formations or chronotopes. In these lost utopian worlds—whether one calls them heroic, organic, or folk societies—the individual is formed only within a mystic or spiritual union with the community. The Burkean tradition stands in opposition to Enlightenment contract theory, in that contract theories overemphasize the will of the individual in forming the social contract and thereby encourage an "atomistic" concept of society as an "artificial, voluntary, legalistic arrangement."[30] Conrad implies the communal nature of identity by the embedding of stories and genres in *Lord Jim*, stories that always cross and mingle with other stories, each story deriving its existence from a community of stories.

The Patusan story, Marlow repeatedly reminds his listeners, is also "the story of his [Jim's] love," although Marlow wishes to distinguish it from the more popular versions of the love genre: "I suppose you think it is a story that you can imagine for yourselves. We have heard so many such stories, and the majority of us don't believe them to be stories of love at all. For the most part we look upon them to be stories of opportunities: episodes of passion at best. . . . This view mostly is right, and perhaps in this case, too. . . . Yet I don't know. To tell this story is by no means so easy as it should be—were the ordinary standpoint adequate" (168).

An "exotic" grand narrative of libidinal gratification typically accompanies the Western discourse of conquest, in which the earth itself is gendered feminine, forests are virgin, and so on. *Lord Jim* hints at the reality of opportunism beneath the myth, and "we" are asked to agree that the grand narrative (if not Jim's little story) of romantic love is hollow. Jim's lover, Jewel, is even named to suggest a fetishized object of trade or conquest, like the gold of *Almayer's Folly*, the ivory of *Heart of Darkness*, or the silver of *Nostromo*. Marlow hovers deconstructively between a complete rejection of such mythologizing and a certain nostalgia for it, figured in his urge to tell *this* story differently, in his desire for there to be a story that escapes the history of opportunism—"the ordinary standpoint."

The question Marlow leaves unanswered is, how, exactly, are "we" as readers (situated in various places and times) to write the story of Jim's career and death in Patusan? Fleishman stresses the extent to which the ideal of the organic community is achieved in *Lord Jim*. To Fleishman, Jim is a success because, despite his lapse in identifying with Brown, he "gives himself back to the group and its justice."[31] Jim has fully engaged himself with others and has demonstrated the viability of a just, ameliorative form of imperial colonization. But it is equally valid to stress Jim's failure and the ruin he brings to Patusan. His identification with Brown, with the worst of his own society, may dramatize the impossibility of a full and just identification with people of other cultural or ethnic groups. Jim becomes at best "bicultural," and whatever ambivalence this implies initiates the destructive effect of even the best-intentioned colonial activity.[32]

Here again, as in the ending of *Heart of Darkness*, is a writerly text that requires "the" reader to question either: (1) the modes of emplotment he or she employs in order to understand or interpret literal stories by translating them into more general and familiar meta-narratives; or (2) the possibility of interpretation without these grand emplotments. This questioning is prompted by the generic self-consciousness—that is, by the way the discourse foregrounds the different possible encodings of Jim's story—that occurs in the latter part of Conrad's novel, the part that has displeased many readers because of its retreat from the realistic mode of the novel's beginning. But *Lord Jim* risks this displeasure so as to foreground the conventional aspect of truth and the way our knowledge of who we are in our temporality is produced by conventions of emplotment.

Marlow's references to stories, legends, myths, heroic stories, romance, and love stories extend his discourse, rhizome-like, into the surrounding culture and its ways of encoding knowledge narratively. The preference many critics have for the *Patna* episode results from modernism's privileging of certain conventions of emplotment and the attendant illusion of truth or reality these conventions produce. But Marlow's search for a genre in the Patusan section underlines the notion that the heart of the subject is unknowable and its freedom unrepresentable, and it shows how different speech genres uttered by differently situated speakers reflect and produce a different reality. However he is emplotted, be it in heroic legend or popular romance, Jim remains "at the heart of a vast enigma" (204). Moreover, the Patusan episode exists as an evocation and critique of the romantic, self-congratulatory myths produced by early capitalism in its narrating of its own encounter with other cultures. Any false note in this section of *Lord Jim* is an echo of what is false in imperialism's dream of itself. The novel risks an aesthetic imperfection—the move from realism to romance—but the imperfection itself carries a powerful social and historical critique.

Marlow's proleptic anticipation of the "legend"—"the time was coming"—is intriguing because, in its generic references, the story glances back in history at older genres as it moves ahead to its own conclusion. One observes a similar reprisal of past genres in *Nostromo*, but Nostromo, reversing Jim's pattern, becomes less "heroic" as he ages. Nostromo is an incarnation of the movement from heroic to capitalistic culture, whereas Jim attempts to move against the flow of history and to recover a past ideal of the heroic self. Historically, the heroic age of legend and myth has passed, as has the moment of the Westerner's first encounter with the Third World peoples who became the colonized. Jim's arrival in Patusan is a sort of historical analepsis in a double sense: it is both an attempt to recover heroic values and a meditation on the West's first encounter with the Third World and on the potential of that encounter for good and for ill. *In Heart of Darkness*, Marlow referred to journeying up the Congo River as a temporal regression. But in both novels the imagined recovery of the primal moment of this cross-cultural encounter is deferred. Africa's heart has already been violated by capitalism, as has Patusan; this violation is figured in Cornelius, who "has his place neither in the background nor in the foreground of the story: he is simply seen skulking on its outskirts, enigmatical and unclean, tainting the fragrance of its youth and of its naiveness" (174). (The fact that this passage sounds like a literary critic's commentary illustrates Marlow's self-consciousness concerning the problematic relationship between narratives and truth.) In *Nostromo*, too, one encounters a "paradise of snakes" where the Fall is already accomplished. The "beginning" recedes and is always already a repetition.

This sense of beginnings as repetitions is conveyed also in Jim's "personal" story. As the opening four chapters make clear, Jim is already fallen before he jumps from the *Patna*, having failed to jump to the rescue of drowning people during his training days and having shown a soft spot in his attraction to the less demanding service in Eastern waters and ports. The repetition of scenes involving jumps, in which the act of jumping is sometimes valued positively and sometimes negatively, creates a sense of cyclical return that works against the notion of linear narrative progression, as do the proleptic and analeptic jumps of Marlow's plotting. According to the narrative paradox, progress is at once real and illusory, and as Jim finally faces his death with the courage he lacked on the *Patna*, he once again fails the community that has trusted him. The irony of these repetitions, in Jameson's words, "is the irony of reequipping oneself better to wage the previous war, for which one was so grievously unprepared, with the result that one is equally unprepared, but in a new way, to fight the following one."[33]

Such themes are the content of Conrad's narrative form as the final episode approaches. At the start of chapter 36 "Marlow had ended his narrative" (204). But his "incomplete story" is recommenced two years later, now transmuted from speech to the writing received by "the privileged man," who has taken an interest in the oral story (205).[34] After characterizing this narratee—his racial and colonial attitudes—in a manner that enables an understanding of the pragmatics of this particular narrator-narrative-narratee relationship, Marlow's letter says that "it all begins with a remarkable exploit by a man named Brown" (209). But before we actually get to those exploits, "the letter proper ended" (214). Now, three chapters after the end of Marlow's oral narration, we hear for a second time that "it all begins, as I've told you, with the man called Brown." This second beginning is found in a second writing by Marlow included in the packet sent to the "privileged man" (214). All of this highly mannered stopping and starting calls attention to the conventionality of our sense of narrative beginnings and endings, and to how these conventions structure our notions of where we have been and are going, creating fictions of who we are and how to be.

In telling the "legend" of Jim in Patusan, Marlow tries to recover something of the early days of imperial expansion, but his skepticism concerning the legend is also a skepticism about imperialist ideology itself, echoing his skeptical response, in *Heart of Darkness*, to the frame narrator's eulogizing of the great "knight-errants of the sea" during the age of exploration. Gentleman Brown is a demonic parody of these chivalric seafarers, and critics who, following Guerard, dwell only on the psychological dimension of Jim's "sympathetic identification" with Brown miss the political implications.[35] Jim and Brown are two sides of the same historical phenomenon, the white man's impact on other races and cultures; something of this parodic kinship is suggested in their respective "titles," Lord and Gentleman. Jim's uncanny identification with Brown is a striking instance of how, in the novel, character and psychology are phenomena in which social contradictions enact their displaced dramas.

Lord Jim encourages a conceptual fusing of Jim and Brown in a way that does not depend on a political deconstruction of the psychology of sympathetic identification, since the political message conveyed with the doubling of these two characters is not buried in the novel's unconscious. Brown's history, as recorded in chapter 38, is a dark version of Jim's story; as an archetypal nemesis figure, Brown is an exaggerated incarnation of the potential evil in Jim's own subject position within the imperialist structure.[36] Brown's story is written to "the privileged man," who believes in colonialism and has "a firm conviction in the truth of ideas racially our own" (206). By "fighting in the ranks" (unlike Jim) armed with these ideas, the European can establish "the order, the morality of an ethical progress" (206). The privileged man's conflation of the ethical and the ethnic establishes him as one who, despite his interest in Jim's story, has failed to understand its implications as a critique of the relationships among selfhood, community, and value in his culture. The privileged man, in short, might be Conrad's own typical reader, a subscriber to *Blackwood's* and *New Review*, taking as stern a view of Jim as the British press in fact took of the crew of the *Jeddah*.

Marlow is careful to voice the beliefs of the privileged man, allowing us to understand the pragmatics of his writings to that man. These pragmatics encourage one to read the entire Brown episode as a dialogic response to this particular privileged narratee, whose belief in fighting for ideas produced by his own ethnic group is darkly mirrored in Brown's "blind belief in the rightness of his will against all mankind" (225). It will be recalled that Marlow began to speak in *Heart of Darkness* in response to a similar idealistic discourse. Now Marlow's response to the man who apparently shares John Cecil Rhodes's dream of unlimited expansion and progress is to rewrite the story of the benevolent white man pursuing "the idea"—to tell the story of white imperialism now from the point of view of Brown, the worst sort of person that Western expansionism can produce.

Marlow's authority as a narrator derives from his first having been a narratee of Jim's narration; now we again have the scene of a prior narration established—Brown's deathbed rather than the Malabar Hotel—and the new story "begins." There are Brown-legends as there are Jim-legends: "You who have knocked about the Western Pacific must have heard of him" (214). Like Jim, Brown came from good English stock, deserted a ship in his youth, and became a wanderer. And even Brown had his love story—"the most wonderful part of the tale" (215). Jim is conveniently absent from Patusan upon Brown's arrival so as to position Brown as the new focus of attention, and Brown experiences initial difficulties in Patusan that parallel Jim's. If Jim wanders the Western Pacific in search of a "shadowy ideal of conduct" (253), Brown's nomadic roaming shows how dark that shadow can be. If Jim is the enigmatic signifier, Brown is one of the dark signifieds—"running his appointed course, he sails into Jim's history" (215).

The packet of writings comes to the privileged man two years after he hears Marlow's oral narrative. As was suggested in the discussion of *Heart of Darkness*, interpretation must account for possible changes in a narrator's intentions during the course of his dealings with an audience or audiences. Here the time gap and the new specification of the privileged man as narratee make this interpretive approach even more necessary. It is as though, in this written version, the Jim-story that survives from the oral narration is a sort of pretense for the blunter, harsher corrective of the Brown-story that this privileged man of Western imperialist ideas requires—the word "privilege" carrying its full social, political, and historical implications. While it may be possible among like-minded friends to make all possible allowances for Jim's error, there are others who have already made too many allowances for themselves and their privileged class. The pragmatics of narrating to such people dictate the narrative expansion of the Brown-story, with its accompanying harsher indictment of Western adventuring.

If the story of Gentleman Brown offers a direct warning to the privileged man and a corrective to his faith in the rightness of the values of his ethnic group, this audience-oriented reading of Marlow's discourse contains a reservation concerning Jameson's reading of this novel. Jameson sees the modernist text, of which *Lord Jim* is an early instance, as implicated in a project of repressing the political and the historical; the text becomes a mechanism for its own misreading, and the critic must recover what the text withholds:

> But if this is what *Lord Jim* is really all about, then it only remains to ask why nobody thinks so, least of all Conrad himself. . . . The burden of our reading of *Lord Jim* has been to restore the whole socially concrete subtext of late nineteenth-century rationaliza-tion and reification of which this novel is so powerfully, and on so many different formal levels, the expression and the Utopian compensation alike. Now we must turn to the mechanisms that ensure a structural displacement of such content, and that pro-vide for a built-in substitute interpretive system whereby readers may, if they so desire—and we do all so desire, to avoid know-ing about history!—rewrite the text in more inoffensive ways. (265–66)

Wimsatt and Beardsley's attack on intentionality is the conser-vative precursor to Jameson's position. Both positions ground mean-ing not in the author's intentions but in the system that is the text's medium. To Wimsatt and Beardsley this system is language, thought of in an abstract and depoliticized sense; to Jameson it is history and more specifically the ideologies of the historical moment of the writ-ing of the text. But whereas Wimsatt and Beardsley argue that one cannot know what an author's conscious intention *is*, Jameson makes the dubious epistemological assumption that he *can* know what an author's intention *is not*. To Jameson, whatever the author's conscious intention is, it is not the reading that Jameson locates only in the text's unconscious. Why what Jameson calls the text's "unconscious" could not have been consciously intended is never clear.

But when Jameson finds in *Lord Jim* both an "expression" and a "compensation," he is qualifying his general contention that it is his own reading that compensates for the evasions of nineteenth-century reification. Is the compensation Conrad's or Jameson's? Is it Conrad or Jameson who, in Jameson's pre-glasnost rhetoric, "interrogates" the conditions that produce the idealistic representations of imperialism? I do not mean to quibble over a fine point of Jameson's analysis. The question of what ideological positions and intentions to attribute to the inferred author or discursive subject—and to his narrator, Marlow— is recurrent in Conrad criticism. Jameson's uneasy opposition between "expression" and "compensation" is not unlike Guerard's notion of the two *Lord Jim* novels: in Guerard's hypothetical first reading the novel expresses certain idealist values, but in his second reading the novel unfolds a compensatory critique of idealism.

Benita Parry points to this phenomenon of double representa- tion by speaking of Conrad as being both consoling and disturbing, the writer of a "double vision" and "divided mind." [37] Parry appro- priately quotes the following portion of a letter Conrad wrote to the *New York Times*: " 'The only indisputable truth of life is our ignorance. Besides this there is nothing evident, nothing absolute, nothing un- contradicted; there is no principle, no instinct, no impulse that can stand alone at the beginning of things and look confidently to the end. . . . The only legitimate basis of creative works lies in the coura- geous recognition of all the irreconcilable antagonisms that make our life so enigmatic, so burdensome, so fascinating, so dangerous—so full of hope.' " [38]

From the standpoint of narratology, these antagonisms are the- matic effects of the discourse/story opposition. In Guerard's first "novel," or reading, we encounter Marlow's discourse, which seeks to make all necessary allowances and which holds out the possi- bility of decent conduct and ordered transmission of values from one generation to the next; this discourse is a consoling (Parry's read- ing) *expression* (Jameson's) of nineteenth-century reifications. In Guer- ard's second reading we encounter stories that qualify and *compensate* (Jameson's contention) for the discourse—we give added weight to the French lieutenant's story, we see Jim's own story as one of egoism and failure, and we see the truth of imperialism reflected in Gentleman Brown's story. The novel's critique of its own discourse is consistent with Conrad's belief that there is "nothing uncontradicted" and that life is a fabric of "irreconcilable antagonisms."

When one confronts such contradictions within a text, it is tempt- ing to privilege one side of the contradiction as a conscious intention and to see the other as unconscious; this is a carryover from formal- ism's need to create totalizing hierarchies and to account for what Wolfgang Iser calls "alien associations." [39] Totality, unity, and harmony are saved within the conscious text, and the unconscious becomes the dumping ground for whatever disrupts that totality. My reading of

Conrad does not require an unconscious text, preferring instead to give conflicting tendencies an equal, shared ontological status.

Conrad's texts, whether or not they possess an unconscious, are nothing if not dialogic, staging as they do encounters among competing social voices and positions. One aspect of this dialogism is the artful placing of discourse in a dialogic relationship to story, each questioning the other rather than each simply supporting the other in a monologic totality. One side of a social contradiction is encoded in discourse, the other side in story. If one equates showing with story and saying with discourse, it is this particular dialogism that Parry is describing when she says that "it is the presence of incommensurable meanings, which are articulated in the dialogue of voices soliciting support for antithetical ideas and principles, and generated by the discontinuities between what the action *shows* and what the narrative *says*, between the fiction's indwelling significations and the formal constructions imposed by narrative exegesis and rhetoric, that displays the text's struggle to escape ideology and the pressures drawing it back into the orbit of the imperialist world-view."[40]

Marlow does not interpret the story of Jim's death in a discourse of redemption, as he did Kurtz's, and much in the ending of *Lord Jim* is a studied inversion of the ending of *Heart of Darkness*. One recalls, too, Marlow's brutally truthful statement to Jewel that Jim "is not good enough" (194). Her retort—"You lie!"—can only be fully read in relation to Marlow's comforting lie to Kurtz's Intended: there a lie was received as truth; now truth is received as a lie. Marlow's greater honesty in *Lord Jim* is found in his refusal to finalize Jim in a familiar metastory or grand narrative; we are not consoled with a story of victory. Jim remains at the end veiled and inscrutable, and the novel closes in an interrogative voice: "Is he satisfied—quite, now, I wonder? We ought to know. He is one of us—and have I not stood up once, like an evoked ghost, to answer for his eternal constancy? Was I so very wrong after all? . . . Who knows?" (253).

Since Marlow withholds judgment concerning Jim's redemption, considerable critical debate has tried to fill the gap left by Marlow's omission. As Jameson argues, the exalted tone of the ending seems to offer an answer that is at odds with "a sober reading of the narrative." Story fails to support discourse, and Jameson is right to say that the resulting ambiguity accomplishes the task Lévi-Strauss describes for myth—the imaginary resolution of real social contradictions, "it being understood that an imaginary resolution is no resolution at all."[41] As I see it, however, the ending of the novel challenges the beliefs of the privileged man in its depiction of Brown's depravity, and it poses a question to all readers for whom selfhood and its relation to social discourses remains a problem. Meaning is in the pragmatics, which is to say that Marlow's meaning resides outside his tale, like a halo, in the actions and responses of his audience. But Jameson wants answers to the question of Jim's redemption *in* the tale: "All of Conrad's artfulness is in this concluding section mustered for a kind of prestidigitation designed to prevent the embarrassing question from being posed in the first place."[42] Jameson confuses the posing of a question with its answer, ending his remarks on Jim's death with the odd assertion that *Lord Jim* avoids the very question that Jameson began by saying it has encouraged critics to ask.

Parry, too, after all that she said in her introduction concerning Conrad's double vision, finally stresses the singularity of *Lord Jim*'s complicity with imperialist ideology. She smuggles Marlow's discourse in *Heart of Darkness* into *Lord Jim* when she says that Jim's death is a "triumph" and a "victory,"[43] and she attributes the victorious conclusion she finds in *Lord Jim* to Marlow's desire to "speak in praise of the ardour impelling the colonial adventurers of old to heroic feats."[44] Although she remains aware that "the fiction's discourse generates its own antithesis," her own discourse is dominated by the current demand to situate the literary text under the domination of the prevailing ideology of its time; she accedes to today's most authoritative critical metanarrative, by which the text, like Jim, must be tried and found guilty. In fact, she sees little real change over the course of Conrad's entire career; he is always an author for whom "the question of goals beyond immediate necessity is expunged."[45]

To be sure, *The Nigger of the "Narcissus"* celebrated work and solidarity without concern for the ends served by that work; it argued that sympathy for a dying man of another race is misplaced, and presented his death and expulsion in the most positive terms. But *Heart of Darkness* more deeply engaged the question of the ends served by Western values and actions as they affect others, and *Lord Jim*, with its numerous glimpses of lost, violent, and aimless behavior, is a profound critique of the subject produced by the dominant bourgeois and imperialist ideologies. When a society's fundamental belief systems are wiped away, the subject too undergoes a radical sense of instability or even unreality. Conrad is the inheritor of God's slaying, as described by Nietzsche's madman: " 'Where is God gone?' he called out. 'I mean to tell you! *We have killed him,*—you and I! We are all his murderers! But how have we done it? How were we able to drink up the sea? Who gave us the sponge to wipe away the whole horizon?' "[46] The word "horizon" has come to mean in our discourse the framework or order in which a person or a society finds its identity, and Conrad's art is filled with dissolving horizons, both literal and figurative.

If Marlow has a nostalgia for fixed horizons and for the values produced within the horizon of bourgeois and imperialist ideologies, he also has his skeptical side, and it is Marlow himself who actively researches and writes the story of Gentleman Brown, which corrects any romanticizing tendencies expressed earlier about Jim. *Lord Jim* reveals a world on the verge of the postmodern, a world of discontinuous stories and of homelessness and opportunism in which the ideological fictions about "us" and our sacred and "fixed" codes no longer withstand scrutiny. As MacIntyre describes our present condition, harmonizing with Lyotard's description of the loss of grand narratives, we base our conduct on "no unassailable criteria" and our morality on "fragmented survivals and implausible modern inventions." [47] No horizons are fixed in the shifting, multicultural world *Lord Jim* so clearly anticipates, and yet Stein's discourse, which speaks not of "us and them" so much as of humankind, points to the need for a cross-cultural rewriting of the discourse on values. Parry criticizes *Lord Jim* for not being "vatic" enough, for not telling us "who the architects of the new age will be or what it is they are striving to construct." [48] But any such prophecy would project onto the future the ideologically freighted desires of yesterday's horizons, and Parry's recourse to the old notion of the vatic denies the major premise of her own critical method, which is that the work must be understood in its dialogic relationship to its own time and place.

Literary criticism in the last quarter of the twentieth century has engaged in a radical critique of the assumptions that have grounded literary and cultural studies in the past, particularly as those assumptions support systems of hierarchy and domination that have an impact on the lives of people who have been selected to know nothing of "our" academic discourses. Many authors once revered under humanism now find their own secret or unconscious political failings brought to public trial, and critics who cling to humanist values—who hope to find nothing shameful in Western traditions—perhaps wish, like Brierly, that the hearing would end. I have tried to show that something like today's debate between traditional humanism and emergent skepticism is staged in *Lord Jim*, distinguishing my reading from those that stress only the novel's affinities with imperialist values.

One place where the story and discourse correspond in *Lord Jim* is in the proposition that values and ethical standards are matters of community, finding their legitimation or critique in real social practices. Marlow says as much, and the action leads to the same

conclusion. An appeal to religious or quasi-religious legitimation—
to notions of redemption and eternal salvation—of the sort found in
Marlow's discourse on Kurtz's death would detract from the emphasis
in *Lord Jim* on the existential community. If Marlow and his author
have not fully imagined the concept of a global community and the
influence this concept should have on values and conduct, *Lord Jim*
nonetheless points in that direction. On the other hand, the novel
withholds any utopian optimism about such a community ever existing, and perhaps the prophetic vision Parry asked for is found in the
novel's images of global dispersion that ironically oppose Marlow's
nostalgia for home.

Values must be thought within a concept of community, but community is an always-receding utopian ideal. *Lord Jim* is suspicious of
utopian grand narratives and other totalizing discourses, a suspicion
permeating a narrative technique that involves the uneasy assemblage
of disperate little stories and viewpoints. MacIntyre's projection for
the future of values is bleak, and he speaks at the end of *After Virtue* (I
take his "after" to designate both belatedness and pursuit) of a world
dispersed into local "enclaves" (like Patusan?), each rediscovering on
its own microlevel the social and communal bases of value and conduct, a world of *petits recits*. MacIntyre is in fact addressing a question
similar to that posed by Lyotard in *Just Gaming:* How can we be just in
the absence of consensus concerning the beliefs in which justice must
be grounded?

This question is everywhere implicit in Conrad's work. Although
the community in which the question is posed in *Heart of Darkness*
and *Lord Jim* is an imperialist community, one of privilege, Conrad's
novels capture this community in moments of dissolution and dispersion. The enclaves of Marlow's scenes of narration are the primary
examples of this dispersion, as are the failed enclaves sought by Kurtz,
Jim, Heyst, and other characters of Conrad's who try to escape the
European consensus. If one recalls especially Marlow's opening tale
of the young Roman in *Heart of Darkness*, Conrad's texts seem to be
a powerful if unstated presence in MacIntyre's concluding thoughts,
although these texts have already critiqued whatever optimism may
be implied in MacIntyre's words:

> It is always dangerous to draw too precise parallels between
> one historical period and another; and among the most mislead-
> ing of such parallels are those which have been drawn between
> our own age in Europe and North America and the epoch in
> which the Roman empire declined into the Dark Ages. None

the less certain parallels there are. A crucial turning point in that earlier history occurred when men and women of good will turned aside from the task of shoring up the Roman *imperium* and ceased to identify the continuation of civility and moral community with the maintenance of that *imperium*. What they set themselves to achieve instead—often not recognizing fully what they were doing—was the construction of new forms of community within which moral life could be sustained so that both morality and civility might survive the coming ages of barbarism and darkness.[49]

MacIntyre is not specific about what new norms might arise within the new structures of community he imagines for our own age, but his writings subsequent to *After Virtue* speak increasingly of the need to return to religious authority. Jameson has said that the post-modern disintegration of the modernist consensus can be evaluated in either a progressive or a conservative manner, and it can also be evaluated from either a secular or a religious perspective.

Lord Jim, the more remarkable because it is an *early* modernist text, pauses on the threshold of such a disintegration. Jürgen Habermas argues that modernism can be characterized in terms of its changed consciousness of time; much of modernist art understood itself "as invading unknown territory, exposing itself to the dangers of sudden, shocking encounters, conquering an as yet unoccupied future."[50] But Conrad's texts do not enter this unknown territory with the avant-gardist's enthusiasm that Habermas is describing. A particular effect of the narrative paradox in *Lord Jim*, the fact that Jim seems not to age in the course of his story, is a symptomatic hesitation before the unknown. Habermas is in fact aware of such hesitation on the part of modernist art, as is clear in his discussion of that art's obsession with the present: "But these forward gropings, this anticipation of an undefined future and the cult of the new mean in fact the exaltation of the present. The new time consciousness, which enters philosophy in the writings of Bergson, does more than express the experience of mobility in society, of acceleration in history, of discontinuity in everyday life. The new value placed on the transitory, the elusive and the ephemeral, the very celebration of dynamism, discloses a longing for an undefiled, immaculate and stable present."[51]

Marlow's nostalgia for a fixed code of conduct and his inadvertent temporal fixing of Jim forever on the doorstep of adulthood reveal a conservative hesitation before the unknown future and a longing for a stable present. Nonetheless, Conrad's privileged reader has come a long distance from the reactionary opposition to labor and to its modern aspirations for justice found in *The Nigger of the "Narcissus."* Conrad's confrontation with history and temporality continues to evolve; it will take new forms in *Nostromo*.

4

Forms of Time and of the Chronotope in *Nostromo*

> Where the soul pretends unification or the self fabricates
> a coherent identity, the genealogist sets out to study the
> beginning—numberless beginnings whose faint traces and
> hints of color are readily seen by an historical eye. The analy-
> sis of descent permits the dissociation of the self, its recog-
> nition and displacement as an empty synthesis, in liberating
> a profusion of lost events.
>
> Michel Foucault, "Nietzsche, Genealogy, History"

I examined *The Nigger of the "Narcissus"* and *Heart of Darkness* from the standpoint of the ideological overdetermination of the narrative voice(s). *Lord Jim* is a meditation on ethics that questions the conduct of an individual in relation to the codes of the communities in which he lives, which is not to say that it retreats from the vision of the discontinuous and displaced subject found in the earlier novels. Furthermore, the ideal of a stable, coherently governed community of seamen with its fixed codes (like one of Alasdair MacIntyre's enclaves) is undermined by Jim's failure and its various effects on people such as Brierly and Marlow. The possibility of such an ideal community is also questioned by the novel's depiction of so many human failures, dropouts lounging and rotting in Eastern ports or turned murderous like Brown. This body of seamen and one-time seamen represents by synecdoche Western civilization in dispersal and deterioration, and contrasts with the less nomadic and more stable community of Patusan.

The theme of community in *Lord Jim* is reflected in the formal feature by which each person's story is inserted in other stories. The stories that precede us constitute a remembered tradition or history that establishes the ethical norms and metanarratives by which our conduct and contributions are measured. The stories of Stein, Bob Stanton, and the French lieutenant are fragments of such a composite history. These remembered stories mingle with more recent stories of people like Jim or Brown to alter, sustain, or debase the tradition as it is projected into the future. The story of the dialogic mingling of such stories—the story of which stories are retained in official memory and which must be recuperated in counter-memory—is the form of history Foucault calls, following Nietzsche, genealogy. Many of Conrad's major works are genealogical in Foucault's sense.

Individuals, Jim and Marlow, are at the center of *Lord Jim*, and we read outward to the communal, global, and historical problematics. The individual subject remains important in *Nostromo*, but no individual dominates as does Jim, and no narrator demands our concern as a character in his own story as does Marlow. At only one point, the start of the eighth chapter of "The Silver of the Mine," do we glimpse a dramatically conceived, first-person narrator—a human subject as well as a discursive subject. This parallels the brief emergence of a first-person speaker at the end of *The Nigger of the "Narcissus"* and of the "I" who occasionally speaks in *The Secret Agent*. Conrad's narrator in *Nostromo* claims to have been in Sulaco before its modernization for reasons of "business or curiosity"—he does not specify which. Furthermore, he says that his knowledge of the modernized Sulaco is secondhand: "The outward appearances had not changed then as they have changed since, as I am told . . ." (108).

The very act of establishing narrative authority problematizes that authority by suggesting an uncertain chain of verbal transmission or shared authorship, a paradox pushed to an extreme at certain moments in *Under Western Eyes*. As in my discussion of *The Nigger of the "Narcissus,"* the word "narrator," deceptive in its suggestion of a single center of consciousness, is retained in this chapter as a convenience, but it should not obscure the fact of the dispersed perspectives within the narrative discourse.

As Eloise Knapp Hay says, in *Nostromo* "historic process" is "the real subject of the story, more important than any of the people in it."[1] But *Nostromo* maintains the sense, developed in *Heart of Darkness* and *Lord Jim*, of history and community as assemblages of micronarratives and individual stories; if *Lord Jim* is bound analeptically to *Heart of Darkness* by the common presence of Marlow, it is bound proleptically to *Nostromo* in its genealogical approach to history as a plurality of stories. But in *Nostromo* transindividual historical "events" figure more largely than in *Lord Jim*. *Nostromo*, with its (usually) omniscient narrator, its large cast of characters, its geo-political themes, and its greater temporal scale, offers a fictional representation of the problematics of historiography and genealogy.[2]

Nostromo, according to Benita Parry, is "a meditation on the meaning of history and produces a perspective on historical narrative," the coherence of which is both "demonstrated and repudiated."[3] To speak of a simultaneous demonstration and repudiation is to speak of the deconstructive relationship between the forces of memory and counter-memory, between history and genealogy, and between grand narratives and individual stories. By questioning the form and possibility of general history, *Nostromo* at the same time problematizes personal narratives of selfhood. Is the legitimacy of the self questioned by the impossibility of its commensurability with a general and knowable form of history? Or do narratives of the self receive their legitimacy only in their opposition to general history?

The question of the exchanges between fiction and history has received considerable theoretical attention. Hayden White has shown how historiography borrows from the tropes and emplotments of fiction and how these borrowings help to form our perception of history. Louis O. Mink has also addressed this problem, and Paul Ricoeur has attempted an ambitious overview in his three volumes entitled *Time and Narrative,* which begin by contrasting the "aporetics" of time in Augustine's thought with Aristotle's treatment of time and emplotment. After discussing the theories of historiography of White, Mink, and others, Ricoeur shifts the focus to fiction, ending his project by examining "the hypothesis that fictional narrative in some way imitates historical narrative."[4] This imitation is presumed to exist in the requirement that fiction posit a "quasi-past" and establish a relation to it:

> The interpretation I am proposing here of the "quasi-historical" character of fiction quite clearly overlaps with the interpretation I also proposed of the "quasi-fictive" character of the historical past. If it is true that one of the functions of fiction bound up with history is to free, retrospectively, certain possibilities that were not actualized in the historical past, it is owing to its quasi-historical character that fiction itself is able, after the fact, to perform its liberating function. The quasi-past of fiction in this way becomes the detector of possibilities buried in the actual past. What "might have been"—the possible in Aristotle's terms—includes both the potentialities of the "real" past and the "unreal" possibilities of pure fiction.[5]

T. Peter Kemp, in his discussion of Ricoeur's theory of narrative, writes that "the grand narrative which transcends the individual biog-

raphy not only towards the past but also towards the future has . . .
a very considerable ethical importance; it is through it that all com-
munality, small or large, thinks itself."[6] Jean-François Lyotard's work,
as I have said, addresses the question of ethics in the absence of
such grand narratives, and these questions are crucial to a discussion
of Marlow, who is the voice of a community's overdetermined and
contradictory self-thinking; both *Heart of Darkness* and *Lord Jim* attest
in their respective ways to the problematic linkage between grand narratives and community. In *Heart of Darkness* we saw Marlow's need to
reassert a grand narrative of redemption as an aspect of his attempt
to maintain a sense of community with his narratees, a variant of
the grand narrative of love and devotion with which he maintained
solidarity with the Intended. In *Lord Jim* the failure to be faithful to
a fixed code or narrative of conduct accompanies the dispersion and
fragmentation of the Western imperial project. *Nostromo* also dramatizes the failure of various grand narratives, while at the same time
configuring its own version of the question of the narrative structure
of history.[7] To represent history in a narrative that at the same time
undermines the grand narratives that give form to historiography is to
write within the aporetics of a demonstration and repudiation of historical coherence, as Parry claims. If the coherence of history freed of
ideologically invested metanarratives is unrepresentable, it becomes
a sort of Lacanian "real" that escapes symbolization; traces of that
escape are apparent in *Nostromo*.

We can begin to understand the problematics of historical representation as configured in *Nostromo* by reference to a confrontation
on the pages of Ricoeur's *Time and Narrative*. Ricoeur discusses the
"Annales" school of historiography, focusing particularly on Fernand
Braudel's *The Mediterranean and the Mediterranean World in the Age of
Philip II*. What is at stake is the nature of the "event" in historiography. Are events "what active agents make happen," and do they
"share in the contingency proper to action"? Braudel's model denies the assumption that "events are what individuals make happen,"
that "the individual is the ultimate bearer of historical change," and
that "the most significant changes are pointlike ones, those that affect individual lives."[8] As opposed to the notion of the event, with
its potential filiation with bourgeois definitions of selfhood, Braudel
speaks of a multiplicity of social times or historical planes. As Ricoeur
says, "For Braudel, history even becomes a geohistory whose hero is
the Mediterranean and the Mediterranean world." From this point of
view "the most superficial history is concerned with the dimension
of individuals" and the unit of historical study becomes not the event
but the "long time-span."[9] Braudel's version of historiography may be

compatible with the ideology of the organic society, which minimizes individualism, but its stronger affiliations are with our poststructural decentered subject.

Ricoeur's own intention, contra Braudel, is to salvage the notion of the event and thus to maintain the centrality of the individual. Without presuming to mediate between Ricoeur and Braudel, I would suggest instead that something like a tension between their two models of history informs the narrative structure of *Nostromo*, an aporetic structure by which various individuals and their stories emerge for a time into the foreground only to recede again into the larger plurality of stories that accompany social change and the even-larger plurality of times in which social change occurs. As Avrom Fleishman says, "Men of varied classes and nationalities are shown caught up in a situation that their acts transform into history, that gives shape to their lives, and—what is rarer still in fiction—that is seen to continue beyond them."[10] And behind them as well, one might add. *Nostromo* reflects the multiplicity of time-spans, ranging from the history of the earth itself and, more specifically, of the Golfo Placido and the land of the Occidental Province, to the short time-spans of individual lives and of decisive moments in those lives. Between these extremes of geohistory and the moments of the individual fall the histories of civilizations, societies, and political units, each with distinct time-spans.

The novel's opening words, "In the time of the Spanish rule . . . ," establish the long time-spans of civilizations and societies in which the political events of the fictional present will be contextualized. The time of the Spanish conquest is past, though its architectural and social traces remain imprinted on Sulaco and Costaguana, particularly in the decaying palazzo with its painted ceilings and its now uselessly formal and expansive space. The time of the Spanish rule is further contextualized within the geohistory of the Golfo Placido, with its "sunken rocks," its "walls of lofty mountains" (39), and its "motionless and opaque clouds" (41). The clouds, always shifting and always the same, overhang the gulf "like a mass of solid silver" (465) in the final sentence of the novel, a paradoxical image of insubstantial permanence. This insistence on environment suggests a quality of ancient epic and drama described by Mikhail Bakhtin in "Forms of Time and of the Chronotope in the Novel": "The time of ancient epic and drama was profoundly localized, absolutely inseparable from concrete features of a characteristically Greek natural environment. . . . In every aspect of his natural world the Greek saw a trace of mythological time; he saw in it a condensed mythological event that would unfold into a mythological scene or tableau."[11]

Until recent improvements in the design of ships, the geography of the gulf and the hostility of its capricious breezes isolated it from "the temptations of the trading world" (39), creating a gap between world time and Sulaco time. The technology of that outer world finally closes the gap, since "the variable airs sporting lightly with the vast semicircle of waters within the head of Azuera could not baffle the steam power" of the Oceanic Steam Navigation Company (43). When Sir John, the economic backer of the new railroad, visits from London, he wonders, "Has anything ever happened here for a hundred years before today?" (63). Despite the intrusion of steamships and the railroad, the slower pace of economic history in the Occidental Province is emphasized by repeated references to the late sunrise over the eastern Cordillera Mountains, specifically Higuerota, which separate the province from the rest of Costaguana.[12] Costaguana experiences its own particular "horizon," with all the figurative value that word has come to possess.

If the Mediterranean space is itself the "hero" of Braudel's history, there is a similar suggestion in the shaping force of geography in Conrad's novel. The way in which space and time seem to conjoin as a single entity in *Nostromo* is what Bakhtin describes under the rubric of the "chronotope":

> We will give the name *chronotope* (literally, "time space") to the intrinsic connectedness of temporal and spatial relationships that are artistically expressed in literature. . . . In the literary artistic chronotope, spatial and temporal indicators are fused into one carefully thought-out, concrete whole. Time, as it were, thickens, takes on flesh, becomes artistically visible; likewise, space becomes charged and responsive to the movements of time, plot and history. The intersection of axes and fusion of indicators characterizes the artistic chronotope."[13]

In addition to the chronotope of the long time-span, Conrad situates the action of *Nostromo* in the chronotopes of folkloric and religious time. The folk legends of the poor have associated the peninsula of Azuera with wealth and evil. In a passage reminiscent of the condensed mythological event or tableau that Bakhtin describes in Greek epic, we are told that "tradition has it that many adventurers of olden time had perished in the search" for this wealth, and that "two *gringos*, spectral and alive, are believed to be dwelling to this day amongst the rocks, under the fatal spell of their success. Their souls cannot tear themselves away from their bodies mounting guard over the discovered treasure" (40). This myth of suspended time intersects with the events in "real" time when Nostromo and Decoud become the "two gringos" on the Great Isabel. The effect of this dissolution of boundaries is to contain the short-term "progress" of historical "events" in a larger framework of stasis or return, as Ricoeur explains:

> In the case where a myth relates unique events, the efficacy of these founding events spreads over a broader stretch of time than that of the action recounted. Here again, ritual assures the correspondence between this longer stretch of time and the founding mythical event by commemoration and imitation, when it is a question of past events, or by prefiguration and preparation, when it is a question of future events. In a hermeneutics of historical consciousness, to commemorate, to actualize, and to prefigure are three functions that underline the scansion of the past as tradition, the present as actual, and the future as the horizon of expectation and as eschatological.[14]

The long spans of geohistory and the mythic time-frames are perspectives from which the individual is diminished, as though seen through the other end of a telescope. The myth of the two gringos announces a folkloric chronotope that will permeate the broader stretch of time of the novel and prefigure future events, as Dorothy Van Ghent and Claire Rosenfield have both shown. Folkloric or mythic time is found in what Rosenfield calls the "traditional" story within the novel, as opposed to the novel's "political" story.[15] As a timeless story, Sulaco is a paradoxical Eden, not a prelapsarian one but rather a "paradise of snakes," as Don Pepe characterizes it (116). Rosenfield sees this phrase as an example of what Northrop Frye calls "demonic modulation," or the deliberate reversal of conventional archetypes:

> What Conrad presents is a demonic paradise, a parody of the Eden of Genesis wherein the only change was the daily rhythms of darkness and light. This "paradise of snakes" is a prophecy of the future, of the constant threat of corruption over the Conradian universe, of the evil influence of the traditional in the political affairs of the area. The jumbled and tangled natural setting which greets Charles and Mrs. Gould—the Adam and Eve who first yield to the temptations of power—represents the irrational of the individual or the prehistory of the new race born of material interests. Unlike our first parents, who were driven from paradise to found the race of man in time, Charles brings his new race into a demonic Eden.[16]

Rosenfield further observes that the spatial location of the mine on the side of the mountain "recalls the tendency of biblical and classical humanity to situate religious shrines in high places." [17] The effect of the demonic modulation comes from the impact of real time and economic history on the chronotopes of Edenic and religious time-space and from the issues of human and environmental ethics raised by that impact. With the introduction of technology into the Occidental Province, the waterfall that once existed has been transformed into a stream of silver. The new grand narrative of material progress, replacing the older folk and religious metanarratives, alters the fictive chronotope by literally transforming the physical world. The older world is now preserved only in the atemporal medium of Emily Gould's watercolor sketch:

> There was no mistaking the growling mutter of the mountain pouring its stream of treasure under the stamps. . . . The waterfall existed no longer. The tree-ferns that had luxuriated in its spray had dried around the dried-up pool, and the high ravine was only a big trench half filled up with refuse of excavations and tailings. The torrent, dammed up above, sent its water rushing along the open flumes of scooped tree trunks striding on trestlelegs to the turbines working the stamps on the lower plateau— the *mesa grande* of the San Tome mountain. Only the memory of the waterfall, with its amazing fernery, like a hanging garden above the rocks of the gorge, was preserved in Mrs. Gould's water-colour sketch. (115–16)

The references to mythic, folkloric, and religious time/space and to the long span of geohistory serve to enhance the impression of the rapidity with which modern people, scripted by metanarratives of technological and material progress, destroy the land. Perhaps the most powerfully ironic echo of sacred time within economic time is the moment when Mrs. Gould consecrates the silver with a laying on of hands:

> On the occasion when the fires under the first set of retorts in their shed had glowed far into the night she did not retire to rest on the rough cadre set up for her in the as yet bare framehouse till she had seen the first spongy lump of silver yielded to the hazards of the world by the dark depths of the Gould Concession; she had laid her unmercenary hands, with an eagerness that made them tremble, upon the first silver ingot turned out still warm from the mold; and by her imaginative estimate of its power she endowed that lump of metal with a justicative conception, as though it were not a mere fact, but something farreaching and impalpable, like the true expression of an emotion or the emergence of a principle. (117)

These words dramatize a moment somewhere in history when the concept of time changes as the organizing metanarrative represented by Mrs. Gould's piety gives way to the silver she touches. Later in the novel her unmercenary hands are shown to be aglitter with jewels. It is difficult to measure the exact degree of irony with which the discourse treats Mrs. Gould, but the sad delusion of her belief that time can once again be filled, as in the Christian myth, with something far-reaching is summed up in the passage above in the words "as though it were not a mere fact," which unfortunately it is.

Other ways the modern abandonment of responsibility for the land is played off against mythic chronotopes include the presentation of Holroyd as a demonic parody of God, removed from the garden, viewing it from on high in his San Francisco office building, and announcing his divine plan for the earth: "We shall be giving the word for everything: industry, trade, law, journalism, art, politics, and religion, from Cape Horn clear over to Smith's Sound, and beyond, too, if anything worth taking hold of turns up at the North Pole" (94).[18] And, by virtue of the power of his wealth, Holroyd, like a deity, is said to be eternally young. He aims to bring a "purified" Protestantism to the darker corners of the world, and he opposes the history conveyed in Catholic iconography, which is the visible and material embodiment of a religious tradition. Mrs. Gould says that "Mr. Holroyd's sense of religion . . . was shocked and disgusted at the tawdriness of the dressed-up saints in the cathedral—the worship, he called it, of wood and tinsel" (90). The irony of the ultimate materialist voicing the old Protestant objection to the material forms of Catholic worship does not escape Mrs. Gould, who observes that he looks on his own God "as a sort of influential partner, who gets his share of the profits in the endowment of churches" (90).[19]

The Casa Gould carries traces of the history of the Spanish rule in its architecture and of religious history in the Madonna it houses—to which the novel repeatedly refers, like the clouds over the gulf, as a motif. The child in the arms of the Madonna invokes a time and place in which human time was filled with a divine presence, and it stands in ironic opposition to the childless loves in *Nostromo*, not only the Gould marriage but the unachieved union of Decoud and Antonia, and Nostromo's failed courtship. The barrenness of Sulaco is a salient attribute of this modern chronotope, an attribute that is also suggested in the opening description of the seaboard and, particularly, of the Azuera as a wasteland haunted by the two gringos.

The absence of generation in *Nostromo* results from the domination of personal time by the form of time imposed by material interests.

Comparing the treatment of time in "pre-class folklore" with its treatment under the novel in developing capitalism, Bakhtin finds that the latter is marked by a fragmentation and plurality of times: "This imminent unity [of pre-class folklore] becomes apparent only in the light of later perceptions of time in literature (and in ideology in general), when time of personal, everyday family occasions had already been individualized and separated out from the time of the collective historical life of the social whole, at a time when there emerged one scale for measuring the events of *personal* life and another for measuring events of *history*."[20] In *Nostromo*, the mine has seduced Charles Gould, and historical time—which is now the time of capital—destroys personal time, as indicated by the absence of procreation.

Thus the insertion of the present-time story of Holroyd, Gould, et al. into the longer span of Christian history and the mythic times of Christian doctrine creates a sense of an ironic Advent or Second Coming in Sulaco. T. McAlindon sees this evocation of Christian time in what he calls "the iconographic style in *Nostromo*" (which is to say that this evocation is encoded in the narrator's discourse as well as in the story). By virtue of this style, found in the many tableau-like descriptions and moments of stasis,

> the world itself is a great temple or shrine filled with images of divinities and saints and their throng of ardent worshippers; it conspires thus with characterization and plot to suggest that all human bonds are essentially bonds of faith between the worshipped and the worshipper, protector and protege. More particularly, the iconographic style establishes a perspective from which we see that the living and the dying are already in the process of being absorbed by history, and that the paradigms of myth, religion and history are all one.[21]

Compare Kiernan Ryan's observation concerning "the pervasive sense of stasis, of almost lifeless reification" in Conrad's description of characters: "Giorgio's face has 'the immobility of a carving' and to the end he remains 'unstirring, like a statue of an old man.' The Sulaco ladies 'looked like white plaster casts with beautiful living eyes.' Mrs. Gould, 'her face powdered white like a plaster cast,' confronts a people 'suffering and mute, waiting for the future in a pathetic immobility of patience.'"[22] Ryan offers many more examples testifying that life itself has become frozen and static in *Nostromo*, perhaps not so much in spite of as because of the rush of historical "events" in which people are caught. Paradoxically, life seems more dynamic in the mythic and timeless chronotopes than in the chronotope of Sulaco;

it is as though the configuring of history in the economic grand narrative of industrial capitalism threatens and diminishes human time.

Other mythic chronotopes besides the Christian are invoked in the novel. Decoud accuses Charles Gould of living on the model of a fairy-tale romance (199), and Mrs. Gould is repeatedly seen as fairy-like. Rosenfield compares Gould to the impotent Fisher King,[23] and Nostromo, prior to his theft of the silver, is the changeless hero of episodic romance. Van Ghent speaks of the novel's archetypal folkoric plot concerning treasure, and she comments more specifically on the folkloric element of "ordeal," comparing Conrad's plot to that of the ancient Irish fairy tale of Conn-Eda.[24] Martin Price compares Hernandez to Robin Hood.[25] One could go on, but it suffices to say that critics have seen in Conrad's plot traces of earlier literary and folkloric structures, just as the fictional geographic space in which this plot occurs everywhere retains traces of lost time.

Within these multiple times and chronotopes—the long spans of Costaguana's geohistory, political history (from the time of the Spanish rule), and religious history, as well as the mythic chronotopes of folklore and Christian eschatology—are inserted the shorter spans of recent political "events" and the biographical and psychological times—the human time—of the people associated with those events. The representation of recent history and events in the novel is highly achronic; these numerous departures from normal chronology provide a skeptical commentary on the myth of progress, suggest the achronic structure of human (as opposed to official) memory, and underline the tension between general historical narrative and the individual's story.

The novel's many proleptic and analeptic shifts bring distant places and events into juxtaposition, and the proleptic glimpses of the future give the reader a knowledge that causes "present" events to be read ironically. Irving Howe refamiliarizes Conrad's text by presenting the historical events of the novel in their chronological order, clarifying the story that the discourse obscures with its emplotment.[26] By virtue of this emplotment we already know of the future revolution of Montero when Charles and Emily agree to marry and take control of the mine, and we have already had Mitchell's tour of the new and independent Sulaco, during which he refers to Decoud's death, before we read the direct description of Decoud's suicide. In fact, rather than allowing our suspense to be maintained during the recounting of the disturbances in Sulaco, the narrator, in one of his infrequent but pointed attempts to situate himself in the future time of the act of narration (rather than the time of the narrated events), tells us that the separation of Sulaco will be—or was, from his temporal position as he narrates—successful. Inserting the future in parentheses, Conrad says of the letter from Father Corbelan concerning Hernandez's role in opposing Montero that "Decoud's idea of the New Occidental State (whose flourishing and stable condition is a matter of common knowledge now) was for the first time made public and used as an argument" (303). These highly mannered proleptic and analeptic dislocations serve to throw the individual story into a problematic relationship with the larger movements of time and history and to question the commensurability of the two.

The narrator, for instance, describes Pedro Montero as a throwback to "primitive mankind," and after a short summary of the values of primitive man—including cunning, duplicity, and bodily strength—he tells us that "we have changed since" (327). Here the short-span changes in contemporary Costaguana's political history, organized by the achronic associations of human memory, recapitulate and symbolize long-span changes from the primitive to the civilized. Montero's individual story is occluded by his being viewed as a summary or culmination of historical conditions. On the other hand, despite the affirmation that "we have changed," the possibility of a grand narrative representing such change is also questioned. *Nostromo* derives much of its power as a meditation on history from its questioning (but not its outright denial) of the idea of progress.

William W. Bonney suggests that the denial of the notion of linear time, the commonsense notion of "the capitalistic and Christian West, founded upon a teleology of linear progress toward material acquisition and metaphysical redemption," results from Conrad's interest in oriental religions and in Schopenhauer, who himself appropriated many oriental beliefs.[27] In *Nostromo* Conrad emphasizes the specifically Western nature of the space-time configurations he scrutinizes by setting the action in what he calls the Occidental Province. His questioning of the linear model of time is implicit in the proleptic and analeptic movements that continually juxtapose past and present, "primitive" and "civilized." Even on the level of style or diction, Conrad's unwillingness to represent time in its supposedly normal, linear aspect is found in sentences such as this one referring to Mitchell, which replicates in miniature the mannered structuring of time in the novel as a whole: "He used to confess afterwards that the events which followed surpassed his imagination" (279).

A particularly good example of the novel's achronic juxtapositions and their thematic effects occurs in chapters 9 and 10 of "The Lighthouse." Chapter 9 moves analeptically (the previous chapter concerned Nostromo's rebirth and his discovery of Hirsch's hanging corpse) to the scene of Sotillo's murder of Hirsch. Chapter 10 then propels us proleptically into the future, giving us Captain Mitchell's famous tour of the thriving capital city of the independent Occidental Republic. This juxtaposition poses questions—certainly the defeat of the Sotillos of the world is progress, but whether this progress is more apparent than real, and whether Sotillo's brutality has merely been exchanged for other forms of oppression, is not clear.

Irving Howe locates a fundamental disagreement in critical responses to *Nostromo* concerning whether the ending is pessimistic or optimistic, whether some form of "progress" has occurred. I concur with Howe, who deconstructs the opposition: "Civil war brings capitalism and capitalism will bring civil war; progress *has* come out of chaos but it is the kind of progress that is likely to end in chaos."[28] The final chapters of the novel, with the many references to new and ongoing political disputes—continuing civil unrest, the possible annexation of Costaguana, and the appearance on the scene of communist organizers—suggest a model of history involving cycles of peace and civilization alternating with war and brutality. This model is like the one Marlow seems to accept in *Heart of Darkness* when he observes that "this also has been one of the dark places of the earth." Marlow speaks of periods of civilization as brief flashes of light in the darkness—"we live in the flicker" (9)—and the mechanical alternation of light and dark is figured in the lighthouse, the dominant image with which *Nostromo* ends.

The narrative discourse calls into question Mitchell's view of linear progress in history when it refers to Mitchell's "more or less stereotyped relation of 'historical events'" (394), and one indication of Mitchell's superficiality, although he shares this error with everyone else in the novel, is his ignorance concerning the secret of Nostromo's new prosperity. Mitchell, the novel's most satirized and discredited historian, represents the view of history, debated by Ricoeur and Braudel, that speaks of "events" (one of Mitchell's favorite words) and their origins in individual action: "Proud of his experience, penetrated by the sense of historical importance of men, events, and buildings, he talked pompously" (395). He lauds the role that "his man," Nostromo, has played in shaping events, but, as Van Ghent observes, Nostromo himself comes to realize "that, in the complication of events, it actually mattered very little whether the silver was saved or whether it sank to the bottom."[29]

Mitchell's view of history is predictably bourgeois, invested in an ideology of individualism. This is not to say that Conrad completely dissociates himself from this view. From the short-span perspective, individual decisions seem to influence history in this novel, although not necessarily in the intended way. *Nostromo* takes the middle ground in the traditional debate (the Ricoeur-Braudel encounter is a recent occurrence) concerning the role of the individual in determining historical change. This debate, of course, is only another version of the question of the nature of the subject.

Despite his fatuous discourse, Mitchell is an accurate observer of surfaces that are readable, and Conrad's narrator cannot claim to be entirely above stereotypical history himself—in fact, he relies on Mitchell to convey crucial information to the reader. Furthermore, the narrator, who visited Sulaco once, perhaps on "business," shares many of Mitchell's racial and aristocratic biases. The views of Conrad's narrator often blend with those of his characters, as when he seems in accord with Charles Gould's sympathetic attitude toward the career of Gould's father. He shares the Blanco disdain for liberalism, discrediting the Montero brothers by referring to their suspected "Negro blood" (328) and by describing the Montero supporters who fill the streets as "a torrent of rubbish" (326). And the gap or boundary between the narrator and Mitchell that at first seems so incontrovertible becomes fluid and unclear at important moments. If Mitchell "was no democrat" (279), this is not to Mitchell's discredit as far as the narrator is concerned. The political position that the Monteros adopt—that Costaguana is being exploited by foreign interests—is mentioned but never acknowledged by the narrator as having any validity, as of course it would not for Mitchell. Here a certain distance exists between the narrator and the author I infer, who reveals what the narrator ignores or minimizes.

Edward Said posits a "sizable distance separating his [Mitchell's] ingenuous record from the reality," but Said does not pause to discuss the problematic nature of the term "reality."[30] If it includes the suffering and legitimate resentment existing in many of the Monteros' destitute followers, then Conrad's narrator also speaks at a certain distance from the whole of "reality," just as grand narratives repress countless little stories. Mitchell and the narrator share a political agreement about what people and events are worth talking about. It is Mitchell, and Mitchell only, who tells us of the fates of Sotillo and the Montero brothers, of Antonia's future life, of Hernandez's installation as Minister of War, of Monygham's position as Inspector of Hospitals, and of the *Porvenir*'s new position, in the inevitable historical slippage of categories, as a conservative journal. Analeptically, Mitchell refers to

Nostromo's famous ride, telling us most of what we know about it, and he informs us of the decisive role played by the new rifles brought by Decoud.

The city Mitchell describes for his "privileged" guest is a modern chronotope, artistically representing the particular intersection of space and time in the imperial expansion of Western economic and political power. As with Marlow's "privileged" reader in *Lord Jim*, the social implications of that word are appropriate. Mitchell moves in a world of privilege, dwelling with pride on the superficial and material accomplishments of the modern international economic system. These things, of course, indicate progress only from the perspective of those privileged to benefit from them. Mitchell's references to the nationalities of the various clubs point to the way the new economic system has fractured the once-separate national boundaries and spaces, and a paragraph beginning "Lot of building going on" and then moving to "Observe the old Spanish houses" (396) shows how historical change is inscribed in the city's architecture, which serves as a sort of archive.[31] Sulaco is a boundary phenomenon in which residual and emergent social formations overlap. The Casa Avellanos, "with all the ground floor windows shuttered" (396), testifies eloquently to change, although there is no regret for lost time expressed on the part of Captain Mitchell. Thus Mitchell's discourse constitutes a "thin" description; the "thick" description of the social and cultural significance of the urban geography—the various forms of power, imagination, and failure to which it is a monument—is left to the reader's imagination.[32] As Mitchell's tour continues from the cathedral to the American bar, Sulaco unfolds as a structure of anachorisms and anachronisms, a disruption of linear time-space.

Sulaco has become an architectural collage of residual and emergent styles and functions, and as a composite structure it anticipates Jameson's description of postmodern architecture: "Postmodernist buildings . . . celebrate their insertion into the heterogeneous fabric of the commercial strip and the motel and fast-food landscape. . . . Meanwhile a play of allusion and formal echoes ('historicism') secures the kinship of these new art buildings with the surrounding commercial icons and spaces, thereby renouncing the high modernist claim to radical difference and innovation."[33] Jameson defines the postmodern in terms of a populist assault on the high culture of modernism. Such postmodern architecture can be taken as a celebration of the very historical process that is inscribed upon Sulaco, and *Nostromo*'s descriptions of the city anticipate more recent crises in city planning.

But the narrator's disdain for Mitchell is at odds with his reliance on Mitchell's eye and information. During the moments of this reliance, the narrator's voice and Mitchell's begin to flow together and to lose their separate identities, the boundaries of selfhood becoming as permeable as national and ethnic boundaries, as fluid as the line between past and future. Furthermore, Mitchell's tour of Sulaco is a sort of analogue for the novel's handling of chronology. The reader's experience of *Nostromo*, with its achronic juxtapositions of disparate times, is not unlike the privileged traveler's experience of Sulaco, with its disjointed historical moments readable in its juxtaposed architectures and its spatial form. When the tour that Mitchell conducts for the traveler nears its end, the narrator's words—"The cycle was about to close at last" (407)—apply equally to Mitchell's spatial tour and to the cycle of history that the novel as a whole has presented and that is now physically inscribed in the city. The content in the form of the novel is the accelerated layering of time that characterizes modern experience. This is registered in the architectural strata of Mitchell's city and contrasted to the stasis of the prerevolutionary gulf described in the novel's opening pages.

Although Ricoeur defines the *Zeitroman* in terms of such novels as *Mrs. Dalloway*, *The Magic Mountain*, and *Remembrance of Things Past*, novels that treat personal, psychological time, time is Conrad's theme as well.[34] *Nostromo* situates itself between cosmic and mythical times on the one hand and personal, psychological times on the other—in that middle time called history.

The presentation of Mitchell as a sort of self-appointed, establishment historian is only one of the ways that *Nostromo* foregrounds the problematic of historiography. Mitchell, with his untroubled view of history as progress, contrasts with another oral historian, old Giorgio Viola. After the first chapter of the novel, which presents the geographical chronotope of the Golfo Placido, the second and third chapters present the opposition between Mitchell and Viola. Viola views history as decline. To him, all significant human action was in the past, during the period of Garibaldi's revolutionary activity, which stands in opposition to the aristocratic revolution of the Sulaco Blancos that Mitchell celebrates. Like the physical monument of Charles IV (which, ironically, is removed as an anachronism from this achronic city), Viola is a relic. And, again ironically, Viola now keeps a hotel catering to the European colonists of Costaguana. (Irony is a function of temporality in Conrad's novel. Things are ironic not so much in their departure from atemporal universals as in their deviation from past or future states; *Nostromo* emphasizes the temporal aspect of irony.)

In addition to offering conflicting views of history, Mitchell and

Viola together illustrate the interweaving of history and fiction discussed by Ricoeur, the way "history and fiction each concretize their respective intentionalities only by borrowing from the intentionality of the other."[35] Mitchell is the historian of a fictional country, while Viola remembers a past appropriated from nonfictional history. Thus fiction makes use of "real" history in its configuring of time.

Furthermore, *Nostromo* contains a written history of recent events in Costaguana, contrasting with the oral historiography of Mitchell and Viola. Don Jose Avellanos's *Fifty Years of Misrule* is an example of what Edward Said identifies as a pervasive concern in *Nostromo:* "Nearly everyone seems extremely anxious about both keeping and leaving a personal 'record' of his thoughts and actions. The anxiety seems to be based upon an extraordinary preoccupation with the past, as if the past, left to itself, given only ordinary attention and no official recording, were somehow unthinkable and without sufficient authority."[36] Said finds in all this record keeping a theme of self-authoring that parallels Conrad's personal habit of idealizing his own past in his written records.

The imperfect nature of the historical records in *Nostromo*, and what we know of the revisionary nature of Conrad's own self-authoring, bespeaks an imperfect relationship between action and its representation in recorded history. In addition to *Fifty Years of Misrule*, another written record is Decoud's letter to his sister, the opposition between Don Jose's writing and Decoud's being one of the public document versus the private. Like *Lord Jim*, *Nostromo* is a structure of interlocking stories, recorded and unrecorded. Even Montero (whose past reading habits are curiously reminiscent of Jim's) came upon his own self-concept while reading "the lighter sort of historical works in the French language" (328). Reading, as we know, is also a form of authorship and therefore of self-fashioning.

Another form of history represented in *Nostromo* is the orally transmitted history inscribed in rumor and public opinion. An example occurs in the first chapter of "The Lighthouse," a chapter Guerard chose to illustrate what he thinks is Conrad's careless handling of point of view.[37] In this chapter the engineer and Monygham touch on the topic of selfhood, the engineer having just praised Gould for being "extremely sure of himself." Monygham has replied, with a sort of postmodern skepticism, "If that's all he is sure of, then he is sure of nothing" (269). The engineer is irritated by Monygham's "paradox" and begins his interior train of thought concerning Monygham. But these thoughts turn out to be not really "his" so much as the community's shared speculations about Monygham's character and past behavior. The engineer is not the sole author of his own thoughts, and his selfhood, as it focuses at this moment on the question of Monygham's selfhood, is a heteroglossia of social discourses. As in *Lord Jim,* this socially circulated discourse is a beclouded, composite story or history: "It lost itself amongst the innumerable tales of conspiracies and plots against the tyrant as a stream is lost in an arid belt of sandy country before it emerges, diminished and troubled, perhaps, on the other side" (270).

The engineer, attempting to fix Monygham's character in his mind, entertains thoughts scripted by society's rumors and innuendos. "Whispers had been heard that years ago" Monygham had "betrayed some of his best friends" who had conspired to overthrow Guzman Bento. But "nobody pretended to believe that whisper; the whole story of the Great Conspiracy was hopelessly involved and obscure." In fact, it is "admitted in Costaguana that there never had been a conspiracy" and that therefore there had been "no one to betray" (271). This is rich in irony and ambiguity. What is "admitted" is a self-defensive denial of the truth, and the "pretending" is the pretending *not* to believe what is in fact true and still whispered. Even though the truth of the rumors is clarified elsewhere in the novel, the representation of the engineer's point of view on Monygham serves to underline the novel's skepticism, since the engineer himself has no place from which to see or hear the truth outside of the shared language of the rumors. The past is relevant, but what genealogy can retrieve it when it is subject to narrative alterations by the needs of those who report it? The namelessness of the engineer further obscures his selfhood amid the rumors and stories that engulf him.

If the recording and telling of history—and the multiplicity of stories this activity gives rise to—is a theme in *Nostromo,* the significance of this theme lies largely in what escapes inscription or speech. Mitchell's ignorance of the truth of Nostromo's wealth is merely symptomatic of the repression of individual stories upon which official history depends. The failure of Gould's idealism, Mrs. Gould's disenchantment, and Decoud's suicide are other realities that escape any of these record keepers, and that therefore can be recorded only in the counter-memory of an omniscient narrator of "fiction," a genealogist who can liberate the profusion of lost events. He "knows" what could not be found in any document or heard from any eyewitness, and the history of Costaguana and the Occidental Republic is completed in the literary configuring of time. Thus the fictional device of narrative omniscience, despite its own potential for totalization, becomes the vehicle for a critique of the totalizing tendencies in "real" historical narratives. The omniscient narrative discourse, with its kaleidoscopic perspectives, is able to present alternate "little stories" that qualify or correct the repressions of the totalizing grand narratives of true believers such as Mitchell, Gould, Holroyd, or Viola.

But this omniscient and aristocratically biased narration is guilty of repressions of its own; the original inhabitants of Costaguana, for instance, live at best only on the margins of narrative consciousness. Any configuring of time, historical or literary, stands in need of correction by that as-yet-unwritten history of the victims it has ignored. If *Nostromo* encourages a critique of totalizing histories, and this is the function of counter-memory for Foucault, this critique is also encouraged by the reader's awareness of the imperfections in the narrator's vision. As in *Heart of Darkness*, the novel undermines official memory but at the same time, by virtue of a transferential relationship, repeats official repressions and therefore does not escape its own critique of narrative authority.

Mrs. Gould's refusal to repeat the secret of the treasure told to her by the dying Nostromo thematizes the dependence of our enabling fictions upon repression and, of course, recalls Marlow's lie to the Intended in *Heart of Darkness*. Her silence stands in opposition to the various recorded or spoken histories, and her refusal to become an author or to correct the flawed record is, she assumes, the higher form of service to her community. The tension between recording and repressing is related to the tension between social criticism and despairing irony in the narrator's discourse, what Ryan refers to as "the mind-snapping tension between subversive unmasking and the occlusive confirmation of the prevailing social order."[38]

The individuals and their personal narratives are placed within the novel's various time-spans and chronotopes, and within a self-referential problematizing of historical recording. It is curious that Charles Gould's manner of experiencing time is unavailable to us, given his central importance. The narration only occasionally employs its omniscience to report on Gould's inner life, which is usually conveyed through Mrs. Gould, who functions as a Jamesian reflector in this regard. But we do find, in passages such as the following, that Gould himself experiences his time as one of corruption and failure, a destruction of his grand narrative of material and moral progress: "To him, as to all of us, the compromises with his conscience appeared uglier than ever in the light of failure. His taciturnity, assumed with a purpose, had prevented him from tampering openly with his thoughts; but the Gould Concession had insidiously corrupted his judgement" (311).

This is an odd passage. Throughout the novel the narrative discourse has suggested that Gould is held by the fixed idea of protecting and working the mine. The bribes and other compromises do not trouble him because they are the necessary means to a valued end. In this passage, he seems to be conscious of them in the first sentence, but in the first half of the second sentence he does not think "openly," and in the second half the opinion concerning his corrupted judgment apparently becomes the narrator's and not Gould's. The point of view of the narrative discourse is, once again, imperfectly differentiated from the character's, in another transgressive dissemination that raises the question of who is speaking.

Gould emerges from a family history of involvement in Costaguana, and on the day of his engagement to Emily he casts himself in the role of his father's avenger in his family narrative. But revenge co-exists with altruism in Gould's grand if vague script, since he believes the success of the mine will improve the lives of all the people of Costaguana: "A vague idea of rehabilitation had entered the plan of their life. That it was so vague as to elude the support of argument made it only the stronger. It had presented itself to them at the instant when the woman's instinct of devotion and the man's instinct of activity receive from the strongest illusions their most powerful impulse" (92).

Here the differentiation of the points of view is clearer, the narrator's skepticism being evident in words such as "vague" and "illusion." Charles is less vague a few pages later when he says that "what is wanted here is law, good faith, order, security. Anyone can declaim about these things, but I pin my faith to material interests. Only let the material interests once get a firm footing, and they are bound to impose the conditions on which alone they can continue to exist. That's how your money-making is justified here in the face of lawlessness and disorder. It is justified because the security it demands must be shared with an oppressed people. A better justice will come afterwards" (100).

Gould's metanarrative invests materialism with spiritual value, turning material pursuits into a religious or moral obligation. As Parry observes, domination of the world becomes the performance of God's work.[39] Gould's belief that religious time can be wedded to economic time, his faith in an economic eschatology, makes his partnership with Holroyd (who is a debased God-figure) especially appropriate, and the unsatisfactory wedding of religious and economic chronotopes in the metanarrative is allegorized in his childless marriage to the pious Emily (who is repeatedly associated with the statue of the Madonna) in the literal story. According to Fleishman, the ideal of the organic society that informs Conrad's social criticisms depends on a contract "in which people of a nation share common experiences and develop common values, bequeathing them to their children," and the underlying metaphor of Burke's social theory is that of the family, rather than of business.[40] But Gould's fixed idea militates against personal development or growth and results in a hardening of his character that destroys the family as a procreative unit, thus destroying the linear time upon which the contract with the future depends. The hardening of character and destruction of generation are functions of the power that politics and economics exercise over human time.

If, for Gould, time is organized by a quasi-religious belief, a belief that precludes the necessity of further thought and therefore of revision, Decoud is at the outset his opposite. Decoud's time lacks an organizing belief, and he has lived from moment to moment as an "idle boulevardier" (151). His return to Costaguana, begun as a mere lark, becomes focused on the trivial romantic gratification he imagines he needs from Antonia. Decoud's personal narrative of flight with Antonia represents a diminished form of the model of the self as a free individual, a model by which "love" becomes a private thing between two autonomous beings. But Decoud is a patriot for whom patriotism is a dirty word, and his role as lover is a necessary mask for his political self.

Decoud's selfhood derives from the community, as his actions prove, even though he has learned the intellectual habit of disparaging this fact, and his personal narrative becomes inescapably wedded to the narrative of that community. Ironically, his apparently subjective and self-indulgent orientation is the start of his involvement in society and history, and he becomes the most courageous of those committed to the Blanco position. A similar plot element occurs in *The Arrow of Gold*, where George joins the gunners during the Carlist revolution out of love for Rita. In both novels, the political cause gains legitimacy in the eyes of the hero by its association with feminine beauty and libidinal gratification.[41]

The opening of *Nostromo* establishes the gulf as a chronotope that stands in opposition to both human time and history, and this opposition is extended later when Nostromo and Decoud slip out onto the water and into the night and fog with the silver. Rosenfield points out that in this night journey Nostromo and Decoud leave social time for mythic time, as they become incarnations of the two gringos and of other mythic characters who harrow mysterious regions that oppose or negate human time.[42] In this regard, the gulf becomes associated with sleep, forgetfulness, and the annihilation of memory: "The enormous stillness, without sight or sound, seemed to affect Decoud's senses like a powerful drug. . . . The change from the agitation, the passions and the dangers, from the sights and sounds of the shore, was so complete that it would have resembled death had it not been for the survival of his thoughts. In this foretaste of eternal peace they floated vivid and light, like unearthly clear dreams of earthly things that may haunt the souls freed by death from the misty atmosphere of regrets and hopes" (231). As Rosenfield says, "the night journey demands a method of understanding beyond that employed by the timed world." [43]

As Decoud slips toward death, "all his active sensations and feelings from as far back as he could remember seemed to him the maddest of dreams" (235). The next ten days, culminating in Decoud's death, are not reported until nearly 200 pages later, when the opposition between gulf and mainland is insisted upon. The tenth chapter of "The Lighthouse" juxtaposes two chronotopes, the independent Sulaco described by Mitchell and the barren Great Isabel on which Decoud dies—a juxtaposition also of public and private time and of recorded and unrecorded history.

Bakhtin's concept of the chronotope is particularly appropriate to the pages devoted to Decoud's death, pages that establish the relationship between physical space and subjective time. In the sterility of the Great Isabel—pregnant only with absence and death—time itself becomes an illusion to Decoud. Human time, these pages eloquently argue, is a function of social activity, but solitude is the overwhelming experience of the Isabels, which even "the sea-birds of the gulf shun" (412). In perhaps the best-known phrase in the novel, the narrator claims that "in our activity alone do we find the sustaining illusion of an independent existence" (413), but in the absence of activity, time for Decoud becomes mere random succession: "He beheld the universe as a succession of incomprehensible images" (413–14). Clifford Geertz bases his ethnographic studies on the premise that "human thought is consummately social: social in its origins, social in its functions, social in its forms, social in its applications." [44] Geertz's credo echoes the organic philosophy informing Conrad's vision, which, as Fleishman says, stresses "the primacy of the community, which gives individual life its possibility and its value." [45] When the narrative discourse depicts the disappearance of Decoud in the absence of this social context, it critiques the illusion of a transcendent, self-determining subject and argues for defining selfhood as a social, ideological, and historical phenomenon.

It may seem a simple irony that the architect of Occidental independence is himself unable to survive independently, but Mitchell's tour of the future Sulaco, with its English, American, French, and Italian presences, has already shown us that Sulaco's "independence" is also an illusion. Sulaco's freedom—its own selfhood or identity—is inevitably lost in other entanglements and other power relations, and the juxtaposition of Sulaco's fate with Decoud's underlines a single proposition, applicable to both individuals and nations, concerning the illusion of independence and individuality.

Frank Kermode writes that for people to make sense of their time, "they need fictive concords with origins and ends, such as give meaning to lives and poems."[46] Previously, a story of elopement and erotic gratification gave fullness to Decoud's time, but now his personal narrative has no structure, no beginning, middle, or end; it is sunk in a silence that "vibrated with senseless phrases" like a "cord to which he clung with both hands" (414). The only narrative Decoud can now compose is the story of that cord's breaking, and the only question his narrative poses is whether or not one would hear the sound of its snap before death. Bonney's provocative discussion of the cord image suggests that Decoud's experience of meaninglessness in the gulf is an extension of his own commitment to "meaningless exercises of journalistic propaganda," which Decoud himself sees as "deadly nonsense" and "intellectual death."[47] When the societal discourse is debased, the self becomes an empty synthesis.

As a chronotope, the Great Isabel is a space where time as *kairos*, time filled with significance, gives way to time as *chronos*, time robbed of significance—or, as Kermode defines it, time as "one damn thing after another."[48] The process of the dissolution of any sense of ordered, significant time for Decoud is counterpointed by the narrator's repeated references to the calendar time in which this dissolution occurs—"at the end of the first day" (412), "after three days" (413), "on the fifth day" (413), and "on the tenth day" (414); the activities of this final day are further specified as beginning when "the sun was two hours above the horizon" (414). This counterpointing of the dissolution of Decoud's subjective time with conventionally measured time is brought home when the reader realizes that time dissolves for Decoud simultaneously with Mitchell's farcical dispute—described at another "time" in the narrative structure—with Sotillo over his stolen chronometer.[49]

The narrator's account of Decoud's final days is framed within Nostromo's return, months later, to the island, and his speculations about how Decoud died. Again, as one story is inserted within another, Conrad's narrative structure of achronic juxtapositions is significant, since Nostromo's "success"—the quality and shape of his time—now depends on the repression of the ending of Decoud's story. Nostromo's new prosperity is not simply a matter of his having appropriated the silver; it grows also out of his having abandoned Decoud to die on the Great Isabel. The "incorruptible" Nostromo feels that he has been "betrayed" by the Blancos who no longer need him, but he is now himself a betrayer who is little better than a murderer. He steals Decoud's time (which, unlike Mitchell's chronometer, cannot be returned) as surely as he steals the silver, and his deathbed "confession" to Mrs. Gould contains no reference to his responsibility for Decoud, as though the crime were only in the possession of the silver and not in the human violence by which it was acquired. Nostromo's independence is paradoxically bound to his guilty secret. Thus, in a new sense, Nostromo remains the "our man" of the "independent" republic in that he personifies the violence, forgetfulness, and repression on which "progress" rests. The phrase "our man" revealed that Nostromo's apparently independent self was only the particular form of his subjugation to ruling interests, and the reborn Nostromo only partially alters this form.

The well-known scene in which Nostromo is reborn after his return from the Great Isabel and after his fourteen hours of sleep in the grass is, like the moment when Emily lays hands on the first silver from the mine, a point of transition from one temporal orientation to another. Until now Nostromo has been a mythic or folkloric hero in his own eyes and in the eyes of those who have used him. Underlining his mythic quality is the fact that he, like Jim, has not seemed to age, and his concern for reputation has been reminiscent of an earlier exchange system of the sort found in *Sir Gawain and the Green Knight,* in which Gawain's reputation alone (or so he thinks, at least) earns him comfort and hospitality. Nostromo has lived in what Bakhtin calls "adventure-time." Bakhtin says of this time in Greek romance: "This most abstract of all chronotopes is also the most static. In such a chronotope the world and the individual are finished items, absolutely immobile. In it there is no potential for evolution, for growth, for change. As a result of the action described in the novel, nothing in its world is destroyed, remade, changed or created anew. What we get is a mere affirmation of the identity between what had been at the beginning and what is at the end. Adventure-time leaves no trace." [50]

Of course, modern economic time swirls around Nostromo from the outset, and the chronotope of adventure time refers only to his own mistaken and romantic sense of himself prior to his metamorphosis. His concern with his reputation further suggests how his outlook reprises an ancient, precapitalistic orientation. In the manner of Sir Gawain, his good name is his capital, and the word "incorruptible" so often applied to him carries traces of the old belief in an incorruptible or immutable realm in opposition to the sublunary world of mutability. An incorruptible self would be an autonomous, transcendent essence escaping the forces of historical and social change. The appearance of "the man" (347) is an awakening into economic time—he will now "grow rich very slowly" (417). The word "grow" marks the end of the stasis of adventure time, but this temporal growth will, of course, also be a process of corruption and decay. In Frye's mapping of the structure of literary history, which has certain similarities with Bakhtin's, Nostromo has changed from a hero in the romantic mode to a "hero" in the ironic mode; in this regard, Conrad's novel offers a partial reprisal of literary history.[51]

The description of Nostromo's metamorphosis from folk hero to economic man consciously reverses the archetypal metamorphosis from man to beast in folk literature. Refusing the traditional association of evil with animality, the discourse emphasizes the specifically human quality of Nostromo's corruption. As he awakens, "a growling yawn of white teeth, as natural and free from evil in the moment of waking as a magnificent and unconscious beast" gives way to the "frown" of "the man" (347). The folkloric motif of metamorphosis—perhaps literature's oldest way of referring to the problem of identity and change—is employed in Nostromo as a sort of farewell to a genre and a chronotope, marking the shift from folkloric or adventure time to modern, economic time. It also underlines the impossibility of material interests ever leading us back, despite the faith upon which the Gould marriage was founded, to an organic society, which exists only in a lost and mythic chronotope.

The following passage, in which Bakhtin describes the development of the novel from Greek to modern times, could as well be a description of Nostromo's change from public to private man—his acquisition of a secret self—a change marked in the novel by his negotiations between the chronotopes of city and island, which give spatial form to the complex dialogic relationship between public and private and between exteriority and interiority in modern experience:

> In following epochs, man's image was distorted by his increasing participation in the mute and invisible spheres of existence. He was literally drenched in muteness and invisibility. And with them entered loneliness. The personal and detached human being—"the man who exists for himself"—lost the unity and

wholeness that had been a product of his public origin. Once having lost the popular chronotope of the public square, his self-consciousness could not find an equally real, unified and whole chronotope; it therefore broke down and lost its integrity. . . . A vast number of new spheres of consciousness and objects appeared in the private life of the private individual that were not, in general, subject to being made public (the sexual sphere and others), or were subject only to an intimate, conditional, closeted expression. The human image became multi-layered, multi-faceted. A core and a shell, an inner and an outer, separated within it.[52]

Nostromo's illicit sexual desire for his fiancee's sister on the island—in the private space—where the treasure is buried enacts an interpenetration of economic and sexual secrets and lends support to Foucault's argument that there existed in nineteenth-century society an "incitement" to guilty sexuality that seeks to avoid surveillance, and that this incitement, paradoxically, was a function of the larger fabric of social control (to have surveillance you need to produce that which must be surveyed).[53] This incitement is only one aspect of the bourgeois subject's cultivation of interior spaces and of the mechanisms for their scrutiny. The buried treasure and the lighthouse establish the subtle relationship between surveillance and secrecy; Nostromo first fears that the lighthouse will reveal his secret, but it soon becomes a device for the protection of the secret.

The lighthouse, with its beam creating an oscillation between light and darkness, becomes a provocative symbol of social contradictions in the capitalist chronotope, its blindness and insight. Nostromo's courting of the two sisters at the lighthouse (one publicly and the other secretly) represents such social contradictions as the public respectability and private guilt that accompany wealth. These light and dark aspects of the courtship plot, to which so many critics have objected, dramatize how social contradictions are registered in what we choose to call our private lives. Furthermore, Nostromo enacts other contradictions of the modern world in his dual or oscillating roles of respectable businessman and patron of radical causes; in this regard he is a reinscription of Charles Gould's initial assumption that one can wed material interests to social progress.

Like *Lord Jim*, *Nostromo* is concerned with the plurality of stories and histories that share the space of social reality. If, to the Western eyes of Jim and Marlow, Patusan is an alternate chronotope, *Nostromo* moves beyond *Lord Jim* in its more complex configuring of the multiplicity of times in which the plurality of human stories exists. In doing so, it problematizes the relationship between time and narration as it interweaves geohistory, mythic and folkloric time, political history, and personal or human time. Various chronotopes share the space and material of Sulaco's architecture and share the language and form of the novel as a whole; the many achronic juxtapositions that occur within the short-span political history that is the novel's primary object of representation are echoed on another level in the way the novel constructs a realistic story on substrata of folkloric and mythic materials. By virtue of this "thick" layering, and in the process of juxtaposing mythic and folkloric times with time as structured in modern capitalism, *Nostromo* reprises the changes in the novel as a literary form as it passes from precapitalist to capitalist society. Bakhtin writes that "a genre lives in the present, but always *remembers* its past, its beginning. Genre is a representative of creative memory in the process of literary development. Precisely for this reason genre is capable of guaranteeing the *unity* and *uninterrupted continuity* of this development."[54] And Frye speaks of the uncanny way modern ironic modes seem to return to mythic and romantic modes.[55] *Nostromo*, a repository and genealogy of cultural memory, returns to these modes in its first two sections in order to then dramatize the movement away from the mythic, the folkloric, and the romantic as material interests tighten their death grip on the hero, and on our time.

5

Shared Words and Western Eyes

A *self* does not amount to much, but no self is an island; each exists in a fabric of relations that is now more complex and mobile than ever before. Young or old, man or woman, rich or poor, a person is always located at "nodal points" of specific communication circuits, however tiny these may be. Or better: one is always located at a post through which various kinds of messages pass.

Jean-François Lyotard, *The Postmodern Condition*

In dialogue a person not only shows himself outwardly, but he becomes for the first time that which he is—and, we repeat, not only for others but for himself as well.

Mikhail Bakhtin, *Problems in Dostoevsky's Poetics*

From the perspective of narrative theory, *Under Western Eyes* looks in the direction of some of today's more provocative issues and problematics, particularly questions of narrative authority, self-referentiality, and intertextuality. Much of the novel is the narrator's paraphrase of other texts, most notably Razumov's diary but also Peter Ivanovitch's book, various letters, and numerous conversations. As a text upon other fictive texts, this metafictional novel foregrounds the scene of writing and recording even more directly than does *Nostromo*, in part because of the narrator's self-consciousness about his writing procedures—especially in his assurances that he has no pretenses to art or imagination—but also because of the central role of writing in Razumov's own self-fashioning. Avrom Fleishman directs attention to this self-referential structure, pointing to the novel's three layers of textuality: the fiction written by Joseph Conrad, the history or biography written by the fictional narrator, and the absent texts that constitute that narrator's primary sources. *Under Western Eyes* at once reflects or imitates the intertextual nature of cultural transmission and reveals the dangers of silence to both self and community.[1]

Although the reader must accept the premise of the existence of the narrator's primary sources, those sources are withheld from our direct examination; they seem to exist nomadically just beyond the horizon, and we cannot measure precisely the narrator's fidelity to them or the extent to which they become altered as they are represented in his composite discourse. But we can be certain that his liberties are legion. He tells us that the diary consists of dated entries, but his own reconstruction occludes that original form. We know that occasionally the diary is the ostensible authority for descriptions that Razumov could not have made, as when Prince K is seen sitting sadly alone in his study or when we are given Sophia Antonovna's inner thoughts about Razumov's character. We also know that the narrator offers other observations he himself could not have made, as when Razumov's mutilation is described as though by an eyewitness or when the narrator reports that Mikulin was a bachelor who liked female dancing (290). Moreover, there is a general omniscience and totality of recall that is not consistent with reasonable assumptions about what could have been in the diary or what would actually be in the narrator's memory of conversations he once had and scenes he once witnessed. Although the narrator is ostensibly a single consciousness, an eyewitness character in the story, the narrative discourse betrays similarities with the fractured, multiple perspective found in *The Nigger of the "Narcissus"* and *Nostromo*. Expanded memory is a convention of narrative fiction, but *Under Western Eyes* calls attention to such conventions in an unconventional and metafictional manner.

Rather than follow Albert Guerard in seeing relatively trivial moments of "clumsiness" in Conrad's handling of narrative conventions,[2] this chapter will argue that *Under Western Eyes* raises the questions of narrative authority and the nature of narrative discourse in ways that can best be understood in terms of Bakhtin's dialogics, specifically the issues involved in shared speech or "reported speech" discussed in Bakhtin's *Marxism and the Philosophy of Language* and the question of the hero discussed in his *Problems of Dostoevsky's Poetics*. And despite the moments of coerced speech and writing—moments of a Foucauldian "incitement" to discourse—*Under Western Eyes* affirms the civilizing power of discourse in the face of silence.

Conrad's decision to violate the logic of his chosen point of view creates a novel that strains at the boundaries of mimetic realism by emphasizing the fissures, gaps, and inconsistencies within textuality.[3] Despite the omnipresence of the first-person narrator, no single voice or viewpoint dominates the text—beginnings are elusive, every word is a shared word, and each iteration is always already a reiteration.

Under Western Eyes foregrounds and problematizes the narrative situation, resisting the reader's totalizing efforts to refamiliarize the text as a single, monologic discourse. To understand the Bakhtinian or dialogic nature of this novel, let us look first at Caryl Emerson's characterization of a crucial aspect of Bakhtin's thought:

> Bakhtin profoundly redefined the Word itself and attempted to infuse it with its original Greek sense of *logos* ("discourse"). For Bakhtin, words cannot be conceived apart from the voices who speak them; thus, every word raises the question of authority. Fully half of *Marxism and the Philosophy of Language* is devoted to an investigation of "indirect" and "quasi-direct" discourse, multileveled speech acts in which more than one voice participates. . . . Words in discourse always recall earlier contexts of usage, otherwise they could not mean at all. It follows that *every* utterance, covertly or overtly, is an act of indirect discourse.[4]

The narrator of *Nostromo* is entirely Bakhtinian when he says that "the value of a sentence is in the personality which utters it, for nothing new can be said by man or woman" (173–74). Everything has been said before, but never in the same place or situation, or with the same accent, which is to say that the pragmatics of the speech and narrative acts are never identical.

In the intertextual, postmodern world of the "always already," as the speaking subject struggles for identity within the ambient social discourse, such questions emerge as "Who Is Speaking?" (Barthes) and "What Is an Author?" (Foucault).[5] If half of *Marxism and the Philosophy of Language* investigates "reported speech" or indirect discourse, most of *Under Western Eyes is* reported speech. Words are transmitted from person to person, and in this sharing the concept of original or unitary authorship recedes. Each word carries the ideological accents and overtones of its past usages, which inhabit the discourse of subsequent speakers so that the sign itself becomes an arena of contestation. In *Under Western Eyes*, we have not so much the mastery of a totalizing narrative as the dialogism of little stories.

A number of critics, following Guerard, have addressed the question of narrative authority in *Under Western Eyes*. Some have felt the need to parcel out responsibilities for speech and authorship between the author they infer and his narrator, the allegedly obtuse middle-aged language teacher who claims to have no art as a writer and no understanding of the Russian character, and who therefore seems to disqualify himself in matters of both form and content. The author these critics infer stands in the background, accepting credit not only for the novel's meaning and significance, but also for its artful structure. By this analysis, whatever is most troubling and profound in the thematics of the novel exists in spite of the narrator, not because of his intentions. The text is saved as realistic mimesis by explaining away and forgiving its occasional deviations from the proper procedures of such a mimesis and by maintaining a strict distinction between two monologic entities, the author and the narrator. Why the subtle structural effects cannot also be credited to the mind and intentions of the narrator—it is the *narrator* as well as his author who decides to end the first part with Mikulin's penetrating question and to initiate the suspended prolepsis of the second and third parts—is, of course, an inconvenient question for this line of analysis.[6]

But the larger difficulty with this analysis lies in its need to totalize the text by locating and fixing its source of authority. An alternate approach is to see the question of the relationships between inferred author, narrator, and the myriad metastories that constitute their discursive materials—relationships that exemplify the larger phenomenon of shared language[7]—as being encoded in the text itself. During those sections of the narrative that purport to be indirect representations of Razumov's diary, the origin of much of the evaluative language of the discourse cannot be located with certainty. For instance, we are told that Razumov began his diary nearly a year after his betrayal of Haldin (55).[8] Our first difficulty, therefore, involves the possibility of something like what Freud called "secondary revision," the way a remembered dream might already be a revision of the actual dream. Does the diary report his feelings as they really were at the time of Haldin's appearance, or has his memory recast that event to suit present needs?[9] If secondary revision occurred (and we must assume it did, insofar as all autobiography is revisionary), the diary itself, which the reader of the novel never sees, is *already* a document of double or divided authority, and this problem is then squared when we factor in the language professor's indirect discourse upon the journal, a discourse that also may contain two or more levels of interpretation—one occurring at the time of his first encounter with Razumov and/or his journal, another occurring at the future time of his act of narration.[10]

The diary is reported not by direct quotation but by indirect discourse, which blends reported speech and reporting speech without demarcating quotation marks.[11] Therefore Penn R. Szittya is wrong to say that the diary "is quoted at length," since in fact it is *quoted* scarcely at all—and the paucity of direct quotation is itself the remarkable fact. Razumov's diary is an absent source like the sun that is missing from the metaphor of moon and haze that describes the story and its meaning in *Heart of Darkness*. Szittya goes on to assert that the distinction between diary and narrator's discourse gives the novel "a schizoid character, in effect dividing the reader between two narrators, two stories, two points of view, two chronologies, two styles." [12] The effect in fact is quite different, one of a deconstruction and subsequent blending of opposites. A certain doubling unquestionably exists—Razumov and narrator, St. Petersburg time and Geneva time, and so on—but it is precisely the work of the narrator's discourse to contain these doubles within the singleness of his consciousness.

If, as Bakhtin argues, any utterance is dialogic, involving reference to and appropriation of others' words, then the narrative situation in *Under Western Eyes* points to the dialogic nature of all speech and narration. What is interesting is not that such dialogism seems "schizoid," but on the contrary that it seems so natural—or if it is schizoid, it is so only in the sense that all speech is schizoid. The speech that we habitually accept in daily life as singular and unitary is filled with disparate echoes. Unity, one might say, is meaningful only in terms of the dialogic differences of which it is constituted. This is as true of personality as it is of texts.

As an example of the undecidable nature of discursive sharing, we find, in reference to Razumov's academic aspirations, the sentence "But a celebrated professor was a somebody" (63)—a sentence from one of yesterday's metanarratives about the academic profession. How many voices participate in this speech act? Did Razumov dwell on this thought before Haldin's appearance? Has this thought loomed larger in his mind only now (at the time of his writing) that the academic career is no longer possible? Or is it voiced because the academic narrator reads it into the diary? Does the sentence express *this narrator's* desires? And these questions say nothing about the absent structures of authority that, even more "originally," create the metastory by which academic careers are made to appear desirable. Gene M. Moore is correct to say that we often are receiving Razumov's Eastern story or *fabula* packaged in the Western narrator's discourse or *sujet*. [13] But the picture is more complicated than Moore suggests because we often cannot be entirely sure *whose* discourse or story we are hearing. The dialogic sharing of language makes such clear oppositions as story versus discourse and narrator's word versus Razumov's impossible to sustain as one addresses specific utterances in the novel.

Another example of shared discourse that raises the question of who is speaking, this time across all three of Fleishman's levels of authorship, is found in those passages in which Geneva is criticized for its stagnant, bourgeois dullness. Literally, the narrator speaks, but how does such a conservative character come by this opinion? One answer is that he is under the influence of Razumov's diary, where he may have read this opinion and given it his tacit consent. But it is also an opinion attributable to the author many readers infer from this text. Tony Tanner, however, wants to attribute the opinion *only* to the author he infers, and to assert—quite contrary to what the narrator actually says—that the narrator finds Geneva "comforting and consoling."[14] According to Tanner's inferences, Conrad rather sloppily placed his own opinion in a mouth where it did not belong. On the other hand, to read the passages on the character of Geneva dialogically is to abandon the attempt to assign ownership to those words and thereby to fix or finalize the narrator with the claim that he could not really have entertained that attitude himself. It is to accept at once the social and the unfinished nature of the subject. Here, too, the opposition between the story of Razumov's words and the discourse of the narrator deconstructs, as does the secondary opposition between these fictive discourses and the inferred author.

The opposition between story and discourse further deconstructs in light of the narrator's own statement that his job is not so much to be faithful to the journal as it is to discover a moral in the story, presumably with whatever Aristotelian deviations from historical truth are needed to discover this higher, moral probability:

> The task is not in truth the writing in the narrative form a *precis* of a strange human document, but the rendering—I perceive it now clearly—of the moral conditions ruling over a large portion of this earth's surface; conditions not easily understood, much less discovered in the limits of a story, till some key-word is found; a word that could stand at the back of all the words covering the pages, a word which, if not truth itself, may perchance hold truth enough to help the moral discovery which should be the object of every tale. (105)

"Rendering," a term that implies the painter's impressionistic or interpretive license, is an appropriate word to describe a verbal portrait in indirect discourse or paraphrase. The narrator's task of rendering the diary so as to discover a moral can be likened to Marlow's task of making the Kurtz story comprehensible within the assumptions, beliefs, and metanarratives of his comfortable yachting companions on the *Nellie*. In both novels the narrator's discourse is not a reflecting but a refracting medium—a problematic window upon the reality of the story. The keyword in the discourse of the Western, logocentric narrator of *Under Western Eyes* is "cynicism," and the monologic intention of his "rendering" is to demonstrate Russian cynicism. The narrator's authorial intention of infusing Razumov's story with the discourse of his own, Western evaluations—evaluations designed to inculcate in his reader the notion of an unbridgeable gap between East and West—exemplifies the politics of reported speech. As Bakhtin points out, "Between the reported speech and the reporting context, dynamic relations of high complexity and tension are in force" as the language of the reporter "devises means for infiltrating reported speech with authorial retort and commentary in deft and subtle ways."[15]

However, reported speech is not at the mercy of the reporter's intentions, and it may in fact override those intentions, inhabiting the reporter's consciousness in equally deft and subtle ways: "The verbal dominant may shift to the reported speech, which in that case becomes more forceful and more active than the authorial context framing it."[16] This could be occurring (some degree of uncertainty is built into the pragmatics of indirect discourse and verbal sharing) in the passages in which the narrator criticizes the bourgeois blandness of Geneva, a criticism, as noted earlier, that may well have originated with Razumov. And elsewhere the narrator's own framing intentions are overridden by the reported speech as the reader inadvertently gains sympathy for the revolution; many of the conversations he reports—especially the stories of Tekla's (169–73) and Sophia's (257) prerevolutionary experiences—are moving testimonials to the origins and necessity of revolutionary commitment in individual lives. And when Sophia begins with the words "Listen to my story," we are reminded of Lyotard's particular defense of dialogics in his assertion of the essential right of each person to have a narrative voice. The *petits recits* of Tekla and Sophia, and ultimately of Razumov and Nathalie, subvert the language teacher's cynical metanarrative of the irredeemable Russian soul.

The narrator's discourse is likewise inhabited by the voices of his interlocutors in Geneva, with their opposing narratives, when he says of Haldin: "But, at any rate, that life now ended had been sincere, and perhaps its thoughts might have been lofty, its moral sufferings profound, its last act a true sacrifice. It is not for us, the staid lovers calmed by the possession of a conquered liberty, to condemn without appeal the fierceness of thwarted desire" (181). Despite his prejudices, the narrator seems at times to be learning something, which is to say he is selecting from what is said to him, allowing himself to share and internalize new words and stories. The presence in the novel of this potential for growth through speech and conversation must seriously qualify any reading that emphasizes only the coercive powers that incite speech—spying, reporting, confessing—as a form of social manipulation.

The intentions of a person reporting another's speech usually fall along a continuum between the desire to represent the speech for one's own purpose by infusing it with one's own evaluations for one's own advantage, to represent it accurately and objectively, or to represent it for the advantage of the speaker. The first intention is present as the narrator represents Razumov's diary by indirect discourse, and it also informs the brief and indirect "rendering" of Peter Ivanovitch's book. But the intention to report accurately and objectively seems to control the language teacher's representation of Nathalie's conversation.[17] That men's writing should receive one treatment and a woman's conversation another is interesting and can be related to the narrator's sense of competition with these males, since all three in one way or another are bidding for Nathalie's affections or allegiances. Moreover, the male writing that the apolitical narrator seeks to dominate with his own discourse is a politically involved or motivated writing, whereas his desire for Nathalie is that she remain free of political entanglements.

Despite the direct discourse or quoted dialogue that represents much of the narrator's Geneva experience,[18] an intertextual sharing is also found in parts of the novel set in Geneva, as for instance in the elaborately detailed account of Nathalie's visit to the Chateau Borel (165–91). Punctuated by the narrator's questions, Nathalie's narration of her visit is rendered by the narrator as indirect citation, in words presumably approximating her own but not directly quoted. Within this indirect discourse, however, the words of people Nathalie encountered are quoted directly, including the lengthy embedded narration by the *dame de compagnie* (later called Tekla) concerning her family origins, her rebellion, and her virtual enslavement by Peter Ivanovitch— another moment in which a certain justice is enacted, as Tekla finds her voice and her story. But are these actually her words, or are the quotation marks a device to lend realism to the narrator's rendering? Formally, we have at this moment the narrator's total recall of Nathalie's total recall of Tekla's story—a story that Nathalie interrupts with questions that mirror the language teacher's interruptions of *her* narration. Both inner (Tekla's) and outer (Nathalie's) stories are elicited dialogically, in response to the questions of a narratee who in turn becomes a narrator, a familiar Conradian situation. This doubling and tripling undermines the reader's desire to attribute individual ownership to the words, and reminds us that the story of Tekla's suffering, once told, belongs to no*body*, but rather to the transindividual space of society's conversation.[19]

Further complicating these levels of transmission and sharing is the problem of the multiplicity of national languages. We know that the sections based on the diary are translations (Razumov's lack of English is explicitly stated at one point).[20] Presumably Nathalie often speaks English with the narrator, since he is tutoring her in English literature. But it is equally certain that many other conversations at the Chateau Borel and in "La Petite Russe" occur in Russian or French. Except when Nathalie can be assumed to have spoken English to the narrator—and these moments are not specifically marked—we are reading translations, but it is not always clear in what language a given utterance began or how many times it has been translated during its migration. The space of cultural conversation is international and multicultural. Given these dynamics, it was from one point of view a simple necessity for Conrad to invent a narrator versed in languages, but this choice gains added significance as we contemplate the extent to which issues of knowledge, truth, and power are implicated in language.

The tangled circuits of the sign's transmission and translation are seen in the narrator's explanation of how he came by his information about Madame de S—'s flight from Russia:

> My informant was the Russian wife of a friend of mine already mentioned, the professor of Lausanne University. It was from her that I learned the last fact of Madame de S—'s history, with which I intend to trouble my readers. She told me, speaking positively, as a person who trusts her sources, of the cause of Madame de S—'s flight from Russia, some years before. It was neither more nor less than this: that she became suspect to the police in connection with the assassination of the Emperor Alexander. The ground of this suspicion was either some unguarded expressions that escaped her in public, or some talk overheard in her *salon*. Overheard, we must believe, by some guest, perhaps a friend, who hastened to play the informer. (179)

By the end of the passage the narrator's faith in his informant has become comical, and it is apparent to the reader that the transmission of the story is ideologically driven; the story as verbal sign arises out of the needs of the community employing it, and its literal truth is not particularly relevant to that community. In his blindness to the dynamics of the shared word as it is translated and embedded in new

contexts, and in his hope to control Nathalie's relations to the revolutionaries, the narrator represents a feeble sort of monologic mentality,
as opposed to the stronger versions of monologism represented by the
autocracy and such revolutionaries as Peter Ivanovitch.

Translation, then, becomes the archetype of all other acts of communication, citation, and even domination. To quote another person
at a future time in a new context to a new audience is a form of translation, and the translated word becomes an arena in which identities
are contested. The language teacher in Conrad's novel is partially correct in asserting that the difficulty of rendering his story for a Western
audience has more to do with psychological and philosophical differences between East and West than with language differences in the
narrow or literal sense. His blindness is in his complacent failure to
see these differences in their ideological dimensions:

> If to the Western reader they [Razumov's thoughts] appear
> shocking, inappropriate or even improper, it must be remem-
> bered that as to the first this may be the effect of my crude state-
> ment. For the rest I will only remark here that this is not a story
> of the West of Europe. (72) To the morality of a Western reader
> an account of these meetings would wear perhaps the sinister
> character of old legendary tales where the Enemy of Mankind
> is represented holding subtly mendacious dialogues with some
> tempted soul.[21] (290)

Even reading and listening are internal acts of translation, the
latter being illustrated by Haldin's translation of Razumov's reticence
as a revolutionary text and by the Geneva group's continual misreading of Razumov's bitter silences and reckless ironies. Fleishman
stresses the potential destruction within these silences and within
the failure to converse: "Silence, far from implying innocence or even
detachment, actually tarnishes what it touches."[22] Reading, writing,
speaking, and listening all stand in opposition to the destructive
silence of which the novel so eloquently speaks, and reading and interpretation, the source as well as the end of narration, are alluded
to in the title, *Under Western Eyes*. Misinterpretation abounds in this
novel (as in many of Conrad's texts), pointing to the relationship between social life and the individual's appropriation or interpretation
of the words of others. Reading and translation represent the problem
of knowing the other; immoral or violent reading and translation objectify others for one's own purposes, whereas moral versions of these
activities respect each person as a "thou." And finally, reading and
translation can stand for the possibility of the individual becoming

more or other than he or she has been, for a contestation within the self—what V. N. Volosinov and Bakhtin call "inner speech"—in which a new ideological formation can emerge.[23] In this sense Conrad's novel is the story of Razumov's translations, of which silence, death's second self, and not coerced speech is the enemy.

At stake in Bakhtin's notion of the dialogic sharing of language, as exemplified in the various scenes of citation and translation in *Under Western Eyes*, is his critique of the false opposition between the individual and the community, an opposition encouraged by capitalism and bourgeois society: "Capitalism created the conditions for a special type of inescapably solitary consciousness. Dostoevsky exposes all the falsity of this consciousness."[24] To Bakhtin the utterance, and therefore the individual who makes it, is not solely an internal phenomenon but instead is organized historically and socially. Utterances "can arise only on *interindividual territory*."[25] If this is so, the entire "work" of Conrad's text, like Freud's dreamwork, challenges the narrator's consciously held belief in an unbridgeable or untranslatable gulf (bridges are a crucial symbol in the novel) separating East and West. It does this by establishing the existence of an interindividual territory—the text itself as bridge—where East and West converse. As Bakhtin says, coincidentally employing one of this novel's dominant symbols, "A word is a bridge thrown between myself and another."[26]

Razumov repeatedly finds himself on one of Geneva's bridges in the pages leading up to his confession, although the bridge to Rousseau Island is an ironic version of the symbol—a bridge to isolation rather than community—reminding us of the opposition between the Burkean tradition of the organic society and eighteenth-century contract theories such as Rousseau's, which legitimated the state within the will of the individual.[27] The narrator denies the possibility of any bridge that would actually make connections between East and West in his many disparaging comments on the irrationality and mysticism of the Russian psyche: "The propensity of lifting every problem from the plane of the understandable by means of some sort of mystic expression, is very Russian. . . . I suppose one must be Russian to understand Russian simplicity, a terrible corroding simplicity in which mystic phrases clothe a naive and hopeless cynicism. I think sometimes that the psychological secret of the profound difference of that people consists in this, that they detest life" (134). This is a position that the text itself deconstructs.

The notion of the radical difference between East and West is voiced by other characters besides the narrator, most notably Nathalie in her statement that some nations have "made their bargain with fate" (142). Presumably, she is referring to the struggles, revolutions, or conquests, in many cases now in the distant past, by which other nations have established their sense of legality and futurity, their social contracts. A comparable founding moment, and the accompanying sense of history and futurity, has not occurred for the Russian people, who therefore gaze at the West as from a different chronotope, a different configuration of time and space.[28] If civilizations are founded in moments of previously unauthorized violence, their future success depends on their ability to engender a discourse that will lend retrospective authority and legitimacy to the originary violence. Such legitimating discourses, such as Rousseau's contract theory in the West, have not been successfully promulgated by the Russian autocracy. Both the narrator and Nathalie posit an irreconcilable difference between East and West, and that difference is compounded in that the two characters explain the difference differently—he with a crude psychologism, she with a historical thesis. And yet the narrator, with his belief in the irrationality of the Russian mind, and Nathalie, with her belief in a radical difference in the historical positioning of East and West, not only communicate but even find a bond of affection.

Nonetheless, the two chronotopes of St. Petersburg and Geneva do exist in opposition to one another. Moore describes the claustrophobic St. Petersburg that is suggested by Razumov's silences and the confined space of his room. Here time is measured in small units, as on the night of Haldin's betrayal, while the larger movement of history seems nonexistent. This chronotope is in part a projection of Razumov's petty and apolitical nature, and one is reminded of Frank Kermode's definition of *chronos* as "passing time" or "waiting time."[29] In St. Petersburg the lack of childbearing that characterized the Sulaco chronotope in *Nostromo* is translated into Razumov's lack of a family. In both chronotopes generational ties are lost, and for Razumov the only available parent is the autocracy.[30] On the other hand, the Geneva chronotope suggests freedom. The narrator is never seen in his own quarters, but always moving about the city, visiting others or encountering them in the streets. As opposed to Razumov's silences, talk abounds in Geneva, although not necessarily productive talk. As Moore says, "The Russian word comes out as if under tremendous pressure, from beneath the terrible weight of a crushing autocracy; while in the rarefied air of Geneva where no such pressure is thinkable, words tend to stagnate and lose what Bakhtin calls their 'power to mean.'"[31] I do not agree with Moore's judgment of talk in Geneva, however, since the conversations in Geneva are inseparable from the self-realizations of at least some of the characters. As Bakhtin also says, in praise of Dostoevsky, "Everything in Dostoevsky's novels tends toward dialogue. . . . All else is the means; dialogue is the end." [32]

Moore accounts for the differences between the diary and its translation by characterizing the two chronotopes that dominate the imaginations of the two writers. But despite the radical disparity between the two chronotopes, they do mingle dialogically within the novel, which is itself a bridge sustaining the possibility of cross-cultural understanding. Not only does the dialogue between the Western eyes of the narrator and the crabbed writing of Razumov's diary create a kind of understanding for the reader, the characters are also able to "translate" themselves from one chronotope to another. Furthermore, these two chronotopes do not stand as dialectical opposites. The stagnant aspect Geneva wears in the eyes of the narrator when he describes the houses as being "comely without grace, hospitable without sympathy" (163) shows that the bargain this bourgeois society has made with history has not been entirely successful. For the narrator, perhaps under the influence of Razumov's writing, the Geneva chronotope is also governed by *chronos*.

Under Western Eyes stages a dialogue between the narrator's cynicism and the revolutionary hope voiced by Nathalie and Sonia, between *chronos* and *kairos*, "a point in time filled with significance, charged with a meaning derived from its relation to the end." [33] Although the narrator's monologic discourse seeks to dominate Razumov's diary with its own "moral" intent, all language in the novel is shared language carrying significance and values that escape the control of any individual. While this observation may seem to deny the individual's freedom, it actually describes the condition of freedom's possibility. That this novel grants its characters freedom—that freedom and futurity are the dominant thrust of the novel—can be seen by taking up the question of the apparent dialogue *Under Western Eyes* enters into with Dostoevsky.

Few readers have failed to remark on the Dostoevsky-like quality of *Under Western Eyes*, a quality deriving particularly from the profoundly intense realization in the first section of the novel of Razumov's consciousness as an arena of struggle and torment. But that our inferred author should attempt a novel in Dostoevsky's key is puzzling in view of the real Conrad's dislike, bordering on contempt, for Dostoevsky's "fierce mouthings." [34] Conrad saw Dostoevsky as an apologist for the autocracy in Russia; in his novels, Dostoevsky's religiosity feeds a political complacency, and in his personal life and journalistic work he grovels shamelessly before political power. And yet, despite

Dostoevsky's unpleasant qualities, Conrad shared with him a suspicion of revolution and an aristocratic outlook that made Dostoevsky a troubling, perhaps an embarrassing, ally.

Aaron Fogel provides a useful summary of the many appropriations and alterations of *Crime and Punishment* in *Under Western Eyes*:

> Raskolnikov commits the murder, and next day visits his good friend Razumihin; Haldin commits the assassination, and immediately visits Razumov. Raskolnikov's mother and sister arrive in St. Petersburg shortly after the murder, and Razumihin falls in love with the sister; Razumov, after in fact betraying Haldin, who is thought to have been his close comrade, goes to Geneva, meets Haldin's mother and sister, and falls in love with the sister. The mothers of Raskolnikov and of Haldin gradually go mad. Raskolnikov, under interrogation by Porfiry, and having taken up with the prostituted, pious Sonia, moves toward confession; Razumov, interrogated by Mikulin, only becomes more implicated in a life of constant betrayal of the revolutionaries, in which he seems to be about to become a perpetual forced spy and forced correspondent. Raskolnikov is accompanied throughout by his companion the prostituted Sonia, whom he loves, and who emerges from the typical Dostoevskian family of Marmeladovs; Razumov at the end does not have Natalie, whom he loves, but only the pathetic, familyless, unappealing Tekla, who leaves her job as a forced secretary just as he leaves his job as a forced spy, and follows and tends him in his last days—which are not, for him at least, romantic.[35]

One might add to Fogel's list the student status of both characters and their writing aspirations—the newspaper article Raskolnikov has published just prior to the events of the novel parallels the essay Razumov is working on at the outset of his novel. Moreover, echoes of *The Brothers Karamazov* are found in the suicide by hanging of Smerdyakov and Ziemianitch and in the satanic imagery in both novels; Ivan converses with his other self in the form of the devil, and Razumov is viewed by others as a devil who beat Ziemianitch. And the priest, Zosim—who is secretly in league with the autocracy and who writes Razumov's letter of introduction to the Geneva revolutionaries—echoes Dostoevsky's Father Zosima.

Fogel's Conrad saw in Dostoevsky the same kind of dialogism Bakhtin describes, but did not share Bakhtin's enthusiasm for it. Instead, Fogel believes that in *Under Western Eyes* Conrad sought to correct the insidious political implications of a dialogism that seems to say not only that people can achieve spiritual freedom and salvation within an autocracy, but that a police autocracy can actually promote such spiritual freedom (since it plays a part in bringing about Raskolnikov's confession). Therefore Conrad, according to Fogel, intentionally denies the freedom and autonomy to his characters that Bakhtin says is Dostoevsky's crowning achievement, creating in *Under Western Eyes* a world of coerced speech and coerced selfhood.[36]

But speech, according to the author I infer, is not inevitably coerced. Conrad, in Fogel's analysis, is a pre-Foucauldian for whom power is everywhere and individual agency is an illusion. Aspects of Conrad's writing support this view. But in *Under Western Eyes*, as in *Lord Jim*, there is a place for agency and free ethical choice within the context of the powerful constitutive forces of social discourses, particularly in a police state. Therefore *Under Western Eyes* is not quite the conscious "revocation" of *Crime and Punishment* that Fogel claims.[37] Whereas Fogel sees a dialectical opposition between the two authors, I hear dialogue. And the Conrad I infer from the novels was also in dialogue with the other, journalistic Conrad who voiced such deep contempt for Dostoevsky. Although Fogel harmonizes the two Conrads monologically, such internal dialogue should no longer be a scandal— every "I," as we now realize, is also a "we."

To what extent, then, does *Under Western Eyes* appear open to the kind of dialogic conception of character that Bakhtin celebrates in Dostoevsky? Crucial to Dostoevsky's presentation of character, according to Bakhtin, is the notion of open-endedness or unfinalizability. The underground man, for instance, is aware of all that others say about him but "knows that he has the *final word*, and he seeks at whatever cost to retain for himself this final word about himself, the word of his self-consciousness, in order to become in it that which he is not." Furthermore, Dostoevsky "does indeed leave the final word to his hero."[38]

From a certain point of view, of course, this is nonsense. Fictional characters are not literally independent of their authors, despite the interesting metafictions generated by fantasies to the contrary. Many novelists have hoped to create in their characters the illusion of free will, and this illusion depends on the author's ability to resist any impulse to dominate the ideas and viewpoint of his or her characters. Dostoevsky represents for Bakhtin the culmination of the literary genre (Bakhtin opposes the dialogic genre, the novel, to the monologic genres, epic and lyric poetry) committed to freedom and difference. In the novel, and particularly in Dostoevsky, characters are free to develop and transcend their roles; they retain a "surplus of humanness." Because of this surplus there "remains a need for the future, and a place for this future must be found."[39] What Bakhtin describes, then, is more than an illusion of Dostoevsky's art; it is his success in achieving the ethical imperative that is the novel's entelechy.

Concern for the future pervades Conrad's "Autocracy and War," in which the crime of the Russian autocracy is precisely its murder of the future.[40] Under autocracy, Conrad suggests, there is no time or history as normally understood. Razumov's broken watch is perhaps a correlative in the novel for the statement in the essay that Russian autocracy "had no historical past, and it cannot hope for a historical future. It can only end. By no industry of investigation, by no fantastic stretch of benevolence, can it be presented as a phase of development through which a Society, a State, must pass on the way to the full consciousness of its destiny." Time is merely *chronos*. Furthermore, reform is impossible because "there has never been any legality in Russia."[41]

This might suggest that the only hope for a future lies in revolution, and in fact words taken almost directly from "Autocracy and War" occur in Victor Haldin's letter to his sister: "Reform is impossible. There is nothing to reform. There is no legality, there are no institutions. There are only arbitrary decrees" (157). When Haldin, the assassin, echoes his author's own ideas, we are in the presence of something very like what Bakhtin describes as the form of the idea in Dostoevsky. This migration of language from the essay of Conrad the journalist to a fictional character of whom he presumably did not approve illustrates the need for the methodological distinction—despite the many instances where the distinction dissolves—between a real author and the inferred author of a specific text.

Conrad's ideas enter his novel in much the same way that ideas found in Dostoevsky's journalism enter Dostoevsky's fiction. According to Bakhtin, "the ideas of Dostoevsky the thinker, upon entering his polyphonic novel, change the very form of their existence, they are transformed into artistic images of ideas: they combine in an indissoluble unity with images of people. . . . It is absolutely impermissible to ascribe to these ideas the finalizing function of authorial ideas in a monologic novel. Here they fulfill no such function, for they are all equally privileged participants in the great dialogue."[42] In Conrad's case, the authorial ideas found in "Autocracy and War" disparage the hope Haldin places in revolution, since Russia lacks the necessary intellectual and moral ground for a constructive revolution: "There is in it no ground for anything that could in the remotest degree serve even the lowest interests of mankind—and certainly no ground ready for a revolution."[43] These same ideas enter the novel in the cynical discourse of the narrator, but *Under Western Eyes* transcends the cynicism of "Autocracy and War," and of its own narrator, in the same way that the polyphonic novel transcends the monologic epic in Bakhtin.

Suresh Raval argues that this cynicism is transcended in Conrad's portrayal of Nathalie Haldin, a portrait that indicates his sympathy for the "revolutionary hope" she embodies, particularly in her decision to return to Russia to serve the poor and the exploited.[44] Indeed, her words in defense of revolution provide the novel with its epigraph: "I would take liberty from any hand as a hungry man would snatch a piece of bread" (158). Claire Rosenfield sees nothing hopeful in Nathalie's decision, which she thinks merely shows Nathalie's inability to love Razumov as apparently she should: "She commits herself to the 'community of mankind' by returning to Russia as a dedicated revolutionary, but she has forgotten all concrete manifestations of that humanity."[45] This charge is difficult to support, and the notion that the higher road for Nathalie would have been to settle down somewhere with Razumov, a notion that privileges the subjective, the personal, and the concrete, has a bourgeois politics of its own. Moreover, Rosenfield seems to equate all forms of concerned social action with revolution, since what Sophia actually says to the narrator is that Nathalie divides her time "between the horrors of overcrowded jails, and the heartrending misery of bereaved homes" (346). To equate this activity with violent revolution and assassination is a deeply reactionary reading of Nathalie's social concern. Nathalie's decision is an act of freedom that the novel respects in spite the cynicism of "Autocracy and War," a cynicism found in the narrator's discourse but repeatedly modified by the speech and stories he reports.

In its highest form, the polyphonic novel enacts an ethic of freedom that opposes objectifying others. Reading Bakhtin in relation to Lyotard, one can say that the polyphonic novel enacts justice by allowing each character his or her *petit recit*, undistorted by the totalizing force of a monologic narrator. Bakhtin illustrates this thesis by staging an opposition between Tolstoy and Dostoevsky. Tolstoy is the monologic author, always controlling his characters for his own ideological purposes. Tolstoy's story "Three Deaths" contains "*only one cognitive subject*, all else being merely objects of its cognition."[46] The one subject is Tolstoy himself.

It may be something more than an interesting coincidence, then, that *Under Western Eyes* contains a character, Peter Ivanovitch, who is assumed to be modeled at least in part on Tolstoy. Peter Ivanovitch is Conrad's embodiment of the monologic tendency to objectify and finalize others. People have merely use value for him, and the specter of Ivanovitch dictating his writings to his coerced stenographer, Tekla, who is not allowed even to move during the sessions, could not be a stronger example of one person's monologic discourse dominating another. Ivanovitch is, within the revolutionary circle, a repetition of the domination that the discourse of the autocracy achieves for a time over Razumov (General T—and Mikulin, too, are interested in Razumov's use), and the subplot of the novel has at stake the question of whether Nathalie will escape Ivanovitch's domination, as Razumov ultimately escapes the discourse of autocracy.

Like Jim, who continually evades the stories that pursue him in *Lord Jim*, Tekla, Nathalie, and Razumov elude the objectifying power of the monologic discourses in which they are caught, escaping even the reservations and outright disapproval of the narrator's discourse, with its cynical charge that all Russians are ruled by cynicism. Herein lies the Dostoevskian commitment to view life as always open and unfinished. As Bakhtin says (employing the "withdrawn" author as a foil very like Conrad's Peter Ivanovitch), Dostoevsky

> affirms the independence, internal freedom, unfinalizability, and indeterminacy of the hero. For the author the hero is not "he" and not "I" but a fully valid "thou," that is, another and other autonomous "I" ("thou art"). The hero is the subject of a deeply serious, *real* dialogic mode of address, not the subject of a rhetorically *performed* or *conventionally* literary one. And this dialogue— the "great dialogue" of the novel as a whole—takes place not in the past, but right now, that is, in the *real present* of the creative process. This is no stenographer's report of a finished dialogue, from which the author has already withdrawn and *over* which he is now located as if in some higher decision-making position: that would have turned an authentic and unfinished dialogue into an objectivized and finalized *image of a dialogue,* of the sort usual for every monologic novel. The great dialogue in Dostoevsky is organized as an *unclosed whole* of life itself, life poised *on the threshold.* [47]

This is a threshold of social possibilities, since consciousness itself for Bakhtin is intersubjective. His argument in *Freudianism: A Marxist Critique* is with what he saw as Freud's internalizing and privatizing of consciousness so as to ignore its dialogic nature. But Bakhtin's belief that consciousness is always social and dialogic is also entirely Conradian. It informs Conrad's description of Decoud's death in *Nostromo* as well as Marlow's meditations on what happens to the self when its only dialogue is with the wilderness ("the wilderness whispered to Kurtz"). It also informs the remarkable opening section of *Under Western Eyes*, in which Razumov's "patriotic" self emerges in dialogue with Haldin and with the larger reality of Russia. Haldin's absolutely unanticipated and unpreventable appearance in Razumov's room destroys the illusion of the strictly private life. Just as Leggatt ("legate": one who brings words from elsewhere) emerges from the sea to share a space and ultimately an identity with the young captain of "The Secret Sharer," so Haldin's appearance in Razumov's room initiates Razumov's experience of selfhood as a shared phenomenon. Razumov's self emerges as an internalization of social discourses, and his subjectivity, as he becomes "subject" to the autocracy, is a boundary rather than an internal phenomenon. Among the social voices that inhabit Razumov's inner dialogue on the night of his betrayal are:

1. The voice of reform. The discourse of the autocracy dominates weaker discourses, specifically the liberal discourse of reform that is never entirely silenced in Razumov: "A murder is a murder. Though of course some sort of liberal institutions . . ." (73). Here the incomplete sentence gestures toward a partially acknowledged voice, one that is quickly silenced, in what Bakhtin calls a "sideward glance" at the discourse of another (the reformer) whose criticisms one hopes to escape.[48]

2. The voice of family. If the discourse of the autocracy dominates the voice of reform, it exploits the discourse that links identity to lineage by offering Razumov a substitute father:[49] "What it needed was not the conflicting aspirations of a people, but a will strong and one; it wanted not the babble of many voices, but a man—strong and one" (78–79). Here the figure of the man, strong and monologic, silences the many voices of the social dialogue, providing Razumov's unformed self an escape from freedom. Again, the credo of the author I infer is like Dostoevsky's, a belief that consciousness is intrinsically multiple, and no one has the right to silence its voices.

3. The voice of religion. The discourse of the autocracy also exploits the voice of religion, which wraps Razumov's betrayal of Haldin in the uplifting rhetoric of conversion and fellowship: "Some superior power had inspired him with a flow of masterly argument as certain converted sinners become overwhelmingly loquacious" (80). He imagines returning to his room and kneeling in an attitude of prayer "to pour out a full confession," and he longs for a "fellowship of souls" (83). In this skeptical characterization of the complicity between the discourses of religion and the autocracy, the inferred author of the novel and the journalist who disliked Dostoevsky agree.

As a result of these dynamics, these discursive confrontations, a new self emerges—Razumov is "translated" or converted. As Bakhtin and Volosinov say, "The individual consciousness not only cannot be used to explain anything, but, on the contrary, is itself in need of explanation from the vantage point of the social, ideological medium"; Razumov's headlong flight to the autocracy illustrates Bakhtin's argument that the inner life must always be understood in its outer, social dimensions.[50] As Razumov, walking the darkened, snow-filled streets of St. Petersburg, arrives at his "conversion," he weaves diverse cliches and formulas concerning reform, parenthood, and religion in an inner dialogue that propels him into the arms of the state apparatus. His inner speech is the selective appropriation of the words of others, and his gaze inward is at once a gaze at and with others. What Bakhtin says of Dostoevsky's Raskolnikov is equally true of Razumov: "The consciousness of the solitary Raskolnikov becomes a field of battle for others' voices; the events of recent days . . . reflected in his consciousness, take on the form of a most intense dialogue with absentee participants."[51]

Because consciousness is dialogic, Bakhtin denies the existence of an unconscious in the Freudian sense, postulating instead an "unofficial conscious," which he defines as those hitherto-unassimilated aspects of the larger social discourse. Razumov's conversion is a process by which the discourse of the autocracy becomes Razumov's own official discourse, and the brilliance with which Under Western Eyes achieves the effect of a claustrophobic, inner struggle only serves to underline the fact that such inner struggles always involve dialogue with and intrusion from the outside—the phantom, or the legate, that arrives in one's room uninvited.

From the time of his conversion and his enlistment by the autocracy as a spy, Razumov is a painfully divided character. His schizoid psychology (here Szittya's word is entirely appropriate) is an internalization of the divisions in Russian society, as he realizes when he tells Peter Ivanovitch that "Russia can't disown me. She cannot. . . . I am it!" (215). His internalization of this divided discourse of Russia takes the form of verbal irony or, as Szittya says, "double talk."[52] A dialogic theory of utterance suggests that all talk is at least double, but dialogism does not mean to Bakhtin that all personalities are necessarily fractured or duplicitous. We internalize discourses selectively, retaining a capacity for freedom and moral responsibility. This capacity is dramatized in Razumov's subsequent confession in Geneva, in his second conversion or translation.

This moment of translation is the culmination (as in other Conrad stories) of a plot involving many of the motifs of adventure literature, and in this regard, also, this novel reveals affinities with Dostoevsky's fiction. Both authors write tales of secret crimes, betrayals, and unexpected fortunes rather than novels of everyday family life. The adventure plot, according to Bakhtin, allows for the presentation of the hero as someone "not predetermined. The adventure position does not rely on already available and stable positions—family, social, biographical; it develops in spite of them. The adventure position is a position in which any person may appear as a person."[53] So in spite of the historical complicity between the adventure plot and imperialist ideology in English society, the adventure tale can also speak to a desire for freedom from totalizing and finalizing discourses.

In *Nostromo*, the adventure plot, if we take Nostromo as the hero, ends when Nostromo decides to grow rich slowly—that is, when Nostromo becomes finalized by material interests. In *Lord Jim*, the adventure elements of the Patusan story are integral to Jim's ongoing struggle to remain free and open to futurity. Razumov's insistence on his own freedom is not unlike Jim's, and his confession before the revolutionaries, like Jim's acceptance of the bullet, is a way of owning his past actions. And like Nostromo, Razumov has been someone else's man. But whereas Nostromo exchanges one form of inauthenticity for another, Razumov achieves a more authentic freedom. Or if one chooses to say that Nostromo achieves freedom in his confession to Emily Gould, then, unlike Nostromo, Razumov is granted life after his confession.[54]

The discourse of the autocracy fails to finalize Razumov, however final Conrad the journalist might have felt Russian darkness was when he wrote "Autocracy and War." Razumov's confession, freely rendered like Raskolnikov's only when he is in no more danger of discovery, when there is no coercion to speak, establishes his freedom. Bakhtin's comments on confession in Dostoevsky's fiction apply with equal force to *Under Western Eyes*: "Confession as a higher form of a person's *free* self-revelation *from within* (and not his finalizing from without) confronted Dostoevsky from the very beginning of his literary career. Confession as an encounter of the *deepest I* with *another* and with *others* (with the folk), as an encounter of *I* and *other* on the highest level of the ultimate instance. But the *I* in this encounter must be the pure, deep *I* from within oneself, without any admixture of presumed and forced or naively assimilated points of view."[55]

It is fitting in a dialogic, polyphonic novel that one of the representatives of monologic coercion among the revolutionaries, Nikita, should rob Razumov of his hearing. Nikita is "saying"—a saying to end all hearing—that if his own revolutionary discourse has failed to objectify or control Razumov, no discourse will. Hearing represents access to the words of others and therefore, because the extrinsic is always also the intrinsic, to oneself. To oppose dialogic encounters, as Nikita does, is to oppose freedom, growth, and ultimately life, since "monologue is finalized and deaf to the other's response."[56] Peter Ivanovitch was a dictator, literally, in his tyranny over Tekla, and now Nikita seeks to control the word through bodily mutilation, a coercion to silence. One aspect of the evolution of Conrad's fiction can be measured in the fact that Nikita is a caricature of the narrative work that silences or ridicules such social enemies as Wait and Donkin in *The Nigger of the "Narcissus."*

Razumov's deafness would be an appropriate form of closure for a novel written in the cynicism of "Autocracy and War." But *Under Western Eyes* forgoes conventional closure in an epilogue that refers to Razumov's ongoing life as a deaf man paradoxically engaged in dialogue with the revolutionaries. He lives again in Russia, and Sophia Antonovna says: "Some of us always go to see him when passing through. He is intelligent. He has such ideas. . . . He talks well, too" (347). The monologic closure that Nikita attempted to inflict (now replacing Ivanovitch as the type of the monologic author looking to end dialogue) has been overthrown by the formal denial of closure in the structure of the novel itself, which leaves us with an image of the ongoing conversation, or what Bakhtin calls "the great dialogue."

Razumov had defended his encounter with Haldin to Mikulin by saying that "he talked and I listened. That is not a conversation" (124). But in Geneva he experiences a "day of many conversations" (238), conversations that are relatively free and unconstrained in contrast to the involuntary interviews of St. Petersburg. This freedom of conversation leads him to his own confession in the den of the revolutionaries, echoing Haldin's confession in his own student quarters some time ago, in another chronotope. His refusal to hear Haldin sympathetically is now answered in his punishment of deafness, but not with his death. Death is the state of being unheard, whereas being is communication, and the novel concludes with an evocation of—and an opening upon—the ongoing conversation of life and culture. Razumov casts off his monologizing deafness; like Oedipus seeing in his blindness, he now converses in his deafness.

Conrad must have considered blindness as a possible punishment for Razumov, which would have been consistent with the ocular imagery of the novel's title, with the secret meeting with Mikulin in an oculist's office, and with the usual visual connotations of spying. Furthermore, Conrad, who was not hesitant to reuse situations and motifs, had made blindness Whalley's dominant characteristic in *The End of the Tether*. But the dynamics of the shared word make deafness the appropriate choice in this novel, where the title's reference to vision is answered in the penultimate reference to hearing—a framing motif that underlines the twin modes of verbal sharing (writing and speech) that inform the novel as a whole.[57]

There may be hints of irony in the references to the conversation of a deaf man; in Conrad's fiction, skepticism, however intricately qualified, is always present. Moore contends that all the talk in Geneva is vapid and pointless. Certainly it would be an error to privilege conversation above all forms of social action and reform, but whatever one thinks of Razumov's later career as a conversationalist, one must acknowledge the real social action taken on by Nathalie and credit her involvement in the conversations of Geneva as having played a formative role. Frederick Karl argues that the ending is unsatisfactory because one cannot imagine the revolutionaries visiting Razumov in his later days.[58] Like Rosenfield in her decision to equate Nathalie's social involvement in the prisons and among the poor of Russia with the revolutionary activity of the likes of Nikita and Peter Ivanovitch, Karl seems to imagine only stark oppositions.

But in the sharing of language between East and West, between the chronotopes of St. Petersburg and Geneva, such oppositions dissolve. Despite the narrator's cynicism, the novel enacts the possibility of living beyond the ruling oppositions of the past, as Nathalie and Razumov, in their separate ways, appear to do in the "end" that is not final, and as Sophia does in her openness to others. Rosenfield may be correct after all in believing in the desirability of a marriage between Razumov and Nathalie. It would symbolize the union of talking and doing, thought and feeling, but such a comic ending would also be something other than we should expect from an author who has been so critical of consoling myths; it would make Conrad's story responsible for the kind of consoling fictionalizing with which Marlow's discourse finalized Kurtz. With this qualification, one must find something positive in the futures of Nathalie and Razumov. We should not need a Marlow to supply the consoling discourse for that future.

The way *Under Western Eyes* grants Razumov an unfinished future of conversation is reminiscent of the "ending" of "Notes from Underground": "The 'notes' of this paradoxalist do not end here, however. He could not resist and continued them. But it also seems to me that we may stop here."[59] Like this self-referential moment in Dostoevsky, Conrad's metafictional novel challenges the reader's desire to totalize the text in conventional ways—particularly the reader's desire, born of a Western ideology of selfhood and individualism, to distribute as private property language that the novel insists is always shared and never possessed. Thus *Under Western Eyes* draws attention to the always open, supplemental, and unfinished nature of the social discourse of which, for Bakhtin, the genre of the novel is an image. To be human and to live freely is to engage in an always unfinished dialogue with an always already spoken language, a recognition implied in this particular novel's unclosed ending as much as it is in so many places in Dostoevsky's art: "When dialogue ends everything ends. Thus dialogue, by its very essence, cannot and must not come to an end. At the level of the religious-utopian world-view Dostoevsky carries dialogue into eternity. . . . At the level of the novel, it is presented as the unfinalizability of dialogue." [60]

Szittya suggests that Razumov's double nature, the tension between his public and private selves, mirrors tensions in the real Conrad's psyche.[61] Conrad was divided between his Slavic and English identities, and this division was compounded by a split between his public and private writing personae—a tension the biographical critic might find reflected in the split between the private diary of Razumov and the public narrative of the Englishman. Most intriguing, perhaps, is Szittya's citation of images of phantoms and hauntings (which are everywhere in the novel) invoked in Conrad's personal letters to describe the painfulness of the writing process. One should find correspondences between real authors and inferred authors, and *Under Western Eyes* may well be an allegory of its author's own identity crisis.

But the novel's work, like the work of myth in Claude Lévi-Strauss's analysis, is to provide a reconciliation of contradictions, even if skepticism requires that we remember it is only a fictional reconciliation. As Razumov's diary is given to Nathalie, then to the narrator, then (indirectly) to us, as Tekla's spoken story follows a similar path, and as the narrator's own judgments and evaluations mingle and are altered by the diary he reads and the conversations he hears, something positive is revealed in the unfinalizability of dialogue and therefore in the always open possibilities of social life, despite the twin horrors of repression and violent revolution. If selfhood is always an unfinished project, the processes I have described in *Under Western Eyes*, despite the uncompromising cynicism expressed in "Autocracy and War," argue the need to embrace uncertainty and openness.

Conclusion:
After Closure

Is conversation not simply a species of music in which first the one takes up the refrain and then the other? Does it matter what the refrain of our conversation is any more than it matters what tune we play? And I asked myself further: Are not both music and conversation like love?

J. M. Coetzee, *Foe*

What matter who's speaking?

Michel Foucault,
"What Is an Author?"

It would not be accurate to say that Joseph Conrad has been either the hero or antihero of my story, since to a large degree I have focused on texts rather than on a biographical person. The hero is a decentered, discursive subject rather than a human one. Within my discourse on this story, the voices of Bakhtin and Lyotard have been prominent. Bakhtin's attempt to define the subject and to analyze the utterance socially and historically and Lyotard's attempt to see the politics of knowledge in terms of a struggle between grand narratives and little stories offer ways of mapping the engagement of Conrad's novels with the problematic relations between subject and community in a time of imperialist expansion accompanied by deteriorating hegemony. This story of Conrad's fiction during his major phase from 1897 to 1911, admittedly "plotted" by virtue of selection and emphasis, is a story of a movement from rigidness to openness, from the monologic to the polyphonic. Like all narratives, mine is enabled by its repressions and silences, but I do not think that analysis of other Conrad texts written during this period would greatly change the impression.

The skepticism concerning liberal or reform values that one finds in many of Conrad's novels occasionally translates into a monologic tendency not unlike that which Bakhtin attributes to Tolstoy, a tendency on the part of a narrator to dominate and control his characters, making them instruments for his own propositions and ideological biases, as in *The Nigger of the "Narcissus"* and, in a more problematic way, *Heart of Darkness*. The voices of these monologic narrators are in turn occupied and appropriated by various extrinsic, nomadic voices originating in discourses and ideologies beyond the texts and their author. In this way, Conrad's fiction repeatedly challenges the notion of the monadic, transcendent, and self-determining subject; his fiction displays the force of Foucault's question, what does it matter who is speaking?

The tendency of Conrad's narrators to exercise a monologic domination, with the possible exception of the narrator of *The Secret Agent*, diminishes during Conrad's major phase, gradually giving way to a freer play of various and conflicting viewpoints. For instance, despite the narrator's identification with the Blancos and his lack of concern for the underclass of Costaguana, *Nostromo* contains, as Benita Parry argues, the radical insight that property is theft and that no moral basis for wealth exists. But this insight, in the always self-modifying internal dialogue of the discourse of these novels, shares its space with a more conservative voice that refuses to allow the appropriation of property by the exploited. As Parry says, "At the very point where the text concedes that no ethical sanction for the ownership of property can be found, it vitiates its own argument by dramatizing theft as a moral transgression."[1]

Conrad's most self-referential novel, *Under Western Eyes*, is also his closest approach to the Bakhtinian ideal of the polyphonic novel, the novel that grants its characters a form of independence from the monologic control of a narrator, although in this regard *Under Western Eyes* was clearly anticipated by such moments as Marlow's refusal to finalize Jim—a shift away from his eagerness to finalize Kurtz. The social nature of the subject is implicitly argued in the many ways *Under Western Eyes* dramatizes the sharing of the word through the acts of reporting another's speech, translating or paraphrasing another's text, and through conversation. Despite its narrator's cynicism, *Under Western Eyes* hints in at least a qualified way at the twin possibilities of cross-cultural understanding and personal growth through conversation, and the multilingualism that this novel takes for granted contrasts sharply with the "babble" of various tongues that is merely an irritant at the start of *The Nigger of the "Narcissus."*

Under Western Eyes refuses to finalize its major characters and is therefore a move to transcend the nihilism with which Conrad's texts so often grapple. In the figure of Peter Ivanovitch, the author who claims to represent feminist concerns but who so crudely dominates and manipulates women, the novel clearly depicts the potential dangers and abuses in any act of representation, particularly the way a representation may reproduce the evil it pretends to oppose. The figure of Ivanovitch is a critique of the monologizing author, and he reminds us not only of Marlow's apparent misogyny but of the authoritarian tendencies in the narrator of *The Nigger of the "Narcissus"* and of the authoritarian strain in the preface to that earlier novel. Further evidence of the difference in *Under Western Eyes* is the way, on the eve of the Russian Revolution, it looks to an open future—a future which, some 80 years after Conrad's novel, may now be at hand. While not overtly optimistic, this rendering of an open future in *Under Western Eyes* contrasts with *Nostromo*'s depiction of Costaguana as a client of capitalism in the aftermath of failed revolution, and with the nostalgia for a stable present built on yesterday's fixed values found in *Lord Jim*. Further, the qualified freedom Razumov achieves contrasts with the inability of Nostromo, "our man," to escape the finalizing power of the forces that own him.

Under Western Eyes gives voice to a political cynicism that is familiar to readers of Conrad's letters and essays, but, in the manner of Dostoevsky, this cynicism is placed in the mouth of a narrator who is also held up to ridicule (much as Captain Mitchell's complacent narration is in *Nostromo*) and who does not manage to repress the accents of revolutionary hope that echo in the novel's many conversations. Furthermore, Nathalie's commitment to a life of social service takes us a certain distance from the rigidly aristocratic biases, and delusions, of the Blancos, from Gould's faith in material interests, from the work ethic that, in other novels, so clearly serves ruling-class interests, and from the attempt to poeticize the exploitation of labor that marked the discourse of *The Nigger of the "Narcissus."* Each novel after *The Nigger of the "Narcissus"* is a meditation on political uncertainty, and each risks charges of inconsistency by staging encounters among rival political values and viewpoints, among discrepant discourses and grand narratives. These novelistic discourses are not assigned to a single subject of enunciation. Instead, we find within each novel, and across the range of these five novels, a nomadic mobility and plurality of discursive positions.

The self-modifying, dialogic way that these texts present ideas—what Bakhtin calls the novelization of thought—is found not only in specific novels, but in the intertextual relations among them. Two parallel moments in Conrad's career highlight this dialogic tendency, although many others could be found. The first occurs in the dialogue between *Lord Jim* and *Heart of Darkness*. Conrad interrupted the longer novel in order to write the shorter, and it is as though he could only complete *Lord Jim* after first writing a text that seems to respond to it, but with differing premises. If *Lord Jim* holds out a qualified hope concerning Jim's ability to internalize a code and act for the good of people outside the horizon of his cultural training, *Heart of Darkness* dramatizes the opposite—the deterioration of all cultural codes in the absence of the policing agents of that culture. The shorter novel speaks of the utter dependence of the subject on a sustaining dialogue with the society in which that subject was nourished; the longer novel speaks in muted tones of the ability of that subject to grow and flourish in dialogue with another culture. Jim was least "himself" on the *Patna*, not in the "uncivilized" other world of Patusan. Thus the novels respond to one another in crucial ways, and it would be a mistake to say that one novel is more true to Conrad's beliefs than the other. The "truth" is in the uncertainty established by the dialogic tension between the two texts, an uncertainty concerning the inner reaches of Western selfhood. *Heart of Darkness* is not unlike an agonistic *petit recit* in relation to the grand narrative of *Lord Jim*, although of course Lord Jim in turn deconstructs the grand narrative of imperialism in its own way.

In the same manner, Conrad interrupted the writing of *Under Western Eyes* to write "The Secret Sharer," with a similar intertextual tension resulting. In the novel the uninvited, nighttime intruder is turned over to the legal system of the society; in the short story he is not. Razumov and the Captain take opposing courses of action in response to a similar event. But here the two texts seem to agree rather than stage a true dialogue; both seem to say that the moral decision lies outside the law—the novel by showing the negative effects of acceding to an illegitimate authority, the short story by showing the positive effects of circumventing legitimate but fallible authority.

A more real tension occurs if one refuses to accept the Captain in "The Secret Sharer" at his own evaluation. His discourse seems to tell us that, as a result of this event and his decision, he has turned out well. But the story shows a man who is extremely gullible—he accepts Leggatt's version of things without seriously hearing another point of view—and who is willing to risk the welfare of his entire crew in order to illegally aid the flight of a man who is being sought by the law. The conversation among Conrad's texts is further complicated when we see the protagonists' responses to Haldin and Leggatt in relation to Jim's response to Brown, Jim's behavior approximating that of the Captain. The Captain congratulates himself for his behavior, and he seems to take the extremely fortunate accident of the hat in the water (by which he guides the ship away from the near disaster he has courted) as a sort of sign that some obscure force or principle has approved of his conduct. He rationalizes his lawlessness as adroitly (so adroitly that many readers see things entirely his way) as Razumov rationalizes his "lawful" response to Haldin. Thus, in the dialogue between the two texts, the question of the relationship between moral behavior and the laws of one's society is left in suspension. A person cannot appeal to universals in making moral decisions, the ongoing dialogue among many of Conrad's texts seems to say; one must instead improvise.

It would be naive to be overly sanguine about the conversational world of *Under Western Eyes*, or about the dialogic tensions that pervade the whole of Conrad's fiction and of which the "day of many conversations" in Geneva is an appropriate symbol. It is possible, under jaundiced eyes, to view all the talk of that day as merely trivial, and such a possibility should not simply be dismissed but should stand as a warning. The notion of conversation has figured prominently in recent discussions of what it is we do as critics and theorists, writers and teachers. To neopragmatists such as Richard Rorty, the whole point is to keep the conversation going, a goal that might seem to empty discourse of moral and political consequences. The skeptical image of this might be Marlow and his friends discoursing forever about Jim on a veranda, perhaps sending someone out occasionally for cigars; or, to alter the allusion, the future as only more of the Chateau Borel— a place where, in Rorty's words, "there are no constraints on inquiry save conversational ones."[2]

Rorty's attempt to justify conversation for its own sake, like Stanley Fish's privileging of performance over truth, is a function of the loss of faith in grand narratives or legitimating beliefs that is, to Lyotard, the most salient characteristic of the postmodern condition. Something of this condition is foreshadowed in the way the world of *Lord Jim* tends to fragment into disparate stories, cohering only in the troubled labor of Marlow's discourse. Or one might recall the Professor in *The Secret Agent*, whose impossible goal is to destroy, with homemade bombs, public faith in legality and conventions without harming people. If Lyotard and Alasdair MacIntrye are correct, this destruction has occurred within the discourses of legitimation and verification, and we are left with something like the sinister freedom the Professor wanted for us, starting again with our "little stories" or our "enclaves."

Despite the descriptive value of Lyotard's work, it may appear to suffer from the problem it diagnoses. How, Lyotard asks, can one conduct a discourse on justice in the absence of founding truths and grand narratives? How can one judge without criteria? His answer, certain to be unsatisfactory to many, is that one begins with "a feeling, that is all."[3] *Transcendent interpretation,* based on a presumably immutable set of norms—norms provided by Marxist, Christian, or some other grand narrative—is no longer valid, according to Lyotard. But what, one might ask in response, makes *immanent interpretation* anything more than the most juvenile celebration of spontaneity? One could argue that Lyotard is the dupe of his own crippling shell game: by attacking traditional grand narratives, removing them as frames that limit and constrain ethical discourse, Lyotard has been forced to hide his own legitimating assumptions from himself under the notion of a gut response that cannot be articulated. If Lyotard's argument sounds like Marlow's attempts to vindicate Jim with references to feelings and sentiments, it is because Marlow is grappling with the same suspicion concerning the grand narratives of his world. Lyotard's (and Marlow's) intuitionism is echoed in Rorty's characterization of the pragmatist who thinks "that by playing vocabularies and cultures off against each other, we produce new and better ways of talking and acting—not better by reference to a previously known standard, but just better in the sense that they come to *seem* clearly better than their predecessors."[4]

But since one cannot derive values from facts, or prescriptions from descriptions, one is left with only performative or aesthetic criteria by which a postmodern but politically engaged discourse is made possible. This performative and intuitionist appeal swings dangerously close to justifying the worst in contemporary political discourse—the White House lie that, since Nixon, everyone takes for granted—the lie that probably (like Marlow's in *Heart of Darkness*) just felt right at the time. Lyotard and Rorty are only two of a number of recent thinkers—one would certainly include Foucault—whose analyses of the constructed nature and regulatory power of traditional moral philosophy and epistemology either fail or decline to confront the question of the grounding of the value commitments in their own oppositional narratives.

On the other hand, the kind of storytelling encouraged by Lyotard's *petit recit* and Foucault's counter-memory can be a powerful tool of contestation, revealing the hidden stories repressed by dominant historical narratives and hegemonic ideologies. In *Nostromo* Conrad reenergizes mythic and folkloric stories as alternatives to a grand narrative of progress, which the novel's achronic structure also constantly resists. And in revealing the hidden story of Nostromo's guilt, the novel subverts the version of his story that serves the grand narrative of material "progress" and Western expansion. *Heart of Darkness* begins as counter-memory, but dramatizes the difficulty of an individual holding to a truly oppositional *recit*. But in *Under Western Eyes* the nomadic stories of Tekla, Sophia, Razumov, and Nathalie override the narrator's cynicism in Conrad's most sustained dramatization of the triumph of counter-memory and little story as reported speech within a dominant, monologizing discourse. *Under Western Eyes*, then, anticipates the concern found in more recent novels such as J. M. Coetzee's *Foe* for the empowerment that accompanies the finding of one's authentic voice. The question in Coetzee's novel of how Friday can be given a tongue is a fitting conclusion to the complicity of adventure literature with imperialism beginning even before *Robinson Crusoe*. From this point of view, of course, Foucault's question must be answered differently—it makes all the difference who is speaking.

If speech is empowering, Rorty and Lyotard challenge us to take complete responsibility for what we say and for the world we imagine, without the convenient alibis of legitimating myths and truths. As Rorty says: "Our identification with our community—our society, our political tradition, our intellectual heritage—is heightened when we see this community as *ours* rather than *nature's, shaped* rather than *found,* one among many which men have made."[5]

From the perspective of the 1990s, "our" community must be defined in global terms. We must abolish outmoded boundaries and learn to position ourselves among others for whom our forms of knowing are alien, and to abandon the use of knowledge as an instrument of domination. Read in light of this imperative, the metaphors of knowledge as conversation or *petit recit* take on the aspect of moral imperatives. Certainly something of "our" responsibility for our stories and therefore for the global community is at the heart of *Lord Jim,* and especially Marlow's repeated reminder that Jim is "one of us." There is a social reality beyond conversation, where talk and "language games" have consequences—a fact to which Conrad's fiction consistently points. The sense in these texts that there is no really legitimating "outside" to our ethical discourse, this emergent postmodernism, expresses at once our anxiety and our hope. The fixed code of conduct Marlow so desperately clings to is not sanctified someplace else; it is our creation and responsibility. The existential necessity continually to invent or improvise moral decisions in a world where ethnic and national boundaries, as well as ideological and discursive boundaries, appear as increasingly less legitimate provocations to our various forms of violence is the most compelling feature of Conrad's moral universe.

It matters what stories we tell about Kurtz and Jim; such stories shape our concept of who we are and therefore of the world that is not really beyond the borders of our narratives and pedagogies—a world structured in the stories of others and in our storied responses. If our grand narratives are hollow, and if our little stories lack legitimacy, we are in the world that Conrad's texts so prophetically anticipate in the uneasy heteroglossia of their narrators, whose voices reverberate with the discordant discourses and accents of an uncertain world. The question of madness in the family in *Heart of Darkness* anticipates the postmodern critique of the ideology of reason—reason as a tool of domination—although Conrad does not go as far as Deleuze and Guattari in privileging madness itself. Madness is still a threat rather than a liberation in *Heart of Darkness*. But Razumov's "reason" (a faculty alluded to in his name) is easily co-opted by the autocracy, and Marlow insists on bracketing reason in order to make allowances for Jim. Furthermore, the uncertainty and injustice of Conrad's world are not simply engendered by skeptical philosophical meditation, but are the monstrous offspring of the union of capitalism and imperialism. In dramatizing the need, not the coercion, to speak and thereby to shape and improvise a community, and in mingling this need with a profound meditation on how to speak or be, these nomadic texts, traversing the terrain of modernism, are part of us.

I ended my discussion of *Under Western Eyes* by saying that this text, as it enacts its many dialogic encounters and tells its many little stories, speaks of the necessity and the possibility of escaping the coercion of grand narratives (of both the Autocracy and the Revolution) and of living with uncertainty and openness. "I" would like to conclude by arguing again for this necessity, this time in the voice of Wlad Godzich, a voice in turn inhabited by the words of the Talmudic scholar Emmanuel Levinas (and perhaps also Bakhtin) and forming a text that, when framed in this place, harkens back to the texts of Joseph Conrad—to the unresolved fates of Jim and Razumov—and therefore back again to our own shadowy narratives of conduct, reason, and justice:

> Levinas argues that there is a form of truth that is totally alien to me, that I do not discover within myself, but that calls on me from beyond, and it requires me to leave the realms of the known and of the same in order to settle in a land that is under

its rule. Here the knower sets out on an adventure of uncertain outcome, and the instruments that he or she brings may well be inappropriate to the tasks that will arise. Reason will play a role, but it will be a secondary one; it can only come into play once the primary fact of the irruption of the other has been experienced. And this other is not a threat to be reduced or an object that I give myself to know in my capacity as knowing subject, but that which constitutes me as an ethical being: in my originary encounter I discover my responsibility for the existence of this other, a responsibility that will lie at the root of all my subsequent ethical decisions. Knowledge and its operations are subordinated to this initial ethical moment, for the responsibility that I then experience is the very ground of my response-ability, that is, my capacity to communicate with others and with myself in noncoercive ways.[6]

In response to the traditional political affiliations of the adventure narrative in Western culture, Conrad's adventure tales have an uneasy, troubled relationship to imperialism. Concerning his own encounter with the other during the height of Western imperialism, Marlow recalls that "you lost your way on that river" (35). Godzich and Levinas, navigating further, speak of an adventure beyond imperialism and the borders of reason and selfhood it has erected. It will be difficult to become a subject of their narrative. The noncoercive conduct they imagine beyond these borders may offer something like a fixed code, but it is also a shadowy ideal. The adventure they propose is perilous, and our instruments of navigation will always and inevitably be forged in the past. But the best of these instruments—like the texts of Joseph Conrad—stand at the heart of the vast enigma of selfhood and futurity, pointing beyond oppression and coercion toward the open and always unfinished project of justice.

Notes

Introduction: Boundaries of the Subject

1. Rene Wellek and Austin Warren, *Theory of Literature* (New York: Harcourt, Brace & World, 1942), passim.

2. Jonathan Culler, "Problems in the Theory of Fiction," *Framing the Sign: Criticism and Its Institutions* (Norman: University of Oklahoma Press, 1988), 206–7.

3. Bette London, *The Appropriated Voice: Narrative Authority in Conrad, Forster, and Woolf* (Ann Arbor: University of Michigan Press, 1990), 3.

4. John Frow, *Marxism and Literary History* (Cambridge, Mass.: Harvard University Press, 1986), 228.

5. Ibid., 231. Throughout, Frow problematizes the relationship between what is external and internal to literary discourse—see especially his discussion of Derrida's "Le Parergon" and the question of the frame (216–35).

6. Jean-François Lyotard, *The Postmodern Condition: A Report on Knowledge*, trans. Geoff Bennington and Brian Massumi (Minneapolis: University of Minnesota Press, 1984), 17.

7. Frederick R. Karl, *Joseph Conrad: The Three Lives* (New York: Farrar, 1979); Jeffrey Meyers, *Joseph Conrad* (New York: Charles Scribner's Sons, 1991); Zdzislaw Najder, *Joseph Conrad: A Chronicle* (New Brunswick, N.J.: Rutgers University Press, 1983); Norman Sherry, *Conrad's Eastern World* (Cambridge: Cambridge University Press, 1966); Ian Watt, *Conrad in the Nineteenth Century* (Berkeley: University of California Press, 1979).

8. Peter J. Glassman, *Language and Being: Joseph Conrad and the Literature of Personality* (New York: Columbia University Press, 1976), ix; Albert J. Guerard, *Conrad the Novelist* (Cambridge, Mass.: Harvard University Press, 1958), 31.

9. Eloise Knapp Hay, *The Political Novels of Joseph Conrad* (Chicago: University of Chicago Press, 1963), 69.

10. Avrom Fleishman, *Conrad's Politics: Community and Anarchy in the Fic-

tion of Joseph Conrad (Baltimore: Johns Hopkins University Press, 1967), 3, 12, 56–57.

11. Watt, *Conrad in the Nineteenth Century*, 112–25.

12. Chinua Achebe, "An Image of Africa: Racism in Conrad's *Heart of Darkness*," reprinted in *Heart of Darkness*, ed. Robert Kimbrough (New York: W. W. Norton & Co., 1988), 251–62; Fredric Jameson, *The Political Unconscious: Narrative as a Socially Symbolic Act* (Ithaca, N.Y.: Cornell University Press, 1981), 206–80; Benita Parry, *Conrad and Imperialism: Ideological Boundaries and Visionary Frontiers* (London: Macmillan, 1983), 99–127.

13. Thomas Moser, *Joseph Conrad: Achievement and Decline* (Cambridge, Mass.: Harvard University Press, 1958); J. Hillis Miller, *Poets of Reality* (Cambridge, Mass.: Harvard University Press, 1965), 12–67; Royal Roussel, *The Metaphysics of Darkness: A Study in the Unity and Development of Conrad's Fiction* (Baltimore: Johns Hopkins University Press, 1971); Daniel R. Schwartz, *Conrad: Almayer's Folly to Under Western Eyes* (Ithaca, N.Y.: Cornell University Press, 1980), xvi–xvii; Murray Krieger, *The Tragic Vision: The Confrontation of Extremity* (Baltimore: Johns Hopkins University Press, 1973), 154–94.

14. Suresh Raval, *The Art of Failure: Conrad's Fiction* (Boston: Allen & Unwin, 1986), 1.

15. Ibid., 2.

16. William W. Bonney, *Thorns and Arabesques: Contexts for Conrad's Fiction* (Baltimore: Johns Hopkins University Press, 1980). I have quoted the titles of the last two chapters. James Guetti, *The Limits of Metaphor: A Study of Melville, Conrad, and Faulkner* (Ithaca, N.Y.: Cornell University Press, 1967), 11.

17. Charles Taylor, *Sources of the Self: The Making of the Modern Identity* (Cambridge, Mass.: Harvard University Press, 1989), 33–34.

18. Ibid., 111.

19. Lyotard, *Just Gaming*, trans. Wlad Godzich (Minneapolis: University of Minnesota Press, 1985), 36.

20. An important essay on the relationship between Bakhtin and Lyotard is David Carroll's "Narrative, Heterogeneity, and the Question of the Political: Bakhtin and Lyotard," *The Aims of Representation: Subject/Text/History*, ed. Murray Krieger (New York: Columbia University Press, 1987), 69–106.

21. In Bakhtin, *The Dialogic Imagination*, ed. Michael Holquist (Austin: University of Texas Press, 1981), 259–422.

22. Bakhtin, "Discourse in the Novel," *The Dialogic Imagination*, 259. Theodor Adorno follows Bakhtin in this regard: "How can works of art be like windowless monads, representing something which is other than they? There is only one way to explain this, which is to view them as being subject to a dynamic or immanent historicity and a dialectical tension between nature and domination of nature, a dialectic that seems to be of the same kind as the dialectic of society. Or to put it more cautiously, the dialectic of art resembles the social dialectic without consciously imitating it." *Aesthetic Theory*, trans. C. Lenhardt (New York: Routledge, 1986), 7.

23. Lyotard, *The Postmodern Condition*, 31.

24. Lyotard, *Just Gaming*, 17.

25. Carroll, "Narrative, Heterogeneity, and the Question of the Political," 79. Justice is the central issue in Lyotard's *Just Gaming*.

26. Ibid., 86.

27. Fredric Jameson, "The Politics of Theory: Ideological Positions in the Postmodern Debate," *Contemporary Literary Criticism*, ed. Robert Con Davis and Ronald Schleifer (New York: Longman, 1989), 418–27.

28. This characterization of the postmodern crisis is offered by Craig Owens, "The Discourse of Others: Feminists and Postmodernism," *The Anti-Aesthetic: Essays on Postmodern Culture*, ed. Hal Foster (Port Townsend, Wash.: Bay Press, 1983), 57.

29. Linda Hutcheon, *A Poetics of Postmodernism: History, Theory, Fiction* (New York: Routledge, 1988).

30. Paul Ricoeur, "Civilization and National Cultures," *History and Truth*, trans. Charles A. Kelbley (Evanston, Ill.: Northwestern University Press, 1965), 278. Quoted by Owens, "The Discourse of Others: Feminists and Postmodernism," 57–58.

31. Raval, *The Art of Failure*, 167.

32. Bakhtin, "Forms of Time and of the Chronotope in the Novel," *The Dialogic Imagination*, 206.

33. See Bakhtin, *Speech Genres and Other Late Essays*, trans. Vern W. McGee (Austin: University of Texas Press, 1986), 60–102.

34. Taylor, *Sources of the Self*, 36.

35. Miller, *Poets of Reality*, 1, 3, 5, 7.

36. Aaron Fogel, *Coercion to Speak: Conrad's Poetics of Dialogue* (Cambridge, Mass.: Harvard University Press, 1985), 10, 220.

Chapter 1: The (De)Construction of the Narrator in *The Nigger of the "Narcissus"*

1. Roland Barthes, *Image, Music, Text*, trans. Stephen Heath (New York: Hill, 1977), 104n.

2. Jacques Lacan, "Of Structure as an Inmixing of an Otherness Prerequisite to Any Subject Whatever," *The Structuralist Controversy*, ed. Richard Macksey and Eugenio Donato (Baltimore: Johns Hopkins University Press, 1972), 189; Emile Benveniste, *Problems in General Linguistics*, trans. Mary Elizabeth Meek (Coral Gables, Fla.: University of Miami Press, 1971), 223–30; Michel Foucault, *The Order of Things* (New York: Vintage, 1973), 386–87; Barthes, *Image, Music, Text*, 111, 142.

3. Although I do not assert simple, one-to-one relationships between social voices heard in Conrad's narratives and political positions he may have taken outside of these texts, it might be useful to recall a few aspects of Conrad's own political beliefs as his biographers have described them. First, he felt a deep aversion to revolutionary socialism and to anarchism, even though his friend, Cunninghame Graham, was a socialist; Fleishman, however, argues that Conrad became more sympathetic to the politics of revolution in his later years. (*Conrad's Politics*, 129–57. Fleishman speaks, for instance,

about "the affirmation of revolutionary politics in *The Rover,*" 154.) Second, Conrad was proud of Poland's progress toward liberal forms of government before its partition at the end of the eighteenth century, but this pride was tempered by another voice, which distrusted democracy and longed for traditional, aristocratic structures and for clear, fixed codes of conduct. Conrad's investment in a conservative grand narrative at the time of the writing of *The Nigger of the "Narcissus"* is unnuanced in a letter concerning the election of 1885. Here he complains, in words that sound like the narrator's discourse on Donkin, that "every disreputable ragamuffin in Europe feels that the day of universal brotherhood, dispoilation and disorder is coming apace, and nurses day-dreams of well-plenished pockets amongst the ruin of all that is respectable, venerable and holy." Gerard Jean-Aubry, ed. *Joseph Conrad: Life and Letters* (London, 1927), 84. This letter of December 19, 1885, is discussed by Fleishman (23). Third, he scorned "material interests," especially the international opportunism represented by the American Holroyd in *Nostromo* and by the Belgian trading company in *Heart of Darkness*, but his celebration of work often supported those interests inadvertently. Fourth, Conrad's subjective and personal valuation of work encourages his indifference, also implied in the above letter, to the conditions of the working classes or to the unemployed. Finally, he believed, as did Bakhtin, that the self is a social phenomenon, but he harbored a deep, Schopenhauerian skepticism concerning our ability to act for the social good. A tension between isolation and social involvement runs throughout his fiction and many of his political essays as well.

This skepticism permeates Conrad's best-known political essay, "Autocracy and War." The nineteenth century, Conrad suggests, began with a fall that anticipated the failure of what Lyotard calls the grand narrative of Emancipation: "The origin of the French Revolution was intellectual, the idea was elevated; but it is the bitter fate of any idea to lose its royal form and power, to lose its 'virtue' the moment it descends from its solitary throne to work its will among the people. It is a king whose destiny is never to know the obedience of his subjects except at the cost of degradation." Joseph Conrad, *Notes on Life and Letters* (New York: Doubleday, 1925), 86.

This passage contains a textbook deconstructive gesture. The idea of overthrowing a monarchy is itself praised in a monarchical figure—democracy is a king who becomes tragically overthrown even as he is coronated. The passage nicely if inadvertently portrays Conrad's ambivalence as it reinstates on the figurative level the very values it denies on the propositional level. Later, in describing the Russian autocracy, Conrad says that it "succeeded to nothing; it had no historical past, and it cannot hope for a historical future. It lies outside the stream of progress" (97). Again, one finds an oddly deconstructive tendency in an essay that, on the one hand, discusses the rapidly approaching Russian Revolution and even speculates as to why it will fail, and on the other hand argues that Russia is so monstrous as to defy understanding in the usual political or historical terms, so monstrous that "it seems to have no root either in the institutions or the follies of this earth" (98). The essay speaks at once of the necessity and the impossibility of political thought about Russia.

4. Patrick Brantlinger, *Rule of Darkness: British Literature and Imperialism, 1830–1914* (Ithaca, N.Y.: Cornell University Press, 1988), 35.

5. John M. MacKenzie, *Propaganda and Empire: The Manipulation of British Public Opinion, 1880–1960* (Manchester: Manchester University Press, 1984), 45. Quoted by Brantlinger, *Rule of Darkness,* 35.

6. Marvin Mudrick, "The Artist's Conscience and *The Nigger of the 'Narcissus.'* " *Twentieth Century Interpretations of The Nigger of the "Narcissus,"* ed. John A. Palmer (Englewood Cliffs, N.J.: Prentice, 1969), 72.

7. Like *The Nigger of the "Narcissus," "*The Waste Land" has a problematic, wavering point of view, and T. S. Eliot's suggestion that Tiresias is the focus of narration of the whole poem is as unsatisfactory to most readers as is the "I" narrator at the end of Conrad's novel. But while Eliot's handling of point of view has been considered an effect of art, Conrad's has been seen as mere carelessness. An excellent study of the modernist theme of the fragmented self is Dennis Brown, *The Modernist Self in Twentieth-Century Literature* (New York: St. Martin's Press, 1989).

8. See Mikhail Bakhtin, *Problems of Dostoevsky's Poetics,* trans. Caryl Emerson (Minneapolis: University of Minnesota Press, 1984), esp. chaps. 1–3.

9. Guerard is consistently critical of what he sees as clumsiness in Conrad's handling of point of view, not only in this novel but in such works as *Nostromo* and *Under Western Eyes. Conrad the Novelist,* 107, 206, 248.

10. R. D. Foulke, "Postures of Belief in *The Nigger of the 'Narcissus,'* " *Modern Fiction Studies* 17 (1971), 258.

11. Susan Rubin Suleiman, *Authoritarian Fictions: The Ideological Novel as a Literary Genre* (New York: Columbia University Press, 1983), 19, 17, 16.

12. *The Birth of Tragedy* (1871) achieved its deconstruction of a totalizing or monologic voice by similarly juxtaposing two grammatical voices. See Paul de Man's discussion in *Allegories of Reading* (New Haven, Conn.: Yale University Press, 1979), 94. Nietzsche was perhaps the most significant of Conrad's contemporaries to challenge conventional faith in the subject as origin. He writes: "The 'subject' is not something given, it is something added and invented. . . . We can set up a word at the point at which our ignorance begins . . . e.g. the word 'I'. . . . However habitual and indispensable this fiction may have become by now—that in itself proves nothing against its imaginary origin." Friedrich Nietzsche, *The Will to Power,* trans. R. J. Hollingdale and Walter Kaufmann (New York: Vintage, 1968), 267–68. Furthermore, Ian Hacking argues that the discourse of psychoanalysis invented the phenomenon of the split personality in the years just before Conrad's novel. Hacking, "Making Up People," in *Reconstructing Individualism: Autonomy, Individuality, and the Self in Western Thought,* ed. Thomas C. Heller et al. (Stanford, Calif.: Stanford University Press, 1986), 223. And E. H. Gombrich quotes Wilhelm Dilthey in a statement that summarizes a significant theme in late nineteenth- and early twentieth-century thought: "The individual is merely a nodal point of cultural systems, of organizations which are inextricably intertwined with its existence." Quoted in Gombrich, " 'They Were All Human Beings—So Much Is Plain': Reflections on Cultural Relativism in the Humanities," *Critical*

Inquiry 13,4 (Summer 1987), 689. The problem of the self as articulated in recent theory has important antecedents in the historical period during which Conrad wrote.

13. Jameson, *The Political Unconscious*, 12.

14. Glassman sees a parallel between the emerging self-awareness of the narrator and Conrad's own maturation as a writer, with the narrator's final farewell to the crew reflecting Conrad's own farewell to the sea: "Conrad wrote *The Nigger* primarily to explore and to reinforce that developing process of reconciliation with his own character." Glassman, *Language and Being*, 176.

15. Watt, *Conrad in the Nineteenth Century*, 99. Watt comes to Conrad's defense against such critics as Guerard and Mudrick, dismissing the idea that point of view must be consistent; he agrees with Samuel Johnson that such rules of unity insult the audience's intelligence and misconstrue the nature of art: "Delusion, if delusion be admitted, has no certain limitations" (quoted by Watt, 102). Watt's defense, however, finds no particular method or significance in Conrad's manipulation of point of view. By contrast, Marion Michael argues that the shift from omniscient to personal narration establishes a thematically relevant dual perspective. "Currents in Conrad Criticism: A Symposium," *Conradiana* 4,3 (1972), 14. John Lester also tries to find method in Conrad's juxtaposition of two narrators, but his commentary simply locates in the text the many changes from one narrator to the other. John Lester, "Conrad's Narrators in *The Nigger of the 'Narcissus,'*" *Conradiana* 12,3 (1980), 163–72. Watt's more open-ended "plurality" brings us closer to Bakhtin's heteroglossia, but none of these critics fixes the problem within the context of larger historical and social discourses, and none sees the structuring of point of view in this novel in relation to social constraints and discursive limits.

16. Bakhtin, *The Dialogic Imagination*, 262, 293.

17. Watt, *Conrad in the Nineteenth Century*, 112–25.

18. In Bakhtin, *The Dialogic Imagination*, 84–258.

19. Ibid., 370–71.

20. Fleishman argues for the influence of the Burkean theory of the organic society on Conrad's political thought in chapter 2 of *Conrad's Politics.*

21. Although we are supposed to disapprove of Donkin's disgust with foreigners, the ethnocentric narrator has asserted the superiority of the "masterful tones" of even tipsy European seamen over the babble and shriek of Eastern languages. The community that concerns Conrad remains primarily, until *Under Western Eyes*, Western European.

22. Bakhtin, "Discourse in the Novel," 370.

23. Sir Philip Sidney, "An Apology for Poetry." *Critical Theory Since Plato*, ed. Hazard Adams (New York: Harcourt, 1971), 168.

24. Terry Eagleton, *Literary Theory: An Introduction* (Minneapolis: University of Minnesota Press, 1983), 20. "Doctrine in Poetry" is found in Richards, *Practical Criticism* (New York: Harcourt, 1929), 255–74.

25. According to Tony Bennett, literary criticism "has played an important role in structuring the field of cultural relations in a certain way, producing

for so-called 'literary' texts a particular position within that field as the supports for the maintenance of bourgeois hegemony at the level of language. The position, it is important to stress, is in no sense natural to such texts. It is the product of a historically particular organization of the field of cultural relations and of the particular way in which the texts concerned are produced for consumption within that field." Bennett, *Formalism and Marxism* (New York: Methuen, 1979), 167. The Salman Rushdie incident unfortunately illustrates that the notion of the disinterested literary text is in no sense natural, but is instead a feature of the way Western culture maps its discursive boundaries. It also shows that, however much the socially committed critic might lament the abuses of the separation of poetics and politics in industrial democracies, the refusal to acknowledge any such boundaries can serve fanaticism and brutality.

26. All general knowledge requires a process of forgetting, a loss of particulars, and this process, when it occurs in the field of social history, can serve ruling-class interests. What Foucault calls counter-memory is the retrieval of the lost or repressed histories of the victimized and the exploited. See Michel Foucault, *Language, Counter-Memory, Practice*, trans. Donald F. Bouchard (Ithaca, N.Y.: Cornell University Press, 1977), especially the essay entitled "Nietzsche, Genealogy, History." By analogy with Foucault, any memory that is offered in opposition to what one assumes to be an official memory (such as the conservative narrator's opposition to liberal or reformist views of history) would be a counter-memory.

27. Bakhtin describes Turgenev's Bazarov as an ideologeme, a character who represents a new class of educated people of lower-class origins as this class appears to the liberal nobility to which Turgenev belonged. Bakhtin, *The Formal Method in Literary Scholarship*, trans. Albert J. Wehrle (Cambridge, Mass.: Harvard University Press, 1985), 21. "Ideologeme" might also describe implied propositions, such as "sailors are like children," that serve an ideological function (here, supporting the prerogatives of management).

28. Jameson discusses resentment in *The Political Unconscious*, 185–205.

29. Hayden White, "The Value of Narrativity in the Representation of Reality," *Critical Inquiry* 7 (1980), 17.

30. Ibid.

31. Bakhtin, *Problems in Dostoevsky's Poetics*, chaps. 1–2.

32. Fogel establishes his belief in Conrad's sympathy for labor via a reading of Conrad's two essays on the sinking of the *Titanic*. Fogel, *Coercion to Speak*, chap. 1. Conrad's *Titanic* essays were written in 1912, by which time his youthful pose of aristocratic snobbery had mellowed.

33. Bakhtin, "Discourse in the Novel," 282.

34. This analysis addresses the difficulty Bonney has with the concluding pages, a difficulty stemming from his decision to hear only the same, unitary voice throughout the novel: "Only with great difficulty, and never with certainty, can the reader decide at a given moment whether the assumptions underlying a particular descriptive mode are exclusively part of the past as the

narrator conceives it or a part of the narrator's completed wisdom and projected from his physically and temporally detached position." Bonney, *Thorns
and Arabesques*, 163.

35. Frow, *Marxism and Literary History*, 223.

36. A letter to Cunninghame Graham written a year and a half after the
publication of *The Nigger of the "Narcissus"* suggests the hazards of identifying
Conrad with the "I" of the novel. While "I" referred to his international crowd
of "brothers," Conrad declines Graham's invitation to attend a conference on
world peace: "I cannot admit the idea of fraternity, not so much because I
believe it impracticable, but because its propaganda (the only thing really tangible about it) tends to weaken the national sentiment, the preservation of
which is my concern." Conrad, *Life and Letters*, 269. This letter, as Eloise Knapp
Hay points out, goes on to pair egoism and nationalism as positives against
the negatives of fraternity and internationalism. Hay, *The Political Novels of
Joseph Conrad*, 23.

Although French abounds in Conrad's personal letters, it is interesting
that here he shifts to French at the moment he entertains his most extreme
and reactionary view, as though to escape into the voice of another self or to
protect the message from inappropriate ears. The second language is a sign of
dialogic differences within the discourse, as Conrad introduces his *petit recit*
on man: "L'homme est un animal méchant. Sa méchanceté doit être organisée. Le crime est une condition nécessaire de l'existence organisée. La société
est essentiellement criminelle,—ou elle n'existerait pas. C'est l'égoïsme qui
sauve tout . . ." (269). This is the disciplinary voice that is heard from time to
time before the introduction of "I" in *The Nigger of the "Narcissus,"* albeit muted
there in the English accents of the novel's intended audience.

37. R. D. Foulke, "Creed and Conduct in *The Nigger of the "Narcissus,"*
Conradiana 12,2 (1980), 113–15.

38. Katerina Clark and Michael Holquist, *Mikhail Bakhtin* (Cambridge,
Mass.: Harvard University Press, 1984), 77.

39. Glassman, *Language and Being*, 171.

40. Ibid., 175.

41. Fleishman's reading of the ending, on the other hand, emphasizes
the theme of group solidarity: "Throughout the novel, the narrator . . . deni-
grates the cowardice, childishness, and mutinousness of the crew. Yet he
closes his narrative with a paean to the class of mariners and the ideal of
courageous service which they represent. As a collection of individuals they
display all the vices of an individualistic society, but as a crew they acquire
virtue through their common experience." Fleishman, *Conrad's Politics*, 74.

42. Bakhtin resisted what he thought were the depoliticizing tendencies
of Freud's theory of the unconscious, replacing it with a theory of the "unofficial conscious" which remains grounded in discourse. See V. N. Volosinov
[Bakhtin], *Freudianism: A Marxist Critique*, trans. I. R. Titunik (New York: Harcourt Brace, 1976). The authorship of this text is disputed. Clark and Holquist
discuss the unofficial conscious in *Mikhail Bakhtin*, 171–85.

43. Bakhtin, "Discourse in the Novel," 365.

44. Karl, *Joseph Conrad: The Three Lives*, passim.

45. It is outside the scope of this chapter to argue the pros and cons of the concept of implied author, a term that I feel mistakenly suggests that there is one such entity that the text clearly establishes and that all readers should therefore see alike. To argue that an implied author, as opposed to the real, biographical author, is a presence *in* the text is to assume with the formalists the autonomy and objectivity of the literary work. But this shadowy author exists instead in the liminal space between the text and the discourses that constitute the reader's interpretive strategies. Perhaps a neologism that indicates both implication and inference would be best, but I will employ the term "inferred author," which requires readers to take responsibility for their creation of this shadowy being. I have not directly presented, with the exception of a few remarks in the third part of this chapter, my own sketch of the author I infer, although my reader may infer it.

46. Wayne Booth, *The Rhetoric of Fiction* (Chicago: University of Chicago Press, 1961, 1983), 3–20, 67–86.

47. Roland Barthes, *Mythologies*, trans. Annette Lavers (New York: Hill and Wang, 1972), 123.

48. In Martin Heidegger, *The Question Concerning Technology*, trans. William Lovitt (New York: Harper and Row, 1977), 149.

49. Fogel's discussion of the preface also focuses on the rhetoric of coercion. Fogel points out that the preface postulates the reader's laziness in opposition to the writer's work, and that this is a displaced version of the theme of rest and work in the novel itself. See Fogel, *Coercion to Speak*, 47–49.

50. Jim's attempt to make Marlow "see" that the jump was not his own responsibility is also an attempt at coerced vision that is not disinterested: "It was their doing as plainly as if they had reached up with a boat-hook and pulled me over. Can't you see it? You must see it. Speak—straight out" (76). And in *Heart of Darkness* Marlow asks, "Do you see him? Do you see the story?" (27). In the next chapter I will argue that Marlow's frustrations over making his listeners "see" cause him to alter his discourse to conform more to their categories of perception.

51. See Eagleton, *Literary Theory: An Introduction*, 24.

52. Brantlinger, *The Rule of Darkness*, 10ff. The relationship between imperial ideology and adventure narratives is also the thesis of Martin Green's *Dreams of Adventure, Deeds of Empire* (New York: Basic Books, 1979).

53. Fredric Jameson, "The Politics of Theory: Ideological Positions in the Postmodernism Debate," *Contemporary Literary Criticism*, ed. Robert Con Davis and Ronald Schleifer (New York: Longman, 1989), 426.

Chapter 2: Discourse and Story in *Heart of Darkness*

1. V. N. Volosinov and Mikhail Bakhtin, *Marxism and the Philosophy of Language*, trans. Ladislav Matejka and I. R. Titunik (Cambridge, Mass.: Harvard University Press, 1973), 12. The extent of Bakhtin's work on this book is disputed.

2. Vincent Pecora, "*Heart of Darkness* and the Phenomenology of Voice," *ELH* 52 (Winter 1985), 993–1015; London, "Only a Voice/Only a Lie: The Novel as Polygraph," *The Appropriated Voice*, 29–58.

3. Steve Ressler, *Joseph Conrad: Consciousness and Integrity* (New York: New York University Press, 1988), 20.

4. London, *The Appropriated Voice*, 54.

5. Watt discusses James and Conrad in *Conrad in the Nineteenth Century*, 200–214.

6. Brown, *The Modernist Self*, 30–36.

7. Didier Coste, *Narrative as Communication* (Minneapolis: University of Minnesota Press, 1989), 5.

8. Bakhtin, *Speech Genres*, 121–22, 136.

9. Excerpted in *Heart of Darkness*, ed. Robert Kimbrough (New York: W. W. Norton & Co., 1988), 207.

10. Brook Thomas, "Preserving and Keeping Order by Killing Time in *Heart of Darkness*," *Heart of Darkness: A Case Study in Contemporary Criticism*, ed. Ross C. Murfin (New York: St. Martin's Press, 1989), 240–41. Note that Marlow's "counter-memory" works in the opposite direction from that of the narrator of *The Nigger of the "Narcissus,"* who is trying to counter liberal and reformist versions of history. Elsewhere I have argued that the plot of *Heart of Darkness* has many elements in common with the mythology of the ancient gnostics, a mythology that also functioned as a counter-memory in relation to the stories about God and Christ taught in the established Church. Bruce Henricksen, "*Heart of Darkness* and the Gnostic Myth," *Joseph Conrad's Heart of Darkness: Modern Critical Interpretations*, ed. Harold Bloom (New York: Chelsea House Publishers, 1987), 45–55.

11. Brown, *The Modernist Self*, 22.

12. Diane Macdonell, *Theories of Discourse: An Introduction* (Oxford: Basil Blackwell, 1986), 34, 35, 47.

13. Richard Koebner and Helmut Schmidt, *Imperialism: The Story and Significance of a Political Word, 1840–1960* (Cambridge: Cambridge University Press, 1964), 230. Koebner's study can be supplemented by examinations of the psychology of colonialism such as O. Mannoni's *Prospero and Caliban: The Psychology of Colonization*, trans. Pamela Powesland (New York: Praeger, 1956) and Albert Memmi's *The Colonizer and the Colonized* (Boston: Beacon Press, 1965). See also Phillip Darby, *Three Faces of Imperialism: British and American Approaches to Asia and Africa 1870–1970* (New Haven, Conn.: Yale University Press, 1987) and Lewis Feuer, *Imperialism and the Anti-Imperialist Mind* (Buffalo, N.Y.: Prometheus Books, 1986).

14. Brown, *The Modernist Self*, 22.

15. Lyotard, *The Postmodern Condition*, 36.

16. Ibid., 41.

17. Raval, *The Art of Failure*, 28.

18. John A. McClure, *Kipling and Conrad: The Colonial Fiction* (Cambridge, Mass.: Harvard University Press, 1981), 132–33.

19. See "Story and Discourse in the Analysis of Narrative" in Jonathan

Culler, *The Pursuit of Signs* (Ithaca, N.Y.: Cornell University Press, 1981), 169–87.

20. The absence of the objectively "true" story of Kurtz's past may also explain the frame narrator's metaphor about the decentered meaning of Marlow's tales.

21. Terry Eagleton, *The Ideology of the Aesthetic* (Oxford: Basil Blackwell, 1990), 23.

22. Quoted in ibid., 20.

23. Raval, *The Art of Failure*, 7.

24. Eagleton, *The Ideology of the Aesthetic*, 27.

25. Ibid., 98.

26. Fleishman, *Conrad's Politics*, 71.

27. In the nineteenth century, "studies" in craniometry and phrenology were used to demonstrate the racial superiority of white Europeans to Africans and Orientals. Michael Adas writes that "the efforts of such physicians as White and Soemmering to quantify physical distinctions between human groups came to dominate scientific thinking on the issue of race. Though measurements of arm length or genital size continued to be made, the skull became the focus of investigation." Adas, *Machines as the Measure of Men: Science, Technology and Ideologies of Western Dominance* (Ithaca, N.Y.: Cornell University Press, 1989), 293. The doctor who measures Marlow's skull—even though he inquires about madness in the family and acknowledges that the real changes in the white man living in Africa will probably be internal—may be testing such theories. His measurements are much less surreal within the context of nineteenth-century "science" than they seem today.

28. Raval's introduction to *The Art of Failure* is an excellent overview of the Conradian problem of understanding as it relates to the inadequacy of language. Derrida's "Cogito and the History of Madness" is found in Jacques Derrida, *Writing and Difference*, trans. Alan Bass (London: Routledge and Kegan Paul, 1978), 31–63.

29. Fogel, *Coercion to Speak*, 19.

30. For Leavis's objections see *The Great Tradition* (New York: New York University Press, 1963), 177ff.

31. Peter Brooks, *Reading for the Plot: Design and Intention in Narrative* (New York: Alfred A. Knopf, 1984), 242.

32. Robert Kimbrough, "Conrad's *Youth* (1902): An Introduction," *Heart of Darkness*, ed. Robert Kimbrough (New York: W. W. Norton & Company, 1988), 408.

33. McClure, *Kipling and Conrad*, 7.

34. Juliet McLauchlan, "The 'Value' and 'Significance' of *Heart of Darkness*," *Heart of Darkness*, ed. Robert Kimbrough (New York: W. W. Norton & Company, 1988), 383.

35. Other well-known studies in this humanistic tradition include Krieger's discussion in *The Tragic Vision*, 154–65, and Schwartz's discussion in *Conrad: Almayer's Folly to Under Western Eyes*, 63–75. Studies more skeptical of this tradition include Achebe's "An Image of Africa: Racism in Conrad's

Heart of Darkness," reprinted in *Heart of Darkness*, 251–62; Bonney's *Thorns and Arabesques*; Parry's *Conrad and Colonialism*; Raval's *The Art of Failure*; Frances B. Singh's "The Colonialistic Bias of *Heart of Darkness*," reprinted in *Heart of Darkness*, 268–80; and London's chapter in *The Appropriated Voice*.

36. Fleishman, making a case for Conrad's growing belief in internationalism while equating Marlow with his author, refers to "the idea" as "a set of cultural values that could provide the basis for widespread public belief in international institutions." *Conrad's Politics*, 34. But Marlow does not tell us what "idea" he means, and fewer and fewer critics since Fleishman have taken for granted Conrad's complete identification with his narrator.

37. Lyotard, *Just Gaming*, 75.

38. Ibid., 16, 93.

39. Fleishman observes that Coleridge was one importer of the Hegelian Idea into English culture. Fleishman quotes J. H. Muirhead, who says that "Coleridge regarded all actual Constitutions, including that of his own country, as temporary and imperfect embodiments of an 'idea' that was slowly revealing itself on earth, if not as a city of God, at any rate as a society of seekers after Him." *Conrad's Politics*, 62.

40. Raval, *The Art of Failure*, 9.

41. See Koebner, *Imperialism*, 215–16.

42. Hay, *The Political Novels of Joseph Conrad*, 147–48.

43. See especially *Just Gaming*, 65–72, for Lyotard's attempt to orient his opposition to terrorism in the basic right of all people to continue to play the "game" of the just and the unjust, which is to say to continue to have a narrative voice. The problem of the Idea versus opinion occurs on page 75 of *Just Gaming*.

44. Joseph Conrad, *Letters of Joseph Conrad to Marguerite Poradowska*, trans. and ed. John A. Gee and Paul J. Sturm (New Haven, Conn.: Yale University Press, 1940), 36.

45. Fleishman, *Conrad's Politics*, 54.

46. Krieger, *The Tragic Vision*, 154–65.

47. Caryl Emerson and Gary Saul Morson, *Rethinking Bakhtin: Extensions and Challenges* (Evanston, Ill.: Northwestern University Press, 1989), 26–27.

48. Hayden White, *The Tropics of Discourse* (Baltimore: Johns Hopkins University Press, 1978), 85.

49. Bonney, *Thorns and Arabesques*, 197.

50. Bakhtin, *Speech Genres*, 78, 89 (Bakhtin's emphases). Speech genres do not correspond with literary genres, although overlap is possible. Mary Louise Pratt's assimilation of the work of William Labov on "natural narratives" to her own theory of the literary "speech act" illustrates such overlap. Pratt, *Toward a Speech Act Theory of Literary Discourse* (Bloomington: Indiana University Press, 1977), 38–78.

51. McClure, *Kipling and Conrad*, 149.

52. Hay, *The Political Novels of Joseph Conrad*, 161.

53. See chap. 2, on the hero, in Bakhtin's *Problems of Dostoevsky's Poetics*.

54. Hayden White, *Metahistory: The Historical Imagination in Nineteenth-*

Century Europe (Baltimore: Johns Hopkins University Press, 1973), 29. The notion of a *master* historian deserves emphasis.

55. Wolfgang Iser describes the act of reading in terms of the need to fill "gaps" in the text and to rationalize "alien associations." See Iser, *The Implied Reader: Patterns of Communication in Prose Fiction From Bunyan to Beckett* (Baltimore: Johns Hopkins University Press, 1974), 274–94. Umberto Eco uses the term "ghost chapters" to name those unnarrated events that the reader must "write" to make the narrated events cohere. See Eco, *The Role of the Reader: Explorations in the Semiotics of Texts* (Bloomington: Indiana University Press, 1979), 214ff. Conrad's own awareness of the reader as secondary writer was expressed in a letter to Graham: "One writes only half the book: the other half is with the reader." Jean-Aubry, *Life and Letters*, I, 208.

56. Lionel Trilling, *Beyond Culture: Essays on Literature and Learning* (New York: Viking, 1968), 20.

57. Brooks, *Reading For the Plot*, 242.

58. Lyotard's discussion in *The Differend* of the silence of many survivors of the Holocaust, owing also to the incommensurability of language games, may be relevant to Marlow's silences, particularly in view of the theme of extermination raised at the end of Kurtz's essay. Jean-François Lyotard, *The Differend: Phrases in Dispute*, trans. Georges Van Den Abbeele (Minneapolis: University of Minnesota Press, 1988), 3–31.

59. London, *The Appropriated Voice*, 44ff.

60. When Conrad began the novel, imperialism, at the height of its acceptance in England in 1889 (Conrad's Congo experience was in 1890), had already fallen under extreme moral criticism (see Koebner, *Imperialism*, 197–249). Marlow's reading of a moral revulsion into Kurtz's final words replicates Britain's own swing toward revulsion during the time between Conrad's experience and his writing of the novel, and Marlow's unease during his narration parallels Britain's growing unease with the rhetoric of imperialism. If England was beginning to glimpse the horror in imperialism, the redemption and victory given to Kurtz may be a displaced version of the partial victory Conrad may have observed in England's waning romance with imperialism.

61. Garret Stewart's comments on this matter are suggestive. See "Lying as Dying in *Heart of Darkness*," in *Heart of Darkness*, 358–74. But while he points to the formulaic quality of Marlow's discourse on Kurtz's death, calling it "the inevitably exacted price of repatriation to the European community," Stewart wants to believe that Kurtz achieved a "tragic vision" (referring to Murray Krieger's famous study) in his death (372). Thus Stewart's reading itself seeks repatriation by accepting the eschatology of redemption that usually accompanies the word "tragedy" in this context.

62. Fogel concludes his study with a discussion of "The Black Mate," the story Conrad claimed was his "first." Since conflicting evidence exists about the date of the story (Conrad's wife, Jessie, insists it was written in 1908), Fogel suggests that we read "first" in a figurative sense. The story concerns a man named Bunter, who is forced to invent a tale about ghosts in order to retain his job, since his employer believes in ghosts. Bunter, whose lie is dialogically

forced by his situation, is treated with sympathy, and Fogel suggests that the story is a representation—a metastory—of Conrad's own sense of himself as a writer. Whether this is so or not, "The Black Mate" overtly represents the sort of storyteller/audience pragmatics that I am suggesting explain Marlow's narrative decisions. The story is "first" because it is the most overt expression of Conrad's understanding of his own position and of a recurrent theme. See Fogel, 250–57.

63. Fogel, *Coercion to Speak*, 225.

64. After apparently studying African customs up close, Kurtz labels the Africans "brutes." This reveals not only his own but perhaps his author's blindness to the complex religious and social systems he would have been presented with in actuality. Marlow's discourse, while sympathetic to individual human suffering, supports the notion of the brutishness of the African. Chinua Achebe's *Things Fall Apart*, which ends with a white colonialist contemplating writing "a paragraph" concerning the customs he sees enacted in response to Okonkwo's suicide, is a novel dialogically opposed to this voice in *Heart of Darkness*.

65. The semiotic Freud—the Freud concerned with structures of signification, the relations between meanings and their mediating symbols, between senders and receivers, between interpretation and power—is an important precursor of contemporary textual theory. He is to be distinguished from the Freud of phallic symbols, sexual obsessions, and family romances who has haunted literary criticism for some time. This older Freud has engendered studies of Conrad emphasizing inner journeys (as in *Heart of Darkness*) and encounters with one's unconscious Other (as in "The Secret Sharer"). This older Freud prompts Frederick Crews to see *Heart of Darkness* as a journey back to the father, Kurtz, who is discovered performing obscene rites in a parody of the primal scene—"Kurtz amounts to a vindictive reconstruction of Conrad's father." See Frederick Crews, *Partisan Review* 34,4 (1967), 522.

66. See Raval's pertinent qualifications of Trilling's assertion that Marlow discovered a "self beyond culture." *The Art of Failure*, 43.

67. Jean-Aubry, *Life and Letters*, I, 268.

68. Hay, *The Political Novels of Joseph Conrad*, 138.

69. A section of Ohmann's essay "The Shaping of a Canon, 1960–1975" is subtitled "The Illness Story." See Ohmann, *Politics of Letters* (Middletown, Conn.: Wesleyan University Press, 1987), 68–91.

70. Ibid., 89.

71. Conrad, *The Nigger of the "Narcissus,"* 145.

72. Fogel, *Coercion to Speak*, 18–21.

73. Culler, "Story and Discourse in the Analysis of Narrative," *The Pursuit of Signs*, 169–87.

74. Ibid., 174.

75. Frank Kermode, *The Sense of an Ending: Studies in the Theory of Fiction* (Oxford: Oxford University Press, 1967), 11.

76, See also Paul Ricoeur's discussion of the consoling plot. Ricoeur says that "Kermode's book ceaselessly oscillates between the inescapable suspicion that fictions lie and deceive, to the extent that they console us, and the equally invincible conviction that fictions are not simply arbitrary." *Time and Narrative,* trans. Kathleen McLaughlin and David Pellauer (Chicago: University of Chicago Press, 1985), vol. 2, 27. It is surprising that Ricoeur does not mention *Heart of Darkness,* where the consoling lie is so directly thematized.

77. Volosinov and Bakhtin, *Marxism and the Philosophy of Language,* 21 (emphasis in original).

78. Culler, *The Pursuit of Signs,* 175.

79. Barbara Herrnstein Smith, *On the Margins of Discourse: The Relation of Literature to Language* (Chicago: University of Chicago Press, 1978), 8.

80. Culler's discussion of Labov in *The Pursuit of Signs* is based on Mary Louise Pratt's initial introduction of Labov's work to students of literature. See *Toward a Speech Act Theory of Literary Discourse,* 38–78. Conrad's protestation, in his note on *Lord Jim,* that all of Marlow's discourse in that novel could be read aloud in a sitting indicates his desire to imitate a natural narrative.

81. Culler, *The Pursuit of Signs,* 185.

82. Ibid., 184.

83. Ronald Schleifer, "The Salutary Discomfort of Writing: Roland Barthes, Literature, and Obscurity," *New Orleans Review* 15,2 (Summer 1988), 23. Another version of this passage appears in Schleifer, *Rhetoric and Death: The Language of Modernism and Postmodern Theory* (Urbana: University of Illinois Press, 1990), 192.

84. Much contemporary criticism, concerned with absences, repressions, and discrepancies, assumes some type of unreliability on the part of the narrator. From this point of view, the question is not the textual one of whether a particular narrator is unreliable but the historical one of why critics ever thought narrators *were* reliable. A typology of the forms of unreliability ("seven types"?) might include the unreliability originating in the tendency of "natural" narrators to translate their discursive evaluations into invented "facts" of the story.

85. Seymour Chatman, *Story and Discourse,* 53–56.

86. See Barbara Herrnstein Smith's discussion of these matters in "Afterthoughts on Narrative," *Critical Inquiry* 7,1 (Autumn 1980), 225–26.

87. Volosinov and Bakhtin, *Marxism and the Philosophy of Language,* 96.

88. Edward Said, *Beginnings: Intention and Method* (Baltimore: Johns Hopkins University Press, 1975), 84.

89. Kermode, *The Sense of an Ending,* 6.

90. Ibid., 13, 93–124.

Chapter 3: *Lord Jim* and the Pragmatics of Narrative

1. Raval, *The Art of Failure,* 45.

2. Fleishman, *Conrad's Politics,* 106–7. Fleishman, however, fails to see the limitations of Marlow's own work ethic in *Heart of Darkness.*

3. For Jameson, the modernist aesthetics of *Lord Jim* serve the "literary" function described in my discussion of *The Nigger of the "Narcissus"*: "to dereal-

ize the content and make it available for consumption on some purely aesthetic level." Jameson, *The Political Unconscious*, 214.

4. Green, *Dreams of Adventure, Deeds of Empire*, 37. Brantlinger draws upon Green's analysis at various points in *Rule of Darkness*.

5. London, *The Appropriated Voice*, 56.

6. Quoted in John Batchelor, *Lord Jim* (London: Unwin Hyman, 1988), 30.

7. Batchelor, *Lord Jim*, 30. In *Rule of Darkness*, 39ff., Brantlinger discusses Stevenson's opposition to imperialism, with occasional comparisons to Conrad.

8. "Devil only knows what the skipper wasn't afraid of . . . of what the law would do to him—or of his wife, perhaps." *Heart of Darkness and "The Secret Sharer"* (New York: Bantam Books, 1981), 153.

9. Batchelor, *Lord Jim*, 33.

10. Ibid., 59–76.

11. Dorothy Van Ghent, *The English Novel: Form and Function* (New York: Rinehart & Co, 1953), 229–44. Reprinted in the Norton edition of *Lord Jim*, 376–89.

12. Fleishman offers an excellent summary of "the Brooke myth" in *Conrad's Politics*, 97–111.

13. Gustave Morf, *The Polish Heritage of Joseph Conrad* (London: Sampson, Low, Marston, 1930), 149–66.

14. In *Language and Being*, Peter J. Glassman explores what he takes to be the covert autobiography in all of Conrad's early novels, concluding with *Lord Jim*.

15. Raval, *The Art of Failure*, 57.

16. Coste, *Narrative as Communication*, 9–11.

17. This passage echoes the deceptive belief in objective, undistorted seeing espoused as an artistic credo in the preface to *The Nigger of the "Narcissus."*

18. Alasdair MacIntyre, *After Virtue: A Study in Moral Theory* (Notre Dame, Ind.: University of Notre Dame Press, 1981), 203–4.

19. Guerard, *Conrad the Novelist*, 126.

20. Conrad, *Heart of Darkness and "The Secret Sharer,"* 146.

21. Chester's certainty that he sees things as they are caricatures Marlows "straight" and "clear" eyes as we first meet him, as it does the credo involving seeing in the preface to *The Nigger of the "Narcissus."* Chester, therefore, becomes a sort of deconstructive gremlin in the text, calling into question claims to objective seeing that his creator elsewhere uses to lend authority to his own practice as a writer.

22. Guerard, *Conrad the Novelist*, 165.

23. Eagleton, *Ideology of the Aesthetic*, 83, 91.

24. Ibid., 93.

25. Ibid., 93–94.

26. MacIntyre, *After Virtue*, 115–16.

27. Flashforwards and flashbacks. Gerard Genette's work on Proust is the basis of contemporary discussions of such matters: Genette, *Narrative Dis-*

course: An Essay in Method, trans. Jane E. Lewin (Ithaca, N.Y.: Cornell University Press, 1980). An excellent summary is found in Chatman, *Story and Discourse,* 63–84.

28. MacIntyre, *After Virtue,* 123–24, 133.

29. Van Ghent, in *Heart of Darkness,* 385, 377.

30. Fleishman, *Conrad's Politics,* 57.

31. Ibid., 110.

32. One might compare Kipling's *Kim* and the false consciousness implicit in a hero who supposedly embraces Indian culture while working for the British Secret Service.

33. Jameson, *The Political Unconscious,* 263.

34. If the movement from speech to writing seems to privilege speech as the originary act, the Derridian reader should remember that Marlow's speech was itself a fabric of citations and repetitions, that Jim's ideal self had been written in holiday literature, and so on. The content of Marlow's speech is an infinite regress of inscriptions, their origin always receding.

35. Guerard, *Conrad the Novelist,* 145ff.

36. Stephen K. Land discusses the common structural features and character types, such as the *nemesis,* in Conrad's fiction in *Paradox and Polarity in the Fiction of Joseph Conrad* (New York: St. Martin's Press, 1984).

37. Parry, *Conrad and Imperialism,* 3.

38. Ibid., 3–4.

39. See Iser's discussion in the final chapter of *The Implied Reader,* "The Reading Process: A Phenomenological Approach," 285ff.

40. Parry, *Conrad and Imperialism,* 7 (my emphasis).

41. Jameson, *The Political Unconscious,* 256.

42. Ibid.

43. Parry, *Conrad and Imperialism,* 95, 98.

44. Ibid., 92.

45. Ibid., 95.

46. Friedrich Nietzsche, *The Joyful Wisdom,* trans. Thomas Common (New York: Frederick Unger, 1960), 167.

47. MacIntyre, *After Virtue,* 8, 239.

48. Parry, *Conrad and Imperialism,* 96.

49. MacIntyre, *After Virtue,* 244.

50. Jurgen Habermas, "Modernity—An Incomplete Project," *The Anti-Aesthetic: Essays on Postmodern Culture,* ed. Hal Foster (Port Townsend, Wash.: Bay Press, 1983), 5.

51. Ibid., 5.

Chapter 4: Forms of Time and of the Chronotope in *Nostromo*

1. Hay, *The Political Novels of Joseph Conrad,* 162.

2. Fogel argues for a specific historiographic antecedent, finding *Nostromo* to be like Thucydides's *The Peloponnesian War* in its counterpointing of

"dense realpolitik and scenes of ironically framed set speeches." *Coercion to Speak*, 98.

3. Parry, *Conrad and Imperialism*, 99, 101.

4. Ricoeur, *Time and Narrative*, vol. 3, 189. Articles by Mink include "The Autonomy of Historical Understanding," *History and Theory* 5 (1965), 24–47; "Philosophical Analysis and Historical Understanding," *Review of Metaphysics* 20 (1968): 667–98; "History and Fiction as Modes of Comprehension," *New Literary History* (1970), 541–58. White's major work is collected in three volumes: *Metahistory: The Historical Imagination in Nineteenth-Century Europe* (Baltimore: Johns Hopkins University Press, 1973); *The Tropics of Discourse* (Baltimore: Johns Hopkins University Press, 1978); and *The Content of the Form: Discourse and Historical Representation* (Baltimore: Johns Hopkins University Press, 1987).

5. Ricoeur, *Time and Narrative*, vol. 3, 192.

6. T. Peter Kemp, "Toward a Narrative Ethics: A Bridge Between Ethics and the Narrative Reflection of Paul Ricoeur," *The Narrative Path: The Later Work of Paul Ricoeur*, ed. T. Peter Kemp and David Rasmussen (Cambridge, Mass.: MIT Press, 1989), 76.

7. The word "configure" is used in the sense intended by Ricoeur in his discussion of the three aspects of Aristotle's mimesis. By "mimesis2" (sic) Ricoeur designates the power of the text not merely to refer to reality but to constitute the real. See his discussion of the threefold mimesis in *Time and Narrative*, vol. 1, 52–87.

8. Ibid., 101.

9. Ibid., 103.

10. Fleishman, *Conrad's Politics*, 161.

11. Bakhtin, *The Dialogic Imagination*, 104. Lothe touches briefly on this topic in a section called "The Interplay of Spatial and Temporal Dimensions," a part of his chapter on *Nostromo.* Lothe, *Conrad's Narrative Method*, 203–5.

12. The sun rising over the mountain in *Nostromo* might be compared to the moon rising over the cleft mountain in Patusan in *Lord Jim.* The opposition between sun and moon suggests an opposition between Western and Eastern experiences of time. See Bonney's discussion of the moon in *Lord Jim* in *Thorns and Arabesques*, 29.

13. Bakhtin, *The Dialogic Imagination*, 84.

14. Ricoeur, *Time and Narrative*, vol. 3, 300n5.

15. Claire Rosenfield, *Paradise of Snakes: An Archetypal Analysis of Conrad's Political Novels* (Chicago: University of Chicago Press, 1967), 48.

16. Ibid., 51.

17. Ibid., 52.

18. What has turned up, of course, is oil. Barry Lopez's account of the exploitation of the Arctic in *Arctic Dreams: Imagination and Desire in a Northern Landscape* (New York: Bantam Books, 1987) documents the final stage of Holroyd's plan.

19. Critics have not failed to note the affinity between Conrad's view and the analysis found in Max Weber's *The Protestant Ethic and the Spirit of Capitalism.* See Rosenfield, *Paradise of Snakes*, 36–38, and Fleishman, *Conrad's Politics*,

179. As Fleishman points out, *Nostromo* was written during the interventions in Panama by the United States that culminated in 1904. Fleishman sees in Holroyd a parody of Theodore Roosevelt and also of the New York capitalist Frederick M. Kelly, who was involved in the early attempts to build a Panama Canal and who wrapped himself in religious zeal. *Conrad's Politics,* 170.

20. Bakhtin, *The Dialogic Imagination,* 208.

21. T. McAlindon, "*Nostromo:* Conrad's Organicist Philosophy of History," *Joseph Conrad's Nostromo: Modern Critical Interpretations,* ed. Harold Bloom (New York: Chelsea House Publishers, 1987), 63.

22. Kiernan Ryan, "Revelation and Repression in Conrad's *Nostromo,*" ibid., 53.

23. Rosenfield, *Paradise of Snakes,* 58.

24. Dorothy Van Ghent, "Guardianship of the Treasure: *Nostromo,*" *Joseph Conrad's Nostromo: Modern Critical Interpretations,* 26–27.

25. Martin Price, "The Limits of Irony," ibid., 76.

26. Irving Howe, *Politics and the Novel* (New York: Horizon Press, 1957), 102ff.

27. Bonney, *Thorns and Arabesques,* 11. Other studies of time in Conrad's work include William Bysshe Stein's "Conrad's East: Time, History, Action, and *Maya,*" *Texas Studies in Language and Literature* 7 (1965), 265–83; and Stein's "*Almayer's Folly:* The Terrors of Time," *Conradiana* 1 (1968), 27–34.

28. Howe, *Politics and the Novel,* 106.

29. Van Ghent, "Guardianship of the Treasure," 28.

30. Said, *Beginnings,* 101.

31. Narratologists often distinguish between description and narration on the basis of the notion that narration is temporal, advancing the action, whereas description is motionless in time. But Mitchell's descriptions, while apparently of spatial objects only, are in fact descriptions of temporal change. In this case, from the viewpoint of the chronotope, description *is* narration. Harold F. Mosher explored a similar effect in *The Secret Agent* in a paper entitled "Towards a Poetics of 'Descriptized Narration,'" delivered at the Twentieth-Century Literature Conference, University of Louisville, February 1990.

32. Clifford Geertz, borrowing terms from Gilbert Ryle, distinguishes between "thin" descriptions, very much like Mitchell's, and "thick" descriptions that try to reveal the "stratified hierarchy of meaningful structures" that give significance to all of a culture's various products and manifestations. See Geertz, *The Interpretation of Cultures* (New York: Basic Books, 1973), 7. The stratification and layering Geertz talks about suggest the layers of time readable in the cityscape of Sulaco.

33. Fredric Jameson, "The Politics of Theory: Ideological Positions in the Postmodern Debate," *Contemporary Literary Criticism,* ed. Robert Con Davis and Ronald Schleifer (New York: Longman, 1989), 426.

34. Ricoeur, *Time and Narrative,* vol. 2, 100–152.

35. Ricoeur, *Time and Narrative,* vol. 3, 181.

36. Said, *Beginnings,* 100.

37. Guerard, *Conrad the Novelist,* 207.

38. Ryan, "Revelation and Repression in Conrad's *Nostromo*," 47.

39. With these points in mind, one is tempted to see George Bernard Shaw's *Major Barbara*, published one year after *Nostromo*, as a response to Conrad's novel. In Shaw's play, Undershaft's faith in material interests is vindicated by its power to bring about a better justice for the common people. Undershaft succeeds according to Gould's grand narrative, which weds materialism to sacred obligation; he is also a God-figure like Holroyd, as underlined by his daughter's conversion to his "religion." Shaw and Conrad met around the turn of the century, and Conrad refers to Shaw in a letter to Cunninghame Graham in 1905, the year of *Major Barbara* (see Fleishman, *Conrad's Politics*, 31).

40. Fleishman, *Conrad's Politics*, 57.

41. Charles Gould's plan for the mine is born simultaneously with his engagement to Emily; Decoud's separatist plan is born out of his attraction to Antonia; and Nostromo's new identity as a successful businessman is linked to his guilty attraction to Giselle. The relationship of a male's social role to his romantic or libidinal interests is a recurrent theme in Conrad. The political self Jim discovers in Patusan is an aspect of his "love story," and Kurtz's depraved "methods" are associated with his African mistress. Razumov's discovery of an authentic and social existence in *Under Western Eyes* is a function of his love of Nathalie. One could also cite the political effects of Willems's attraction to Aissa in *An Outcast of the Islands* and the destructiveness born out of the dead captain's illicit relationship in *The Shadow-Line*.

42. Rosenfield, *Paradise of Snakes*, 65.

43. Ibid., 64.

44. Geertz, *The Interpretation of Cultures*, 360.

45. Fleishman, *Conrad's Politics*, 56.

46. Kermode, *The Sense of an Ending*, 7.

47. Bonney, *Thorns and Arabesques*, 206.

48. Kermode, *The Sense of an Ending*, 47. That Conrad sees this emptying of time as an effect of material interests is suggested in "Karain: A Memory," where Karain, seeking to free himself from his guilty memory, wishes to go with the whites "to your people, who live in unbelief; to whom day is day, and night is night—nothing more." *Tales of Unrest* (New York: Doubleday, Page, & Co., 1925), 44.

49. Images of the measurement of time recur at key moments in Conrad's fiction. A partial survey would include:

1. "Karain: A Memory," where "the steady tick of chronometers" accompanies Karain's confession and the mock absolution given him by the gun-runners. The charm that silences the voice of Karain's guilt is a coin carrying the image of Queen Victoria, and the story creates a metonymic link between clock time and Western economics.

2. *Lord Jim*, where Jim bides his time repairing a clock before mustering the energy and courage to escape like Christ on the third day of his imprisonment in Patusan, subsequently reorienting himself in time and history.

3. *The End of the Tether,* where Whalley races with the calendar to finish out his contract before his blindness is discovered.

4. "Il Conde," where the Count's timepiece is emphasized with an apparently irrelevant plot element. At the time of the robbery his expensive chronometer is being repaired, and he has with him only a cheap watch, which the young Camorra does not condescend to steal. Nonetheless, his time is being stolen by a historical process that replaces the old aristocracy with a new criminal elite, and in the end he goes away to die. (Mitchell successfully defends his watch against theft by Sotillo in *Nostromo,* Mitchell being one of those to whom the future belongs.)

5. *The Secret Agent,* where Verloc's dying is apparently accompanied by the sound of a gradually slowing clock—a ticking that turns out to be the dripping of his blood.

6. *Under Western Eyes,* where Razumov is maddened by his broken watch as he awaits the moment of Haldin's arrest. During this period he hears for the first time the chiming of a clock from across the city; the shift of Razumov's attention from the watch to the city clock marks his move from private to public time.

50. Bakhtin, *The Dialogic Imagination,* 110.

51. Northrop Frye, *Anatomy of Criticism: Four Essays* (Princeton, N.J.: Princeton University Press, 1957), 33–35.

52. Bakhtin, *The Dialogic Imagination,* 135–36.

53. See Foucault's *History of Sexuality,* trans. Robert Hurley (New York: Vintage Books, 1980), vol. 1, esp. 17–49. Mark Seltzer discusses the "fantasy of surveillance" in Henry James's *The Princess Casamassima* in terms of a general paranoia concerning secret crimes in turn-of-the-century London. Mark Seltzer, *Henry James and the Art of Power* (Ithaca, N.Y.: Cornell University Press, 1984), 25–39. I have noted the mechanism of surveillance within the form of *The Nigger of the "Narcissus,"* and surveillance is more directly thematized in *The Secret Agent.*

54. Bakhtin, *Problems of Dostoevsky's Poetics,* 106 (emphasis in original).

55. Frye, *Anatomy of Criticism,* 65.

Chapter 5: Shared Words and Western Eyes

1. Avrom Fleishman, "Speech and Writing in *Under Western Eyes,*" *Fiction and the Ways of Knowing: Essays on British Novels* (Austin: University of Texas Press, 1978), 123–35.

2. Guerard, *Conrad the Novelist,* 249.

3. This book began by discussing such discontinuities in *The Nigger of the "Narcissus."* There is an ongoing experiment in Conrad's fiction involving point of view. *Nostromo* is predominantly an omniscient narration, which shifts only momentarily (I exclude Mitchell's reported narration, since he is not the primary storyteller) into first-person narration (108). This shift is so intrusive that inconsistency itself seems to be a matter of principle, and it is found again in the occasional first-person pronoun in the narrative discourse

of *The Secret Agent*. *Under Western Eyes* reverses this procedure, announcing itself as a first-person narration but smuggling in omniscience at various turns.

Bonney offers an excellent discussion of Conrad's "discontinuous narrative perspectives." Especially intriguing is his analysis of the three tales in *Youth—A Narrative and Two Other Stories* as a single experiment in point of view. Bonney argues that the bleakly omniscient narration of *The End of the Tether* is a studied, skeptical opposition to Marlow's subjective narration in *Youth* and *Heart of Darkness*. See *Thorns and Arabesques*, 151–94.

4. Caryl Emerson, "Outer Word and Inner Speech," *Bakhtin: Essays and Dialogues on His Work*, ed. Gary Saul Morson (Chicago: University of Chicago Press, 1986), 24.

5. See Barthes, *Image, Music, Text*, 11, 142. Foucault's "What Is an Author?" appears in *Language, Counter-Memory, Practice*, 113–38.

6. One might extend the objection to the notion of an artless narrator, a notion encouraged by his own pose, as follows: It is not logical to attribute the narrator's presence in Geneva to his art as a storyteller, since his presence there preceded his discourse and provided the material for the story. Nor are the raw facts about what the various characters did attributable to his art— they "really" happened, and he reports on this fictional reality. These matters, in other words, are attributable to the inferred author's *story*, not the narrator's *discourse*. But it is the narrator whose powers of observation, memory, and selection tell us what we know about the Geneva revolutionaries. The "story" is the author's, but all matters of selection, emphasis, and emplotment are elements of discourse for which the fictional narrator must receive credit.

An example of criticism that distributes praise and blame neatly into the author-narrator categories is Tony Tanner's "Nightmare and Complacency: Razumov and the Western Eye," *Critical Quarterly* 4 (1962), 197–214. Within a single paragraph we are told of the narrator's "impenetrable complacency," that he is "impercipient," "stupid," and finally an "idiot" (200–201).

7. See Ronald Schleifer's "Public and Private Narrative in *Under Western Eyes*," *Conradiana* 9 (1977), 137–54. Schleifer discusses the "double authority of the narrative" (149) arising from the split between the narrator's discourse and Razumov's journal. In a similar vein, Penn R. Szittya sees Conrad's novel as a piece of "reflexive and often self-doubting" (817) metafiction resulting from Conrad's various doublings of viewpoints; see Szittya, "Metafiction: The Double Narration in *Under Western Eyes*," *ELH* 48 (1981), 817–40. Gene M. Moore also takes up the problem of the split or double authority engendered by the relation between the narrator and the journal. Moore, employing Bakhtin's concept of the chronotope, attempts to focus "less on what Razumov and the narrator 'mean to say' than on the temporal and spatial conditions surrounding their discourse" (11). See Moore, "Chronotopes and Voices in *Under Western Eyes*," *Conradiana* 18 (1986), 9–25. See also Jacob Lothe's chapter in *Conrad's Narrative Method*. These, along with Fleishman's study noted above, are the best discussions of this novel within the context of recent narrative theory.

8. Moore, however, shows that the narrator is subsequently inconsis-

tent on this point, most noticeably in the statement that Razumov began to write (but write what?) immediately after his interview with Mikulin (286). "Chronotopes and Voices in *Under Western Eyes*," 18–19.

9. If Razumov began the diary a year after Haldin's betrayal, he would probably be writing of the betrayal in Geneva, under the pressure of his acquaintance with Nathalie. But it is spring in Geneva and the betrayal occurred in December, suggesting that less than half a year has passed between the betrayal and the confession. This would make the narrator's statement about the year interval between the betrayal and the start of the diary impossible. For a slightly different analysis of this question, and for discussion of other temporal quandaries, see Moore, "Chronotopes and Voices," 17–23.

10. The interval between the narrator's story time in Geneva and his act of writing is not specified, but its relatively great length is suggested in his allusions to intervening events such as Mikulin's fall into disfavor and Nikita's betrayal.

11. I can quote my son, who said, "I really loved that game. It was awesome!" Or I can report his speech in indirect discourse by telling you he said that he liked the game very much. The relation of the indirect reportage to the original is approximate and involves slight alterations (as my own discourse mingles with his) that remain unknowable if you have no access to the original.

12. Szittya, "Metafiction: The Double Narration in *Under Western Eyes*," 821.

13. Moore, "Chronotopes and Voices," 15.

14. Tanner, "Nightmare and Complacency," 200.

15. Bakhtin, *Marxism and the Philosophy of Language*, 119, 120.

16. Ibid., 121.

17. The conventions of the novel demand that we assume these conversations are reported accurately; without such an assumption reading would not be possible. In literature, if not journalism, the quotation mark is our guarantee of reliability unless the quotation occurs in a larger discourse that has itself been called into question. We can, on the other hand, assume inaccuracy or distortion in the indirect reporting of the diary because the narrator himself makes it clear such distortion has occurred. Narrative unreliability or distortion must always be marked in some way.

18. Dialogue is quoted in the parts of the novel based on the diary, but here we can legitimately wonder about the literal accuracy of the quotes, since they occur in what on the whole is professed to be an impressionistic rendering.

19. Yet another version of such embedding, here suggesting the autocracy's need to occlude the origin of words—or the political advantage of creating the effect of multiple origins—is found in the letter inviting Razumov to meet Mikulin at the oculist's. The note is in an envelope that is in another envelope, each of the three inscribed in a different hand (289).

20. Moore offers a summary of the roles the narrator plays: "In principle the narrator's control of his text is absolute, and this control is exercised (sic)

through his multiple roles of *translator* (interpreting his material through his choice of equivalent words, deciding what will be 'lost' or kept in the translation), *editor* (paraphrasing, inventing transitions, censoring, adding comments or explanations), and *plotter* (determining the order in which the chronological events of the story will be told, or how Razumov's *fabula* will become his own *sujet* as he rearranges Razumov's dated entries to form not a chronological sequence but a *progression d'effet*)." Moore, "Chronotopes and Voices," 12–13.

21. This passage glances at Ivan's talk with the devil in *The Brothers Karamazov*. More will be said below about this novel's relation to Dostoevsky's writing.

22. Fleishman, "Speech and Writing in *Under Western Eyes*," 113. Fleishman's thesis is diametrically opposed to Fogel's, which argues the destructiveness of coerced speech.

23. Bakhtin, *Marxism and the Philosophy of Language*, 22. *Freudianism: A Marxist Critique* is entirely devoted to refuting notions of a transcendent, inner self that precedes experience and social formation.

24. Bakhtin, *Problems of Dostoevsky's Poetics*, 288.

25. Bakhtin, *Marxism and the Philosophy of Language*, 12.

26. Ibid., 86.

27. The question of the relation of Rousseau's thought to the Burkean tradition is complex. Burke and Rousseau took opposing positions on the French Revolution, and Burke branded Rousseau an enemy of civilization. Nonetheless, it is possible and reasonable to read Rousseau's version of contract theory, particularly its emphasis on an originary surrender of the individual will, in a way that minimizes differences between it and organicism. Fleishman's discussion reflects these difficulties. *Conrad's Politics*, 57–59.

28. Bakhtin's term derives from his reading of Einstein on relativity. In more recent cosmology, the "event horizon" establishes a boundary past which no data or information can pass; an example is a "black hole," a gravitational force from which not even light can escape. In the view of the narrator of *Under Western Eyes*, Russian history and Western history often seem to exist on opposite sides of an event horizon.

29. Kermode, *The Sense of an Ending*, 47.

30. Conrad had originally planned to have Razumov and Nathalie marry and have a son.

31. Moore, "Chronotopes and Voices," 15.

32. Bakhtin, *Problems of Dostoevsky's Poetics*, 252.

33. Kermode, *The Sense of an Ending*, 47.

34. Jean-Aubry, *Life and Letters*, vol. 2, 140.

35. Fogel, *Coercion to Speak*, 200.

36. Bakhtin, whose *Problems of Dostoevsky's Art* ("art" was later changed to "poetics") was first published in 1929, has little to say directly about Dostoevsky's politics. Since "free speech" (a possibility some would deny in any circumstances) was not possible under Stalin, literary and academic positions were often encoded political positions (there was not a coercion to speak, but to speak differently). Thus Bakhtin's academic celebration of the disruptive

and the carnivalesque was politically courageous in the repressive atmosphere in which he worked. Similarly courageous was the celebration of a writer whose religion and czarism were notorious, despite Bakhtin's skirting of the overt political content of Dostoevsky's work. (Bakhtin would not have admired Dostoevsky's cringing before the autocracy in any case, but he did share Dostoevsky's Christian faith.) Furthermore, the specific terms of his praise of Dostoevsky—for granting a radical freedom of consciousness to his characters and for refusing to objectify and categorize them within his own discourse—carry a powerful political message and protest. Not surprisingly, therefore, Bakhtin was placed in internal exile for many years.

37. Fogel, *Coercion to Speak*, 201.

38. Bakhtin, *Problems of Dostoevsky's Poetics*, 53.

39. Bakhtin, "Epic and Novel: Toward a Methodology for the Study of the Novel," *The Dialogic Imagination*, 37.

40. This essay was briefly described in my opening summary of Conrad's political attitudes; see chap. 1, n. 3.

41. Conrad, "Autocracy and War," 97, 101.

42. Bakhtin, *Problems of Dostoevsky's Poetics*, 92.

43. Conrad, "Autocracy and War," 100–101.

44. Raval, *The Art of Failure*, 143.

45. Rosenfield, *Paradise of Snakes*, 159.

46. Bakhtin, *Problems of Dostoevsky's Poetics*, 71.

47. Ibid., 63.

48. Ibid., 205–7.

49. Anthropology describes cultures in terms of their kinship systems, and the depiction in this novel of missing or collapsing kinship relations (note also the absence of a male parent of Victor and Nathalie, the deteriorated relationship between Kostia and his father, the narrator's apparent lack of wife or children, the unmarried status of the feminist, Ivanovitch, and so on) must be read as cultural commentary.

50. Bakhtin, *Marxism and the Philosophy of Language*, 12.

51. Bakhtin, *Problems of Dostoevsky's Poetics*, 88.

52. Szittya, "Metafiction: The Double Narration in *Under Western Eyes*," 829.

53. Bakhtin, *Problems of Dostoevsky's Poetics*, 104.

54. What Nostromo omits in his confession is his abandonment of Decoud and therefore his responsibility for Decoud's death, precisely the sort of deeper crime that Razumov acknowledges.

55. Bakhtin, *Problems of Dostoevsky's Poetics*, 294.

56. Ibid., 293.

57. J. M. Coetzee's *Foe* speaks of the ethical imperatives of conversation and the *petit recit*. In Coetzee's novel, Friday's tongue (in contrast to Razumov's hearing) has been mutilated and thus his story is lost: "The story of Friday's tongue is a story unable to be told, or unable to be told by me. That is to say, many stories can be told of Friday's tongue, but the true story is buried within Friday, who is mute. The true story will not be heard till by art we

have found a means of giving voice to Friday." *Foe* (New York: Penguin Books, 1986), 118.

58. Frederick Karl, *A Reader's Guide to Joseph Conrad* (New York: H. Wolf, 1960), 233.

59. Discussed in Bakhtin, *Problems of Dostoevsky's Poetics*, 235.

60. Ibid., 252.

61. Szittya, "Metafiction: The Double Narration in *Under Western Eyes*," 831–38.

Conclusion: After Closure

1. Parry, *Conrad and Imperialism*, 105.

2. Richard Rorty, *The Consequences of Pragmatism* (Minneapolis: University of Minnesota Press, 1982), 165.

3. Lyotard, *Just Gaming*, 15.

4. Rorty, *The Consequences of Pragmatism*, xxxvii (his emphasis).

5. Ibid., 166 (his emphases).

6. Wlad Godzich, "Foreword: The Further Possibility of Knowledge," Michel de Certeau, *Heterologies: Discourse on the Other*, trans. Brian Massumi (Minneapolis: University of Minnesota Press, 1986), xvi.

Index

A Note on the Author

BRUCE HENRICKSEN is a professor of English at Loyola University in New Orleans. He is the editor of *Murray Krieger and Contemporary Critical Theory* and a co-editor, with Thaïs E. Morgan, of *Reorientations: Theories and Pedagogies*.